Kindness Matters

Chicken Soup for the Soul: Kindness Matters
101 Feel-Good Stories of Compassion and Paying It Forward
Amy Newmark

Published by Chicken Soup for the Soul, LLC www.chickensoup.com
Copyright ©2022 by Chicken Soup for the Soul, LLC. All Rights Reserved.

The publisher gratefully acknowledges the many publishers and individuals who
granted Chicken Soup for the Soul permission to reprint the cited material.

Front cover photo of goose holding sign courtesy of iStockphoto.com/Sonsedska
(©Sonsedska), photo of row of ducks courtesy of iStockphoto.com/sidneybernstein
(©sidneybernstein), image of traffic sign courtesy of iStockphoto.com/clintscholz
(©clintscholz) and image of road courtesy of iStockphoto.com/hallojulie (©hallojulie)
Back and Interior photo of chipmunk with acorn courtesy of iStockphoto.com/hallojulie
(©hallojulie), other photo of chipmunk courtesy of iStockphoto.com/GlobalP (©GlobalP)

Cover and Interior by Daniel Zaccari

Distributed to the booktrade by Simon & Schuster. SAN: 200-2442

Publisher's Cataloging-In-Publication Data
(Prepared by The Donohue Group, Inc.)

Names: Newmark, Amy, compiler.
Title: Chicken soup for the soul : kindness matters : 101 feel-good stories of
    compassion and paying it forward / [compiled by] Amy Newmark.
Other Titles: Kindness matters : 101 feel-good stories of compassion and paying it
    forward
Description: [Cos Cob, Connecticut] : Chicken Soup for the Soul, LLC,
    [2022]
Identifiers: ISBN 9781611590883 (print) | ISBN 9781611593259 (ebook)
Subjects: LCSH: Kindness--Literary collections. | Kindness--Anecdotes. |
    Compassion--Literary collections. | Compassion--Anecdotes. | LCGFT:
    Anecdotes.
Classification: LCC BJ1533.K5 C45 2022 (print) | LCC BJ1533.K5 (ebook) |
    DDC 177.7--dc23

Library of Congress Control Number: 2021948157

PRINTED IN THE UNITED STATES OF AMERICA
on acid∞free paper

28 27 26 25 24 23 22   01 02 03 04 05 06 07 08 09 10 11

Kindness Matters

101 Feel-Good Stories of Compassion and Paying It Forward

Amy Newmark

Chicken Soup for the Soul, LLC
Cos Cob, CT

Chicken Soup
for the Soul

Changing your life one story at a time ®
www.chickensoup.com

Table of Contents

❶

~Miracles of Kindness~

❷

~Role Models of Kindness~

3

~The Kindness of Strangers~

4

~The Right Words~

5

~Friends & Neighbors~

❻

~One Good Turn Deserves Another~

❼

~Compassion & Understanding~

8

~Ever Grateful~

9

~Worth the Effort~

10

~Small Things, Big Impact~

⑪
~The Joy of Doing for Others~

Miracles of Kindness

Fire!

*The greatness of a community is most accurately measured
by the compassionate actions of its members.*
~Coretta Scott King

ovember 11, 2005 was a day off for me, so I was in no hurry to get out of bed. As I rolled over and stretched, my husband called up to me from the kitchen where he was brewing coffee and putting out bowls for cereal.

"Get down here. Quick!"

There was no mistaking the urgency in his voice. I hurried down the stairs.

He pointed to the TV in the corner where a newscast showed flames devouring a building. I stood beside him and shook my head.

"What a shame. Is it local?"

"It's your office."

The medical practice where I worked as a nurse had caught fire in the night. We found out later that a spark in the attic, perhaps from old wiring, had ignited and spread through the whole building. The TV camera captured the firefighters' silhouettes, black against orange, as they aimed useless streams of water at the blaze. By dawn, the building was destroyed.

"I've got to get over there," I said. I threw on jeans and a heavy sweater and drove to the site.

Crews from several fire stations had cordoned off the street and stood in groups talking among themselves. Their hoses lay soggy and flattened in the gutter and across the trampled lawn. I stepped through puddles of blackened water to gaze at the smoking, hissing remains of my place of work. The landscaping was burnt and shriveled. Stray scraps of paper skittered into the street from paperwork we'd left unfinished the night before, tattered, singed, and soggy. I gathered up what I could. Half a block away lay our mangled portable oxygen canister. It had exploded and flown that far before coming to rest against the curb.

I stood with co-workers who had arrived when I did. We hugged, unsure what to do — dazed, horrified at the sight, and feeling helpless. I pictured my desk and the photos of my four-month-old grandson buried under the caved-in roof. Through a smashed front window, I caught a glimpse of the rows and rows of medical records, scorched and ruined, dripping from the jets of water sprayed onto them. It was a devastating loss. Because the fire preceded the move to electronic medical records, those file folders were irreplaceable histories of our patients, some going back more than twenty years.

"We've got to get the charts. Maybe we can store them in our basements and dry them out," I told the other staff members who stood beside me gaping at the disaster.

I jogged across the parking lot, sidestepping the debris, lifted the yellow caution tape and ducked under it. I hadn't taken two steps when a firefighter's shocked voice stopped me.

"Hey, you can't be in here."

"It's all right. I work here."

"No."

"I'm one of the nurses," I explained, certain that my job would give me access. "I'm going in to retrieve the charts. We've got to save them if we can."

He stared at me, stunned at my stupidity. "Absolutely not. One, it's very dangerous. Two, those charts are gone, lady," he told me. "Nothing is going to save them. Sorry."

"I can try." I took another step.

"Stop. I mean it." The expression on his face changed from compassion to no-nonsense authority. I backed off.

As the reality of the disaster sank in, all of us, doctors and staff, gazed at the smoldering rubble, numb with shock. We looked on as firefighters worked to ensure the fire was out and secure the area. There were hot spots that could flare up in an instant. The roof had collapsed, and the jagged ends of rafters stuck out at odd angles, a hazard to anyone who might climb around the site. Then, too, there were controlled medications inside, narcotics no doubt ruined but still needing to be accounted for as they were possible targets for drug seekers, even in our safe, little town.

Three acts of kindness got us through that first day — offers of help from people in the town who considered the mess we were in and understood what we needed. Those three gestures meant everything.

The first came almost immediately, before we'd even gotten our heads together as a team to make a plan. One of our patients, a woman we knew well, matriarch of a large extended family who had plenty on her plate already, came up and put a gentle arm around me as I stood gawking at the ruins.

"I came over to see how to help. I can imagine how much you'll have to do to get this sorted out. What about a letter to all the patients explaining the situation?" she said. "If you tell me what to say, I can write it, get copies made, and stuff envelopes. We can send it out right away. That might save you several thousand phone calls."

I was still marveling at her gracious suggestion when one of the doctors walked over with the news of a second helpful offer. A business owner down the street had called. He was going to empty out a couple of offices in his small building and make them available to us. They would not be suitable for exam rooms, but the practice would run largely by phone for the near future. We nurses could be headquartered there to field phone calls about prescription refills, manage what we could, and take messages about the matters that only the doctors could handle.

We spent a few hours brainstorming our next steps while standing out in the cold rawness and damp of a dreary winter day, shaken and discouraged by the immensity of the undertaking ahead of us. We had to keep the practice open. Could we do it?

A third, and welcome, outpouring of generosity occurred about noon. It brought big smiles to our faces, and we were short on smiles that day. An SUV drove up, and the manager of the local McDonald's restaurant climbed out. He scurried around to the back and opened the hatch. Inside were stacks of boxes containing fresh, hot Quarter Pounders and fries for everyone as well as soft drinks.

"I figured you could do with something to warm your bellies and restore some energy," he said. "It won't fix what happened, but it might help for now."

We gathered around the truck and scarfed down the food, our spirits raised. He was right. It did help.

Of course, nothing could undo the fire, but our good-hearted community stood beside us in the weeks that followed as we struggled to keep the practice open. And none of us will ever forget the kindnesses that made such a difference on that first day.

—Holly Green—

The Opportunity to Help Someone

Christmas is the spirit of giving
without a thought of getting.
~Thomas S. Monson

I didn't think anything could compare to our normal family Christmases, with everyone squeezed into Grandma's living room. But I was invited to another very special Christmas party in 2020, and it was held on Zoom. There was no family, no squeezing into a small living room overflowing with gifts, but it was the most "Christmassy" Christmas party I'd ever attended.

Since November, my mom and I had been collecting Christmas gifts for local foster children using our workplace as the hub of the gift drive. Our customers and staff joked that it was starting to feel like Santa's workshop at *The Devine News* office. It got to be pretty chaotic in a busy news office on press day with gifts crammed into every available space. I didn't mind it, though. Every time I tripped over a gift bag, I smiled, thinking about how happy a kid was going to be when he saw that gift sitting under the tree.

We live in a small town and are proud of it. People in our community really pour out their hearts for these kids each year. It's our hope that we can make these gifts for foster kids just as exciting and awesome as the ones sitting underneath our own Christmas trees at home.

It is a big project but a joy to do. In November, we had at least two big gift bags full of awesome stuff and huge stockings for thirty-two kids.

Toward the end of what was our biggest gift drive ever, I got a call from Lanisha, the director of another program that helps foster youth. She was hoping and praying we could help them with Christmas gifts for foster kids who had recently turned eighteen and were starting life out on their own.

The program she works for provides these kids with a small apartment, stove, and bed as they begin working or going to college. She had been turned down by most of the other organizations that year, because they were looking to sponsor younger children, not teenagers.

Our community had gone "all out" and donated so much already. I couldn't imagine asking for more. Plus, there wasn't much time. I figured that I would just go to the store myself and get each of Lanisha's kids a little ten-dollar gift. It wouldn't be much, but it would be something.

"How many kids are in your program?" I asked.

"There are twenty kids placed in the San Antonio area and twenty in Austin," she said. "We have forty kids."

I sat there on the phone, thinking silently for a minute, and tried to imagine what we could do. I told her we would do our best to get something together for at least twenty of her forty kids, but it would probably just be something small. She was so grateful, and that motivated us even more.

Most of their fundraisers had been cancelled due to COVID-19, and I hated the thought of giving something so small to these kids who deserve and need our love. So, we reached out to our readers online, and their response was amazing. One lady, Lisa, had already brought several gifts, but she was so excited to be able to help more children.

After a few weeks, we had big gift bags full of Christmas joy for twenty of those kids. However, I couldn't stop thinking about the other twenty kids in that program, and how the director had said they'd also be grateful for any used furniture and hand-me-down Christmas trees.

Not only did these kids have nothing to unwrap on Christmas morning, but they didn't have a tree to put a gift under.

About that time, a lady whom I'd never met contacted me and said, "Kayleen, how can I help? I'll do whatever you need. Just let me know, and I'll take care of it."

Her name was Heather. I was overwhelmed at that point, and she sounded like an angel.

Shyly, I told her, "Well, I would love to get them all Christmas trees. I have five, and we could use about fifteen more."

My heart skipped a beat as she said, "Sure, no problem." She planned to get all fifteen, plus a few gifts.

A few minutes later, I called Lanisha and told her to go ahead and send us the list of the other twenty foster kids. Time was short, but I knew we could make it happen because of people like Heather.

Before I had received those twenty names, another lady, Amanda, volunteered to make giant stockings full of goodies for all sixteen girls in one of those groups. That was on Thanksgiving Day.

That same evening, another woman, Roxanne, contacted me and said her family would make a gift basket for all the boys in that group with a basketball and snacks.

And that wasn't the end of it. Person after person continued contacting me. "How can I help? What can I do? I'll take care of it."

A lady named Angela volunteered to collect another twenty-five Christmas trees. Now every single one of those kids had a tree to put a gift under. Another resident, Tricia, sent $400 to help with that and buy more gifts. She also picked up a pair of basketball shoes and a special toy that had been forgotten.

My husband, who I thought would be irritated when he saw our bank statement, went out and bought nine large tool sets for all the young men… the same tool set that his daddy had bought him when he was starting out.

Before we were done, people had donated a jumbo-sized gift bag full to the brim for each one of those forty kids (to go along with the awesome stockings and gift baskets). So many angels helped that I wouldn't dare try to name them all.

As it got close to Christmas, I sat at the kitchen table going over the wish lists and re-reading the messages of the many angels who had made this possible. When I looked up at a refrigerator picture that my daughter had colored, I couldn't help but cry. It was a beautiful quote, and she had colored all around it with sunshine and flowers. It says, "When you have the opportunity to help someone, be glad to do it, because that is God answering somebody else's prayers through you."

And that's exactly what was happening.

We collected gifts for seventy-two kids that holiday season. My favorite thing was knowing that those gifts weren't just *a* gift for a boy or girl aged ten or fifteen; they were *the* gifts that each child had wished for. And when they opened them, those kids were going to know there were families out there who loved them.

After the gifts had been picked up, Lanisha called and said that since her foster youth weren't minors, we could join them for their online Christmas party.

It was not held on December twenty-fifth but seeing the faces and hearing the voices of Ace, Devon, Shyla, Gloria, Jeremie, and all those kids truly felt just like Christmas morning. One of the first things one of those kids asked was, "How could you… when you didn't even know us?" We had only known these kids by their Christmas wish lists and names, but we loved them so much already. And they knew.

— Kayleen Kitty Holder —

Santa Drives a Truck

As we express our gratitude, we must never forget
that the highest appreciation is not to utter words,
but to live by them.
~John F. Kennedy

I was thirty-four the first time I saw the real Santa. He drove a big, charcoal-colored truck, not a cherry red sleigh, and he was out and about in the August heat in Georgia. I'm about ninety-nine percent sure there was no white beard, long or otherwise. He wasn't what I expected at all.

My husband had lost his job on my birthday early in July, and we'd been cutting back on expenses everywhere we could. He'd been working with recruiters to find a job and interviewing often, but the process was excruciatingly slow. There were unexpected disappointments along the way, and he was feeling defeated.

I'd been doing what I could to keep up his spirits and encouraging him to step away from the computer periodically to take advantage of the time he had to spend with our nine-year-old daughter. It was summer vacation so he took her to the neighborhood pool. It got them out of the house and gave me time to complete a few extra work projects. I knew those weren't enough to solve our financial problems, but they were something.

I think we were hoping that something better than the job he'd had was on the way but fearing that he wouldn't find anything before everything fell apart.

One afternoon, we were feeling particularly low, so we decided to treat ourselves to a meal from Chick-fil-A. Just a quick drive-through run, no big deal. It was an excuse for us all to get out of the house, too. Plus, the waffle fries were calling our names. I don't remember if it felt like a reckless splurge or a way of showing that we had faith that better days were coming, but I do remember feeling conflicting emotions while we sat in line.

When we got to the window to pay, the employee said our meal had been taken care of by the car ahead of us. People do this all the time (they did that year, at least), and it's always a lovely gesture, but don't think this was just a cliché — for lack of a better word — pay-it-forward type of chain that started.

This time, it was different. We attempted to keep the chain going by offering to pay for the order for the car behind us, hoping they didn't have a family of eight who all wanted extra sides or anything like that.

"No, that man just paid for them, too," the employee at the window said. She gestured toward the truck that was slowly pulling away to exit the parking lot.

"Behind them then?" my husband asked. We really didn't want to just take the gift and run.

"Nope, he got them, too. He paid for everyone in line." There were probably about five cars behind us.

We had no choice but to get comfortable with the fact that a stranger had just done something kind for us, and there was no way (in that moment, at least) to repay it, pay it forward, etc. We just had to accept it. Sometimes, that's harder than it sounds. We were grateful but felt an immediate need to extend a nice gesture to someone else, and we couldn't.

I looked toward the truck that was still trying to get out of the parking lot. I thought I could see the man's grin in the driver's side mirror. He stuck his hand out the window and gave a cheerful wave, and it instantly reminded me of the illustration at the end of the 'Twas the Night Before Christmas poem where Santa was flying away into the night, gloved hand up in a goodbye wave, as he said, "Merry Christmas to all, and to all a good night!"

I'm sure that man — "Santa" in my mind — had no idea how much we needed that little reminder that we'd be alright. I bet there were similar stories behind us in line. Maybe not someone who'd lost a job, but perhaps someone suffering with a different kind of disappointment or grief.

My husband found a wonderful job shortly after that. We've gone on to do random acts of kindness for others, remembering the effect this free meal had on us that sweltering day in August when St. Nick drove a truck through a Chick-fil-A drive-through line in Georgia and left with a big grin and a little wave.

— Crystal Schwanke —

One Soggy Night

The more that you trust and believe in angels,
the more they will pour their blessings upon you.
~Denise Linn

It was our first day to explore the city of Jerusalem on our own, without a friend or tour guide leading the way. We had completed a week-long tour and felt confident that we could navigate the ancient streets by ourselves now. With a map in hand, we left confidently on our excursion. We had enjoyed a full day of exploration when we suddenly realized that the sky had turned from clear blue to an ominous gray. Dark clouds were moving in above our heads. "It's time to head back!" we said simultaneously.

As we proceeded along the Hebron road to our apartment, the storm clouds covered the entire sky, and the first raindrops began to hit our heads. As we looked around, it was apparent that everyone had taken cover.

"Should we grab a cab?" I hollered to my husband, the rain being so loud I had to raise my voice.

"No, we can make it," he boomed back. "It's only a twenty-minute walk, and we will go fast."

As the rain and wind increased, so did our footsteps. The streets had turned into roaring rivers that quickly soaked our shoes. Suddenly, amidst the wind and sheets of rain, the biggest eruption of thunder I had ever experienced sounded directly above us! I think my heart truly stopped for that moment. Dusk had turned into total darkness, which was only interrupted by the sudden flash of lightning from the heavens followed by more intense thunder. We looked at each other in shock and couldn't help but laugh, observing how silly we looked and the predicament we had managed to get ourselves into.

We forged ahead, but it wasn't long before we realized that we had been walking much longer than it should have taken us to arrive home. How in the world did we manage to take a wrong turn? We had not purchased cell phones, so we couldn't call for help (something we learned to do on our future trips), and the streets were empty.

As we trudged along, we noticed some lights on at a gas station in the distance. *Great*, we thought, *at least we can call a taxi from there!* As we approached the gas station, two men appeared, glaring at us. We stood back a bit, asking them loudly if we could use their phone. It just took a few minutes for us to realize that this was not a friendly neighborhood, so we quickly spun around and headed back down the street. If all else failed, we figured that we could backtrack and at least get to a safer neighborhood.

Our unfriendly encounter left us on high alert, and as soon as we were safely out of sight, we stopped a moment to say a prayer. It was simple and went something like this: "Please, God, lead us back to our apartment and send us your angels for protection."

It was still pouring when my husband paused, detecting what appeared to be a pathway off the main road.

"I think we should take this path," he announced.

"Here?" I was skeptical.

I followed his lead as we made our way through overgrown brush until we entered a slight clearing. Peering out into the darkness from behind the shrubs, we realized that we had come to a residential neighborhood.

"Now what?" I asked my trail-blazing husband.

"Let's just wait a minute," he said.

As we stood under the trees, some headlights appeared. A car pulled up to the curb just below where we were huddled. Soon, a woman got out of the car.

"I will ask her for directions…" I half-stated, half-asked my husband. (I was feeling a bit more timid since our gas-station experience.)

"Okay," he agreed. "She would be more likely to respond to another woman."

I attempted to be inconspicuous as I meandered out from behind the shrubbery, dripping and squishing my way to her car.

The woman immediately turned toward me and was noticeably shocked to see such a sight.

"Hello, I am sorry if I scared you. We are visitors and must have taken a wrong turn when this storm came. Can you give us some directions? This is my husband," I said, pointing to him as he poked his head out from behind the trees. He managed a friendly nod and smile. The woman seemed to relax as she inspected us and asked us where we were trying to go. She proceeded to give us directions in passable English. As we listened intently, it became clear that the Hebrew names of the streets only confused us more. My husband had twigs sticking out from his backpack and rain dripping off his long white beard. My mascara was now on my chin, and we were soggy, dripping Americans, lost and desperate.

The woman suddenly stopped mid-sentence and began to laugh.

"Get in my car. I am taking you home," she said.

"We don't want to get your car all wet," we responded.

But our rescuer insisted and repeated for us to get in her car.

We were both so grateful and tired that we didn't argue further. Once inside, we explained our predicament, which seemed to ease her curiosity.

"Where does the road lead just above your neighborhood behind the tree line?" I asked.

"That road leads to a very dangerous area. You don't want to be walking there, especially on a night like this!"

As the car turned into our neighborhood, a sense of relief filled me.

I looked at this stranger driving us home, knowing that she had rescued us from what could have been a much worse situation. I thanked her profusely, telling her that she was the angel we had prayed for just moments before.

She looked at me in amusement and said, "Your prayers must be highly favored! My last name is Angel. My family owns all the Angel bakery stores in Israel!"

As we sloshed into our apartment that stormy winter night, it was apparent to us both that miracles do occur.

— Miryam Howard-Meier —

You Have No Idea

The fragrance always stays in the hand
that gives the rose.
~Hada Bejar

ome years ago, when the General Motors plant closed in our city of 75,000 people, there was a feeling of sadness and doom. Combine that with gas prices that skyrocketed to over $4 a gallon and flooding from the river that went through town, damaging homes and businesses, and we had a recipe for depression.

Our church youth group decided to breathe some life back into our city by doing something nice with no strings attached. So, we went before our congregation and told them of our ideas, and an offering of $1,700 came in for us to use.

One of our ideas was to buy $25 gas cards and bouquets of roses and "randomly" give them out to people all around the city. I put "randomly" in quotes because our group knew it really wasn't left to chance. Before we distributed them, we all gathered in our youth room to pray that God would lead us to the people He wanted them to go to. After our prayer, about twenty-five teens and youth leaders piled into vehicles and our church van and started driving through the streets to find people who might need some encouragement.

Our high-school students had many great interactions as they gave roses to people working in their yards or out walking on the sidewalks on a beautiful day. And our middle-school students gave out the free gas cards to the customers at a gas station.

One interaction really stood out. Two middle-school boys watched as a young woman in her mid-twenties pulled up to the gas pump. The students were told not to approach anyone until they got out of their cars to pump their gas.

The young woman didn't get out of her car. Instead, she began looking through her purse, then her glove compartment and then frantically under her seats.

Then she put her hands and head on her steering wheel and began to sob. The thirteen-year-old boys weren't sure what they should do so they asked one of our youth leaders. He told them to politely knock on the window and offer a free gas card to her, which they did.

Upon hearing the knock, the young lady wiped away her tears, tried to compose herself and then rolled down the window. They said to her, "Here is a free twenty-five-dollar gas card for you, no strings attached. We just want you to know that God loves you."

The young woman began to cry again. After composing herself a second time, she accepted the gas card and then told them her story.

She was a single mom who had been out of a job for a long time. She was having trouble making ends meet but was optimistic about a job interview that she had that day. In fact, she was on her way to it. Her gas gauge was on empty, but she'd thought she had one last ten-dollar bill in her purse. Then she couldn't find it.

When it occurred to her that she wasn't going to be able to get to her job interview (a job she desperately needed to feed her kids), she broke down and began crying out to God.

"God, you know how badly I need this job. I can't find my last ten-dollar bill, and now I am going to miss my interview. Oh, God, I don't know what to do. I am so weary and tired, and I just feel like I have lost all hope."

She looked at the boys and said, "You have no idea what you have done for me. Thank you so much!" They watched tears of joy stream down her face as she began pumping her gas.

The boys went back to the youth leader and told them what had happened, so he gave them four more gas cards and a bouquet of roses to give to the young mom.

She couldn't believe it when they returned. "You all have done enough for me. I can't take anything else from you."

They insisted, and she finally accepted the gifts with new tears streaming down her face.

We have continued the tradition of handing out roses and/or gas cards once or twice a year for the past twelve years now. And every time God leads us to people who desperately need to know that they are loved.

Not only does it make a difference in the lives of those who receive the gifts, but it also makes a difference in the lives of the teens who get to see that God is never random. And they get to take part in something that is bigger than themselves.

—Michael T. Powers—

My Alpine Angel

Unexpected kindness is the most powerful, least costly,
and most underrated agent of human change.
~Bob Kerrey

I was already grumbling on my way to work. My husband Fred had told me I had to drive to our restaurant in Alpine and open it because he was playing in a golf tournament.

Fred and I had bought a little hamburger restaurant in Alpine, a small mountain town east of San Diego. Over the years, the one thing I'd said I never wanted to do was own a restaurant. Yet, here we were, owning Fred's Old-Fashioned Burgers, a true mom-and-pop establishment. If Pop wasn't there, then Mom was, seven days a week.

So, I grumbled all along Interstate 8, through El Cajon and Crest, and starting the incline toward Alpine, hoping to get there in time to let the employees in to begin the day's food prep. It started to rain, which is unheard of in southern California in August. Then there was thunder and lightning, which is even more unheard of. The higher up I drove, the harder the rain came down, making visibility difficult.

I drove on, mad at Fred for making me go up to the store in bad weather just so he could play golf in San Diego where it was dry and sunny. As I drove, I imagined our crew waiting for me to unlock the door so they could start work. I normally close the restaurant, but the one benefit of opening is the smell of bacon and onions frying to be ready for the day. That aroma gets my mouth watering.

I was vaguely aware that the interstate going into Alpine had a slight ditch on the left-hand side and a steep drop-off on the right with few guardrails. Halfway up the hill, I found myself suddenly sliding on the wet road. Before I knew it, I was hydroplaning and lost all control of the car. One second, I was driving north toward Alpine, and the next horrifying second, I was heading south facing oncoming traffic. Then the car, without any help from me, completed its 360-degree spin and thankfully went north again.

But Mother Nature wasn't through with me yet. The next thing I knew, I was moving sideways across I-8 heading toward the dangerous edge of the highway. Then I saw a pickup truck in the lane on my right. Since my brakes were useless, I heard the sound of metal against metal as I struck him. The collision bounced me across the road to the left and into a ditch where my car mercifully came to a bumpy, grinding stop.

I sat behind the wheel, dazed, and looked up only when I saw a police car pull over. The rain had let up, and the sun was now peeking out from the clouds. "Too little, too late," I mumbled to myself. The officer walked over and asked if I was hurt.

"No," I said. "I'm just shook up. And I have to get to work."

"You're not going anywhere in this car," he said as he took my license and registration information and then went over to see the driver of the truck, who had also pulled over. I glanced at my watch and saw that I was late for opening Fred's. I couldn't reach any of the employees to let them know what had happened as I had none of their phone numbers with me, so I called Fred and explained the situation.

"You'll have to come up and open the store," I said. I got out of the car on shaky legs and approached the truck owner to check on him and apologize for crashing into him. He stood outside his truck while his wife sat in the passenger seat. He explained that it was her birthday, and they had been on their way to do something to celebrate. I'd felt bad enough for hitting him, and now I felt even worse if that was possible.

And then something happened that was totally unexpected. He smiled at me and said, "I'm glad I was there for you to hit, or you would have gone right over the edge of the road."

I was speechless. How do you thank a stranger who says he's glad you crashed into him and damaged his truck? On his wife's birthday?

The tow truck came and took my totaled car away. Fred, after letting the employees in, came back and picked me up. He took me to the restaurant so I could finish my 10:30–8:00 shift.

My achy body may have been on the job, but my mind was on the sharp drop I could have careened over and the kindhearted driver's words: "I'm glad I was there for you to hit."

May I show even half that compassion to others.

— Linda Hemby —

Renewed Hope

*An effort made for the happiness
of others lifts us above ourselves.*
~Lydia M. Child

s I sat gently rocking and singing, my two and a half-year-old son, dressed only in a diaper, was lying on my chest. Eyes closed, blond curls damp and curly with heat, he looked so angelic. He was suffering from respiratory syncytial virus and had been in an oxygen tent for the last few days. It was Dec. 22nd, and we were staying at the Children's Hospital of Eastern Ontario.

As I rocked, my mind was working overtime. I worried about my nine-year-old daughter at home being looked after by her father. He and I had separated recently, and this was to be the first Christmas the kids would have without their dad at home. My daughter was having trouble relating to her brother who was taking up a lot of Mommy's time and energy. Add to that her mom and brother were in the hospital and might not make it home in time for Christmas.

I was also worrying about money. I was working as a manager for a retail chain, and it was the most hectic time of the year. I had already taken almost all my vacation time and knew I would not be paid for the days I was now taking off. This would put even more of a financial burden on me, and I had only a couple of hundred dollars in the bank. My ex was not able to help us financially so money was a big worry.

But my main concern was my son. His health had not been good.

He had had meningitis the year before, had missed all his baby and toddler milestones, wasn't talking, and still could not walk. His doctors feared he was developmentally delayed, and I wasn't sure what that might mean for the future. I didn't know how I would be able to manage, working full-time and looking after him and a headstrong nine-year-old girl. I had no family close by. I was feeling very low and very scared, a bad mom, guilty for failing my kids and not being able to solve all our issues. Feeling overwhelmed, I felt the tears well up and spill over.

And that's when Lorna arrived. She had been my assistant at one of the stores I had managed. Quickly blinking back the tears, I welcomed her in and lay the baby back into the tent. She had come to offer some support after her shift and had brought a card signed by the store managers and some of the office and warehouse staff as well, about fifteen people. I was touched they were thinking of me and that she had thought to organize this during a completely crazy work week. But as I read the card, I discovered there was more. Inside the card was this note. "Dear Alina. We want to help. Each person who has signed this card has donated one vacation day into your account. We know you need to spend some time with your son and don't want you to worry about having to take time off without pay."

Even the company owner had donated a day to me. I was speechless and got quite choked up. The tears quelled earlier now threatened to spill over again. I was so overwhelmed and touched by the gesture, the pure kindness with no thought of compensation. We sat and chatted for a little while, she, offering words of encouragement and reassurance that all would be well, and me wanting desperately to believe her.

After she left, I stood by the window. Darkness had fallen and a sprinkling of Christmas lights was visible. I took several calming breaths. I felt an inner peace just then, and a deep gratitude. I had been given some respite, some paid leave to catch my breath. If only we could get home in time, I felt sure I could pull some sort of Christmas celebration together for my kids.

I went to sleep on my cot that night with renewed hope. The next day we received a lovely blanket made by some kind-hearted ladies in the community; some local radio station DJs brought plush toys and played us Christmas music. We had a visit from CHEO Bear, the hospital mascot, and were entertained by a volunteer dressed as a clown. I felt so blessed by these gestures that gave a little bit of joy to children who were hurting. We did make it home on Dec. 24th. Christmas, although a little different that year, still had the decorations, tree, and lights of past years. There were gifts to open and a dinner to enjoy, and I had invited the kid's dad to join us.

In the years following, I wanted to pay forward the blessings I had received. I organized several fundraisers for the hospital, raising a total of $30,000. I manned the phones at CHEO telethons and did interviews about my son's various conditions to inspire viewers to donate to the hospital foundation. From one of our company suppliers, I organized the donations of hundreds of plush toys for the emergency department and pediatric wards at the hospital, and more for my local Children's Aid society and paramedic service. I enjoy making baby blankets to donate to programs for young mothers and lap blankets for seniors in long term care.

My life has been full of challenges. I've been a single mom for twenty-one years. It turns out my son, now twenty-three, is severely physically and intellectually disabled and will need 24/7 care for the rest of his life. Now, no matter how overwhelmed I am, at the end of each day, I look back and pick out at least one positive thing that happened and allow myself to feel good about it. I always try to practice gratitude and thankfulness for the blessings we have. I used to try and be supermom and do everything myself, but now I let others help, which makes them feel good, too.

My company awarded me a handsome volunteer medal to recognize my fundraising efforts. I was touched by the gesture but felt I didn't need to be thanked. I truly believe that nurturing kindness and love for the people in your community is the greatest reward you can receive. And the love will come back to you tenfold.

— Alina Ottembrajt —

Chicken Soup for the Soul

Advent Angel

*We are not put on earth for ourselves, but are placed
here for each other. If you are there always for others,
then in time of need, someone will be there for you.*
~Jeff Warner

We hardly knew her even though she lived just down the country road from the parsonage where we lived. "I'd like to meet the twins," Charlotte said over the phone. "How does this evening sound?" Church members popped in unannounced, but our neighbor's formality piqued our curiosity. Erik and I got busy cleaning the parsonage to within an inch of its life.

Late that afternoon, after the children were fed, I wrestled the diapers into position around the twins' spindly, little legs. I giggled as Erik skipped down the stairs with three-year-old Isaak and two-year-old Sam each dangling from an arm. He settled the boys on the floor in their footed sleepers and handed them trucks from the toy box while I swaddled Ben and Dom together in a single, handmade quilt. Born six weeks early and not yet five pounds each, they were an adorable, two-headed baby bundle, as content as could be.

Erik plopped down beside me. "Now all we have to do is stay awake until our mystery guest arrives."

I laid my head on his shoulder and yawned. "And pray the peace holds until after she leaves."

"Tell me more about her," Erik said, building Isaak and Sam a

Miracles of Kindness | 25

tower of blocks.

"I don't know much," I replied, cradling the twins. "Charlotte's a retired grade-school teacher. That's all I know."

The boys revved their engines. Crash! Bang! Blocks flew in all directions, giving the twins a start.

Erik gathered the colorful rubble and piled it into a front loader for a return trip to the toy box. "Where'd you two meet?" he asked, on all fours.

"That's the funny part," I said, bouncing the twins as they squirmed. "It was our first December in the parsonage. I was putting up holiday decorations when she knocked on the front door and invited herself in. She said she was a Baptist and wanted to learn how we Lutherans observe the Season of Advent."

I paused, remembering the excitement of that chilly December morning. I'd just assembled our Advent wreath with its blue tapered candles and evergreen sprigs and encircled it with my angel collection. I was so proud of my decorating prowess. The winged figurines, illuminated by candlelight, shimmered against the backdrop of the dining-room mirror and leaded glass cabinets.

My cheeks flushed as I remembered what came next. "Her visit was so unexpected. I fumbled through my Advent lesson like a child playing *Chopsticks* on the piano for the very first time." I shook my head. "I haven't seen her since and figured I'd scared her off."

Just then, we heard footsteps on the front porch followed by a firm knock on the wooden door. The sound reverberated through the timbers of the venerable old parsonage like a clap of thunder.

Isaak and Sam put down their trucks and padded over to see what was going on.

Determined to make a better impression this time around, I handed Erik the twins and hurried to the door.

Charlotte stood there dressed in pink with a halo of silver hair. She peeked at me over an enormous laundry basket. I could barely make out her impish grin.

"Welcome. Please, come in." I still wasn't quite sure what to expect.

She set down the basket. "I brought a little something for your family." She chuckled and put her arms around the boys.

I couldn't believe my eyes. The laundry basket was filled to the brim with presents of every shape and size.

She handed everyone a package, waiting for each of us to open our gift in turn. Isaak and Sam received coloring books. Erik got a bottle of wine. She gave me some scented lotions. For the twins, she brought diapers, booties and teething rings in sets of two.

When we were done admiring our gifts, Charlotte spoke directly to me. "You know, I'm the mother of twins. Of course, they're grown women with children of their own now."

At that, Erik brought the twins close so Charlotte could look at the babies she'd come to meet. She touched their delicate noses and hands and watched as they slept. Her eyes twinkled as if remembering earlier times. "How do you tell them apart?"

"It's really quite easy," I said as I caressed their cheeks with the tip of my finger. "We rub our hands across their heads. Ben's downy hair stands on end like a dandelion clock. Dom's silky hair lies flat. At night, we don't even need to turn on the light."

Charlotte nodded. "My girls were fraternal twins. They looked so different we never mixed them up."

I wanted to sit beside her and share more twin stories, but Charlotte kept looking around.

"I imagine your parishioners are helping you out," she said, gathering her things.

"Well," I chose my words carefully, "the women delivered some meals right after the twins were born." My gratitude sounded anemic, even to me.

She stopped in her tracks. "Is that all?" She scowled. "A few meals? I had assistance for an entire year."

Once again, she'd caught me off-guard. "They're giving us our privacy," I said, sounding more appreciative than I felt.

Charlotte would have none of it. "You need help." She grabbed her basket and headed for the door. "I'll be here tomorrow. How does 10:00 sound?"

Our bleary-eyed smiles were her answer.

From that day on, Charlotte came by the parsonage several times a week. She folded mountains of laundry, cuddled the boys, and read them countless stories. She made sure Erik and I got out for walks or took much-needed naps. On days she couldn't stay, she'd sneak in by way of the back door and leave a gift: a doily for the kitchen table, a plate of cookies, or a craft project for the boys. She witnessed firsthand our life in the parsonage as harried parents of four little boys. Never once did she express disapproval or offer unwanted advice; she allowed us to find our own way.

To this day, our grown boys refer to the kind and generous woman they remember from their childhood as Gramma Charlotte. Erik calls her Saint Charlotte. To me, she was my helper, confidante and friend. Each year, as I light the Advent candles, I'm reminded that Charlotte was my Angel of Kindness.

— Mary T. Post —

Mr. Overstreet

No one has ever become poor by giving.
~Anne Frank

I was seventeen years old and didn't have enough money to go to college. My mom, a single parent, was working as a secretary for Mr. R.T. Overstreet, then eighty-one, and president of the Overstreet Investment Company.

Over the years, Mr. Overstreet had often asked my mom to type up checks for various charitable contributions. Seeing this, Mom suggested that I meet with Mr. Overstreet and ask if his company would consider making a charitable contribution to help me pay for my college.

My gut told me to do it, but I was nervous. I walked into his large office, and he offered me a seat. I cut to the chase. I told Mr. Overstreet — with all the passion I could muster — that I wanted a college education so badly, and I promised him that I would graduate #1 in my class, with a perfect 4.0 GPA, if his company would only take a chance on me and help with college.

He told me that he would have to run my request by the board of directors. He asked me to come back next Tuesday.

I couldn't sleep the night before the big day. I went to his office and awaited the decision. Mr. Overstreet informed me that his corporation would not be able to pay my college tuition. He said if the corporation paid for my education, they would have to do it for all the employees.

I thanked Mr. Overstreet for at least trying. And then, uncontrollably, tears started to run down my face. It hit me at that moment that my dream of getting a college education would never come true.

Mr. Overstreet then leaned over toward me, and said, "Son, you can wipe the tears away. I said the company couldn't pay for your college; I didn't say that I couldn't." With that, Mr. Overstreet cut a check and sent me to college.

Four years later, I had the happy privilege of keeping my promise to Mr. Overstreet. I graduated first in my class, with a 4.0 GPA. I then went on to Vanderbilt Law School, and Mr. Overstreet lived just long enough to see me graduate.

Eight years later, on November 7, 2000, I was elected to the United States Congress. In my victory speech that night, I thanked Mr. Overstreet. As I spoke from the stage podium, I imagined Mr. Overstreet looking down from heaven. I hoped he would be proud of me. I know I was proud of him.

I couldn't possibly know it that night on stage, but I would eventually become Chairman of the House Higher Education subcommittee, which increased college financial aid for low-income students (called Pell Grants) by 62 percent.

Mr. Overstreet's single act of kindness to one poor kid who needed a break ended up helping over five million students from low-income families go to college.

— Ric Keller —

10

Chicken Soup for the Soul

Think Positive

Gratitude is the inward feeling of kindness received.
Thankfulness is the natural impulse to express that feeling.
Thanksgiving is the following of that impulse.
~Henry Van Dyke

A few years back, we found ourselves in a financial pinch. We were a one-income family with two small children; making ends meet was hard. People around us kept saying, "Think positive," "One day, you'll get there," and "You'll be okay."

It's difficult to do that when you think there's no end in sight, but my husband and I decided not to be depressed about it and to make the most of what we had. After all, we were all healthy and happy; that was important, too.

But, one Tuesday, we hit rock bottom. My husband said we needed groceries and asked me for some money. I did not have any; we were broke. He said he would put it on the credit card. No money there either. But it was Tuesday, and payday was not until Friday. How were we going to feed the kids?

I told my husband I had to go to work, and I would think about it on my way there. I knew I had to think positive and somehow it would work out.

I was getting a ride with my co-worker, Jeff, since we were a one-car family, and I contemplated asking him if I could borrow a twenty-dollar bill until Friday. But he was already nice enough to give me a ride every day, and I did not want him to think I was trying to take advantage.

So, when I arrived at work, I was in a bit of a panic. Who should I ask? What if no one could help me? What would we do? I knew I had to think positive, so I decided to swallow my pride and ask another co-worker for some money. I would write an IOU, be thankful, and hope this situation would never happen again.

But before getting to my co-worker, Alan, I went first to our locker room. I was surprised to see envelopes in each employee mailbox. What was that all about?

I opened mine and almost passed out. It was a fifty-dollar Visa gift card, and it was attached to a letter from our CEO. He thanked all the employees for the hard work we'd done and announced that since we had met our company goals, everyone was the recipient of this present. How did he decide to distribute the cards on that very day? I'll never know....

After the surprise had passed, Alan walked in the locker room. He said he was looking for me. He then handed me his envelope and gift card. I was shocked. He said he knew we were in a pinch, and he thought we could put it to good use. He wouldn't take no for an answer and told me to accept it. I started crying. But then Ali and Minerva came in the room. They both gave me their cards, too. They said they had watched my husband and me work so hard and make many sacrifices for our family, and they wanted to help. They made me promise to put the gifts cards to good use.

I was in tears and did not know what to say besides "Thank you" a million times. I could not believe how we went from nothing to $200 in one afternoon. I called my husband and told him to start the grocery list because we were going to the store in the morning.

He said, "But how?"

I replied, "Think positive. Think positive. Everything is okay now."

— Betty Farkas-Hart —

Chapter 2

Role Models
of Kindness

Three Months of Thursdays

*Just being there for someone can sometimes bring hope
when all seems hopeless.*
~Dave G. Llewelyn

One December, I was stranded with one-year-old Gail and three-year-old Bruce in a tract house on the side of a small mountain. Our car, which I had no license to drive, was buried in a snowbank, and my parents were ninety icy miles away. My husband Morrie had just signed himself into the psychiatric ward of the veterans' hospital in New York City, forty-five miles away.

My visits were supposed to be part of Morrie's therapy. Visiting hours were limited to the afternoon, and the train was my only option for getting there. But how? I had the kids and no car, and I didn't know anyone who could help.

We had moved into our "dream home" barely three months before, and I had met only two of our neighbors. The closest, about a city block away, had eleven children and was pregnant with the twelfth. She was too busy with the cleaning, cooking and taking care of her family to notice me or my problem. Other neighbors, Jane and Chet, about two blocks away, had four children. One of their children was Bruce's age, and they hit it off right away. Play dates had become a highlight for all of us to get together.

Jane was an excellent manager/mother, and when she heard about my plight, she said immediately, "Now, how can we solve this problem? I could pick up you and the kids, drop you at the railroad station, and then take Bruce and Gail back to my house until you come back. Then I could pick you up at the station and bring you and the kids home."

"Jane," I said, "that is a huge responsibility for you to take on with all you have to do with your own family."

"The kids love to play together, and I can manage the transportation with Chet's help," she answered confidently.

I was overwhelmed by her kind offer, but it was my only solution. Thursday was the day she was most comfortable with, and the following Thursday she picked up the kids and me, dropped me at the train station, and said cheerfully, "I'll pick you up at 6:30."

The visit was a nightmare. My husband was belligerent and violent, and I wondered whether my visit had been helpful at all. It certainly wasn't for me. His psychiatrist, however, said it would help. I tried to pull myself together on the long train ride home so that Jane, her family and my kids would not know what an ordeal it had been. Jane, however, was marvelously perceptive. She took one look at me and said, "I have a great dinner. Won't you please stay?"

The kids were all happy and boisterous, and she and Chet were wonderful hosts. Their love for their family and each other was obvious in the interactions between them and the children. It spilled over to me and the kids. My misery subsided, and by the time she drove us home, the love and kindness in her family had me believing everything was going to be okay.

For the next three months, every Thursday at 12:30, Jane showed up, no matter the weather. Often, the roads were icy or slushy, and getting down the mountain to the railroad station was hazardous. She never mentioned the road conditions, but after we settled the kids in the back seat and I got in the passenger seat, she made the sign of the cross, kissed her finger and touched it to the Saint Christopher rosary hanging on the rearview mirror.

I boarded the train each week with a mixture of apprehension and hope about the visit. As I looked out the window on the ride into the city I wondered if the people in the great houses I saw, surrounded by picture-postcard snowy lawns, were happy in their beautiful surroundings. When the train became elevated in upper Manhattan, the tenements were at eye level, and I could peer into the long, dark hallways and shabby apartments. Curtains on the windows were tattered and torn. Gratefulness for my little, sunlit house filled my heart.

Some of the visits went well, and Morrie would show interest in the kids' antics and achievements. Other times, he became angry at me for "putting me here." I learned to duck when he tried to punch me. I spoke softly when he yelled.

Jane, always perceptive, could tell how the visit went without me saying a word. When the visit went poorly, she always had a "great dinner" waiting at home and made sure I was okay before she or Chet drove us home.

Morrie did not progress, and when he signed himself out of the hospital against medical advice, his psychiatrist told me to take the kids and go as far away as I could to make a new life for my little family. We left suddenly, with no forwarding address, and I never saw Jane, Chet and her wonderful family again. Without her kindness, I never could have survived those awful three months. Her love and the way she conducted her life have been an inspiration to me.

— Joy Feldman —

12

The Unexpected Visitor

A single act of kindness throws out roots in all directions,
and the roots spring up and make new trees.
~Amelia Earhart

We were joyfully awaiting the birth of our first child. As August approached, our excitement (along with a certain amount of nervousness) increased.

I had been terribly ill the entire time — not simply with first-trimester morning sickness but with intermittent vomiting for the entire nine months. So, I was happy to hear "Just a few more days" when we visited the doctor for a checkup. With my aching back, swollen ankles, and an overwhelming sense of fatigue I was ready for this journey to end.

Since we did not know the gender of our little one, we had designed the nursery in shades of yellow and green with an animal décor. The crib was made, the closet was filled with outfits, and the dresser was overflowing with diapers, undershirts, receiving blankets, and other miscellaneous items for a newborn. We had not decided on a boy's name, but I had chosen the name Heather if we had a little girl. I remembered seeing the wind blowing through fields of wild heather when visiting England, and that name was especially meaningful to me.

Three days after the last doctor visit, I sensed something was wrong. There was suddenly no movement and a physical sense of heaviness.

I called my mother, a nurse, and she could hear the concern in my voice. She reminded me that babies often quieted down near delivery time. She suggested I call the doctor and ask her to check me — just to allay my concerns.

The next thirty-one hours were a blurred nightmare as I dealt with the unexpected, horrifying words, "I'm so sorry, but there is no heartbeat."

My world collapsed as I entered the hospital and endured twenty-nine hours of labor — knowing each hour that I would never hold my baby alive. My arms already ached, and I felt my heart had broken into pieces and was scattered from east to west. My dream of holding Heather had turned into a terrifying nightmare. A six-and-a-half-pound girl was born who never took her first breath. Tests later revealed no known cause for Heather's death, which made her loss even harder to bear.

I did not know that the worst pain was yet to come. Since all our friends were our age and beginning their own families, I was surrounded by little ones and toddlers. I waited for the comfort these friends would provide, but it never came. Not a single new-parent friend came to us in our greatest hour of need.

I had become good friends with a single lady in our church who had been on a mission trip to Africa during the last weeks of my pregnancy. I learned later that she had been led to pray for my husband, myself, and the baby for several days. Then, suddenly, she was prompted to pray simply for Dave and myself. Upon exiting the plane, she immediately asked her family, "What happened to Dave and Carol's baby?" Unknown to us — or anyone — Mary had been being prepared to be God's messenger to us — two brokenhearted people whose world had been completely shattered.

Mary called two days later and asked if she could come for a visit. I did not know how I could deal with anyone, but I agreed. When she came to the door, her swollen eyes told the story of her fountain of tears.

And, in her hand, she held a single red rose.

The afternoon went by. There was no advice on how to go forward. There were no words of encouragement for the days to come. There were rivers of tears from both of us, hands held in support, and shoulders hugged in deep friendship.

The shared tears of grief, I later realized, were the beginning of a long healing process.

I also later realized that our friends who did not come around did not do so out of a lack of caring but out of discomfort. They were so frightened of saying the wrong thing that they chose to say nothing. They were so fearful that seeing their young ones would upset us that they chose to stay away altogether. They did not realize their absence made our grief deeper.

And yet there was Mary — a single lady with no children of her own — who stepped forward at the most hurtful time in our lives to lend a healing hand and heart. She could not say she knew how we felt, yet she was willing to give of herself to another. Perhaps she even felt that her gesture was insignificant.

That August afternoon occurred in 1972, forty-nine years ago. An entire lifetime to some folks — and to myself at times. Yet the power of that visit remains as fresh in my memory as if it were yesterday. I kept that red rose in my Bible for so many years that it eventually fell apart.

Mary's act of kindness and thoughtfulness is a reminder in several ways. It reminds me that we do not need to experience the same situation as another to be of help. It reminds me that an act of kindness can transcend years and continue to bring healing long after. It reminds me that what may seem like a small gesture of kindness can dramatically change a life forever.

I am certain Mary had no idea how much her visit and flower meant to Dave and me. Yet she followed her heart and was willing to share in the pain and grief of another. She was willing to experience the cost to herself.

The reminder of her willingness to share of herself has prompted me many times over the years to do likewise. May it be a reminder to each of us to share of ourselves, even when it may seem small at the time.

— Carol Goodman Heizer —

13

A Grandpa to More Than 200 Kids Every Year

How far that little candle throws his beams!
So shines a good deed in a weary world.
~William Shakespeare

I first met Mr. John Southwell when I was covering County Court as a reporter for the local newspaper. That Monday, the county was donating surplus funds to a group named HANK, which I'd never heard of.

HANK, which stands for Helping Abused and Neglected Kids, is a small organization started up by Mr. Southwell and his wife, Debbie. They run it from their home office along with a board of volunteers.

For many years, they had been CASA volunteers, who are like mentors for foster children. During that time, Debbie told me she had seen firsthand that the State Services did not provide everything these foster children needed to be comfortable and happy. Things like band instruments, Christmas gifts, or birthday gifts for kids in State care. Or a set of bunk beds, cribs, clothes, and other necessities for an elderly grandmother who takes in four young grandchildren removed from their home due to abuse or neglect. If a non-offending relative cannot care for them, these children have to be placed in an unfamiliar group home that's miles away from everything they know.

So, HANK steps in to buy these things for all local foster children, taking requests straight from caseworkers when these kids need something the State won't provide.

After the County meeting, I asked Mr. Southwell for an interview. I was so impressed by the things he told me. The first thing he said is that there were 100–200 foster children in our little three-county area at any given time. I was the editor of the local newspaper, and I had absolutely no idea there were so many foster children right here in our community.

The next thing he explained is that more than 99 cents of every dollar donated to HANK goes straight to kids. He wouldn't put up with any nonsense. HANK volunteers take nothing for operating expenses. The only expense was the $100 a year spent for postage and office supplies, etc.

From that first meeting, I knew right then and there that this was the best charity in Medina County. Being in the newspaper business, we see and help promote them all. In a small town like ours, there are a lot of great groups helping neighbors with just about anything. They are all beautiful. But this organization was unique and really spoke to my heart.

So, I wrote article after article, doing everything I could to educate our community on how many local foster children there are and what we could do to help them.

One of the Southwells' goals was to raise enough money to build a community foster home in each of the local towns because finding a warm bed for a foster child was difficult. The local judge told me they often have to send kids to foster homes four hours away or even farther because there is simply no available bed for them in our area.

HANK began to see great support from our hometown, and that dream to build community foster homes soon came true. In 2016, they built their first community foster home in Devine, just a block away from our newspaper office, in large part due to an awesome grant from The Greehey Family Foundation.

"The Devine community has shown us great support, and so that's exactly where we are going to build our first foster home," Mr.

Southwell told me, excited to announce the news. In 2017, they were able to build a second home in the neighboring town of Hondo, Texas, which is where the Southwells live and where HANK, Inc. began.

One of the coolest projects HANK does is the Christmas shopping trip, where they buy a special $50 gift for every local child in foster care. Instead of getting a random gift for a ten-year-old boy or a twelve-year-old girl, these children all receive that special toy they've been dreaming of.

Mr. Southwell is an inspiration to me and everyone who meets him. To see this husband-and-wife team working side by side just blows me away. She had a dream and, boy, did he run with it! Their "little" organization, run out of their home office, has purchased some 15,000 Christmas gifts, birthday gifts, and sets of school supplies. They have built two community foster homes with twelve warm, comfortable beds. That's not to mention the thousands of other things HANK has purchased for kids in need over the past ten years.

Mr. Southwell is growing older and battles many health problems nowadays. All the while, he is doing more good and helping more kids than most of us will do in our lifetime.

The Southwells were both hit by COVID-19 in December 2020. The virus left one of the strongest, best men I know simply too weak to stand. Mr. Southwell was hospitalized for a week but is home and back to helping kids.

He called me soon after getting home from the hospital to give me an update on HANK, which is expanding to serve a five-county area due to the generosity of people in our community. He also mentioned that some of the kids in the HANK homes had turned eighteen.

"When children age out of the foster-care system at eighteen, they often have nowhere to go. Statistics show that one in five of these children end up homeless in the U.S. With no way to make a good living, many of these kids turn to drugs or prostitution. But that isn't going to happen to any of my kids in our HANK homes!" he said matter of factly.

He wasn't two days out of the hospital, and he was already making plans to help these kids in more ways.

And I knew he was going to make sure of it, somehow, some way.

Mr. Southwell's love for these kids is so honest and obvious, and he has surely been a loving "grandpa" figure to hundreds of kids over the years, always making sure that their care providers have what the children need and deserve, and that they have something to unwrap on their birthdays and Christmas.

Before we got off the phone last week, he mentioned that they had just celebrated his birthday. "I think I'm eighty-eight now or something like that," he said with a chuckle.

I just about fell out of my chair because I would never have guessed. It's hard to believe that an eighty-eight-year-old is running this awesome, homespun, non-profit organization, raising tens of thousands of dollars a year and providing for every need of every precious child. Every time we talk, he proudly reports, "We have never had to turn down a caseworker's request for help, thanks to the generosity of this community."

I'm thirty-three years old right now, and I hope that I'm doing as much good as he is in the year 2075!

— Kayleen Kitty Holder —

For the Love of Pete

A little thought and a little kindness are often
worth more than a great deal of money.
~John Ruskin

I'll call him Pete because I didn't take the time to ask his name. A nameless hero who forged his way into my heart.

I had taken Robert, my eight-year-old son, to a taco joint to celebrate his birthday. Lil' Bob, we called Robert, wore his brand-new cowboy boots into the lobby, his face shining with pride and joy. This was Lil' Bob's special day.

We approached the counter, where Pete greeted us with a palpable warmth. His brown eyes twinkled with kindness.

"Welcome," he said with a smile. "Wow, don't you look happy, little fellow." Pete brought his face close to Lil' Bob's level.

"I got cowboy boots," Lil' Bob boasted. "I picked them out myself." Lil' Bob lifted his right foot in the air so Pete could see the hand-stitched leather.

"Smell them," Lil' Bob demanded.

"Robert," I said, attempting to correct his unsocial demand.

Pete came around the counter and dropped to his knees. Lil' Bob almost kicked Pete in the head as Pete brought his nose to the boot. He took a long whiff and then closed his eyes as he pulled away.

"Those boots smell amazing, like fresh leather," Pete said. He opened his eyes and looked directly into Lil' Bob's eyes. "Thank you for sharing your special smell with me."

Lil' Bob beamed at Pete's reaction. Then, Pete returned to the register.

"What does the birthday boy want to drink? It's on me," Pete offered.

Lil' Bob shuffled back and forth in excitement since soda was a rare treat in our home. Now, he could order any soda he wanted. Lil' Bob considered the many possibilities, taking more time than a fast-food customer should. Eventually, he settled on root beer.

"Excellent choice, my friend. It's what I would have picked myself."

Pete's validation brought a massive smile to Lil' Bob's face. We ordered our meals and watched as Pete assembled the drinks and food on the tray before us. When everything was on it, I reached for the tray, but Pete said, "Let me carry it out for you." Pete followed us to the lobby as the birthday boy took a considerable amount of time picking the perfect table. Pete patiently held our tray until we were seated.

"Wow, he is nice," Lil' Bob observed after Pete had walked away. I had to agree — something about Pete emanated love.

As Lil' Bob and I enjoyed his birthday lunch, Pete worked dutifully behind the counter. I observed him with each customer who came in, watching Pete treat all customers with extreme respect and courtesy. He looked everyone in the eyes, gave each person a kind smile, and spoke with them about their day. And when their food was ready, he carried it to their table.

I had been to that taco joint plenty of times in the past. It wasn't their policy to carry the food out for the customer. I imagine Pete did that out of the love he felt for everyone.

Toward the end of our stay, Pete came to our table and gave Lil' Bob a coupon for a free meal to use in the future.

"Happy birthday, little man," Pete said. "And I love the boots."

My mother's heart swelled with thanksgiving for this man who made my son feel marvelous.

Pete taught me a great deal about love that day. Although his service might sound small and insignificant, it changed me for life.

Pete had a simple job without any prestige. Yet, he served everyone he encountered with a genuine love all could feel.

I think about Pete often when I encounter people. What impression do I want to leave with them? How do I want to make them feel? I look people in the eyes, like Pete did. I smile and validate all they have to say and offer. I want to be like Pete.

I talked with Robert, no longer Lil' Bob, today about Pete. Robert's face lit up.

"He was such a nice guy," Robert said. "That was my favorite part of the day." Eight years later, Robert still can feel Pete's kindness. For Robert, the memory of Pete managed to surpass his picking out the cowboy boots, which he wore for two years straight. Pete left a phenomenal impact.

In life, we often judge and rank people by material worth or university degrees. However, the true value of a person comes from how they treat others. Pete taught me that day how to love and care for all I encounter. Pete was a mighty man.

Thank you, Pete.

— Stephanie Daich —

15

Everyone Loves Donuts

Donuts. Is there anything they can't do?
~Matt Groening

Her birth name was Elizabeth, but a friend said a long time ago that she had the "presence of Buddha" and that description, shortened to the moniker, Budd, stuck. She was my friend, as she was friend to many: those who knew her and many who never met her at all but whose lives were improved because of her unselfishness and kindness.

It was a brisk November day when she and I traveled to a conference for children's rights in Washington, D.C. We often traveled together for work, and I treasured those trips. We had wonderful talks and met fascinating people, all working for the causes of children, single mothers, or underprivileged people who just needed a little help. It was fascinating to see the world through her eyes.

She was much older than I was, and, in those days, she walked with a cane. So, I felt privileged to watch out for her and know she was watching out for me. While we were both accustomed to traveling alone, it was always more fun to explore together. I learned so much, and she appreciated my contributions to her work in a way that was unusual in my experience.

We always took adjoining rooms, and since we were both early risers, we usually had a quiet breakfast together before we started our long days of meetings and presentations.

That morning, I awoke a little late and was surprised that she had not already woken me. I hurriedly got dressed and knocked on her door, calling her name. No answer. I checked her room and found it empty and her bed made. Curious, I wondered where she could be before 6:00 A.M. I was a little worried.

I decided she must have gone for coffee without me, so quickly throwing on a sweater, I headed for the hotel coffee shop. There was no one around, not even at the front desk. It was eerie. The all-glass coffee shop at the front of the lobby overlooked the quiet Capitol Hill street. I could see the wind blowing leaves around and wondered how cold it was out there. I hurried over to speak to the man behind the counter, the only person I had seen.

I said, "I'm looking for my friend — an older lady with a cane..."

His face lit up in a big smile, and he said, "Oh, yes, she was here. She had a cup of coffee, and then she bought every donut I had this morning!"

Then I knew where to find Budd. So, pulling my sweater tight against the wind, I opened the door and headed out into the pre-dawn light. As I turned the corner from the hotel, I could see her bright purple coat about a block away. She was talking to a man wrapped in a blanket. I hurried toward her and, with a bit of alarm in my voice, called, "Budd, what on Earth are you doing out here? It's barely daylight. I was frightened."

As I reached her, she turned toward me with that peaceful smile she so often wore and said, "I'm okay. I am sharing some donuts. You know everyone loves donuts." Then I saw them up and down both sides of the street: about a dozen homeless people, all biting into a warm donut and smiling.

— Glenda Wood —

16

The Cup of Coffee

Kind words can be short and easy to speak,
but their echoes are truly endless.
~Mother Teresa

It was supposed to be a normal trip to the supermarket. My son was little, and it was getting close to naptime, so I was rushing through the aisles trying to avoid a meltdown. I remember feeling a sense of accomplishment as I got him into the car without any tears. Then I went to start the car and realized my keys were gone. After a few minutes of checking around, I realized that I must have locked them in the trunk with my bag.

I wasn't sure what to do, so I took my son out of his car seat and went back inside the store with my cart still full of groceries. I had to use their phone to call my husband for the spare key because my phone was in the bag I had locked in the trunk. After multiple calls and messages with no answer, I was getting frustrated. My son was tired and getting fussy. I was exhausted from a sleepless night that all moms go through when their kids are teething. When he went into full-on crying, I felt the tears come down my face, too.

An employee at the store tapped me on the shoulder and asked me to come with her. I was panicked for a moment, thinking that I was going to be scolded and thrown into the storage area to keep us quiet. The employee — whose name I would later find out was Kelly — took me, to my surprise, to the Starbucks café that was inside the store. She asked me if I drank coffee. When I said yes, she walked over to the counter and came back with one for me.

She said that it looked like I was having one of those days and that, as a mom, she had them, too. I told her how stupid I felt locking my keys in the car, and she assured me it happened to a lot of people. As we talked, my son settled into a sound sleep in my arms. After about fifteen minutes, she said her break was over, and she had to get back to work. She said if I couldn't get in touch with my husband, they would call someone to come out and get the trunk open. Also, my meat and dairy groceries would be replaced with new ones free of charge.

After I got home that day, I kept thinking about what she had done for me and wanted to do something for her. When I saw her working again at the store, I told her how grateful I was. She would accept nothing in return and just told me to pay it forward. The store has since closed, and I never saw her again, but I never have forgotten the kindness she showed me that day.

So, Kelly from the Safeway in Delaware, these are the things that *you* have done because I was thinking of your kindness as I did them:

Multiple doors held for people, letting someone ahead of me in line, picking up trash that someone tossed on the ground, hitting "yes" on the donation button at the checkout, helping a woman with heavy bags, food donations, helping a stranger find her glasses, and many others.

I am so glad I locked my keys in the car that day. I am a better person because of my encounter with Kelly. Who would have thought one act of kindness could have so much of an effect on a person?

— Kelly Okoniewski —

17

The Kind Clerk

If you really are thankful, what do you do? You share.
~W. Clement Stone

Not too long ago, I was at the grocery store, and an elderly man in front of me was using a Supplemental Nutrition Assistance Program (SNAP) card — what we used to call food stamps. The card reader kept rejecting his payment. He had apparently gone over his limit for the month. He was confused about how it had happened and more than a little distressed about the situation.

While I was trying to decide if the man would be offended or grateful if I offered to step in and pay the difference, the young man checking him out (who looked to still be in high school) said, "Sir, this happens all the time. It's not a problem. I bet we can figure out a solution together."

The line behind us was growing long, but the young man didn't show an ounce of impatience or irritation. He confirmed that the man was, indeed, over his limit for the month and found the amount of the overage. Turned out, he wasn't over by much, so the checker helped the customer determine which two or three items that he could make do without until his account was replenished.

"You'll definitely want to keep the milk and the butter and the eggs and the bread," I remember him saying as he looked through the already bagged groceries. Then the clerk, who had clearly done this before, pulled out a jar of salsa, a bottle of juice and some crackers that he and his customer agreed could wait until the beginning of the new month.

The young man assured his older customer, once again, that this was a common occurrence and not a problem at all. The man left with his dignity intact and, no doubt, with a renewed sense of loyalty to that grocery-store chain.

When it was my turn, I told the young man that he had done an extraordinary job of handling the situation. The kid looked at me kind of funny when he said, "Thanks." It was obvious that he didn't understand what I was talking about. He didn't see that he had done something that others might not have done in his position.

I made note of the name on his nametag, and when I got home, I sent an e-mail to the manager of the store commending the employee for his kindness and customer service. I got a return e-mail that day with thanks from the manager, letting me know that my note would be included in the employee's file and noted each time he was up for a raise or promotion.

While his act of kindness made a positive impact on the life of someone who was struggling that day, I hope my act of kindness at least had a positive effect on that young man's career — and possibly his paycheck.

— Anne Russ —

The Grocery Store Trip

Small acts of kindness can make a difference in other
people's lives more than we can imagine.
~Catherine Pulsifer

My two-year-old daughter was lovingly squished between a stack of groceries in one of my two shopping carts. Holding a frozen pizza, she smiled and giggled happily, poking at the pepperonis through the cellophane wrapper.

Shopping once a month was a well-planned process. My list was organized so that I wouldn't miss even one item. I knew the aisle, order, and cost of each item. Budgeting was important to me. Times were lean as we adjusted to the financial responsibility of our new house.

A gentleman in a suit stood behind me with three items. He looked up at his watch, then at me and smiled.

I'd already let two people ahead of me with single items. While my daughter was behaving well, I knew I'd pushed her longer than her endurance promised to last. Still, I felt for the man; he obviously had to be somewhere, and he'd be behind me a good long time.

"Why don't you go ahead of me?" I said shifting the cart backwards. "You only have a couple of items."

"Thank you," He replied appreciatively stepping ahead of me.

My daughter gave him a flirty smile, "Heh wo," she said in her sweetest voice. She then showed him her pizza.

"Hello," he replied, taken off guard by her friendliness. His face lit with pleasure.

As the belt moved forward I started unloading my cart. His few items were ahead of mine separated by a red marker with the store name on it.

I was only halfway finished unloading the first cart when a realization hit me. My husband had borrowed my bank card the night before and I couldn't recall him putting it back in my wallet.

I hurriedly dug out my purse and opened my wallet, My heart dropped. He hadn't returned it.

The gentleman in front of me had paid and was picking up his groceries.

"I've forgotten my bank card; will you take a credit card?" I asked the cashier hopefully.

"I'm sorry ma'am. We only accept debit or cash." The cashier looked down the lane, disgusted at the amount of groceries I'm sure she was predicting she'd have to put back on the shelves.

"It will take me an hour to run home and an hour back. Can you just put my stuff on the side please?" I was discouraged. All my careful planning hadn't helped. The hour and a half of shopping left me exhausted and I wasn't sure how my daughter would handle another two hours in the car.

"Let me." The gentleman in front of me said. "I'll pay for her order."

"I couldn't let you do that!" I protested, having over $250 worth of groceries.

"You can just send me a check." He smiled warmly. "That's too much of a car trip for the little one."

I hesitated. I was always one willing to help another. There was a new humility I experienced being the recipient of being helped.

Afterward the gentleman walked me to my car, helped me with my groceries and gave me his business card.

"I'll send the check tonight; you have my word." I shook his hand. "I can't thank you enough."

"No rush." He smiled at my little girl.

"Buh buh." She waved her fat little hand.

"Bye bye." He waved back.

Later that night, my husband returned from work. He was shocked that a complete stranger would trust another with a loan of that amount.

"Thank God for small miracles." he said as he held our daughter.

— Nicole Ann Rook McAlister —

Kindness Is Often Quiet

Do things for people not because of who they are or
what they do in return, but because of who you are.
~Harold S. Kushner

When I was in the first grade, my mom worked, but her employer allowed her occasional afternoons off to be room mother for my class. This often meant baking cookies and buying milk in little cartons for a party.

That year, there were twenty-two children in Mrs. Olson's first-grade class. We were mostly farm kids at our school, but there were a few families whose dads worked for the steel mills. That year, the mills had been on strike the entire summer before I started first grade. My dad was the letter carrier for our town, and he knew everyone well.

When it was time for Mrs. Olson and Mom to plan the Christmas party, Mrs. Olson mentioned the pair of twins in the class. Their dad had not worked for several months, and she was concerned about their Christmas. My dad said there were two younger children in that family, so Christmas would probably be scant. My parents talked about what to do when they thought I was in bed sleeping, but I was sitting on the stairs eavesdropping. They wondered how to give those children something without hurting their feelings.

Dad and Mom went shopping and bought coloring books, soft-cover storybooks, and crayons for the entire class. The night before the school party, they wrapped the gifts and put on name tags. The day of the party, my dad borrowed Aunt Ruby's great red coat and put it on over his post-office uniform. When my class was coming back from the cafeteria, Dad made sure he was seen entering our classroom. He had a bag over his shoulder. And, of course, we saw him leave in a hurry. Even I didn't know then it was Dad in Aunt Ruby's great coat. We all thought it was Santa Claus. When we got to the room, the bag was sitting on Mrs. Olson's desk. Such excitement.

Mom showed up a few minutes later with cupcakes and milk, and the party began. Everyone, including Eddy and Edith, got gifts of books, crayons, and coloring books. But that wasn't the end of my dad and mom's kindness.

Eddy and Edith lived at the edge of town in a tidy, well-kept little house. On Christmas Eve, Dad borrowed Aunt Ruby's great red coat again. Back in those days, the letter carrier didn't drive a post-office Jeep. He drove his own car. After he had finished his mail route, he put on the bright red coat. He parked just around the corner from Eddy and Edith's house. He and Mom had bought stuff for all four children. I had seen some of it at home and thought it was for cousins or my little brothers. None of it was wrapped, and nothing was labeled.

Dad carried the bag over his shoulder and around the corner. When he got to their gate, he shouted, "Ho, ho, ho! Merry Christmas!" As soon as he was sure he had been heard, he put the bag inside the gate and ran around the corner to his car. When he drove past the house a few minutes later, Eddy's dad was taking the bag into the house.

He came home and told Mom that the delivery had been made. They hugged each other, and when I came into the kitchen, Dad told me that he was so glad I was his little girl. He sure hoped Santa would bring me something nice.

When school resumed after the holiday, Edith confided in me on the playground that Santa had come even though her mom had told them that he might miss them because they had moved. She got two big storybooks, pajamas, socks, and a doll. She described the doll. It was just like the one I saw at my house that I thought was for my cousin.

I didn't realize all this at the time. I was six. I believed everything I was told. I think I was about eight when I realized that I had witnessed a very special kindness when I was in the first grade. And, as I got older, I saw my parents do other kindnesses. Almost always, they were done secretly so no one's feelings were hurt.

Mom used to invite a couple of neighborhood families to supper every week. The dads all worked in the steel mills. My dad looked out for the older people on his mail route, even picking up their groceries when they couldn't venture out.

When my parents retired, they moved to Arizona where they were recognized for the kind and wonderful people they were. They were voted Arizona Senior Citizens of the year twice in the 1970s. My dad was embarrassed, and my mom cried. I was delighted that, finally, someone other than my brothers and I knew what kind and wonderful people they were.

— Charlotte Lewis —

The Kindness of Strangers

20

A New Orleans Welcome

*Most travel, and certainly the rewarding kind,
involves depending on the kindness of strangers,
putting yourself into the hands of people
you don't know and trusting them.*
~Paul Theroux

This would be our second trip to New Orleans. My husband and I were excited to return to the historical city and enjoy its music, trolley cars, fine restaurants, chicory coffee and beignets. For several weeks, I had been checking and rechecking our vacation to-do list. In the guest room, I had placed our luggage, airline tickets, hotel reservations, and a pair of tickets to a Black Gospel play.

Finally, the big day arrived, and we boarded our flight. It took us a few minutes to adjust to the extreme heat and humidity when we landed. Our taxi driver said his air-conditioning was on the fritz. But he laughed and promised, "I will go as fast as I can so you at least get a breeze."

Appreciating his sense of humor, we got in and enjoyed the conversation and the ride. At the hotel, we hurried in to register and unpack before going to the play. Then we got a taxi to take us to the play, but when my husband read the address to the driver, he turned around and advised us: "You may not want to go there. This past week, our city experienced a front-page racial incident that has caused quite a bit of tension. However, I'm sure the box office will refund your money under the circumstances."

Not knowing anything about the conflict, my husband said to me, "You bought the tickets. What do you want to do?"

After quickly thinking about it, I replied, "Well, I'm sure the cast and orchestra have put in a lot of time rehearsing, and quite a bit of money has been spent producing it. We just want to enjoy the play and music. Let's go in good faith and hope for the best."

"There's your answer," my husband told the cab driver.

Sitting in the back seat holding hands, we looked forward to the evening before us. We found the theater lobby empty and quiet when we arrived. The only person we saw was in the ticket booth. As my husband slid the tickets toward him, he told us, "Half the audience has asked for a refund or just didn't show up. Do you want a refund?"

"No," my husband answered.

Looking hopefully at each other, we turned around and went to the double doors on our right. Our seats were down front in the middle of the fifth row. Everyone turned to look at who was entering the half-empty theater. It was a bit awkward, but we calmly found our seats as those already sitting in row five silently stood up to let us by. Fortunately, the orchestra started playing, the lights dimmed, and we forgot about the state of affairs outside in the city.

The play was about the hardships in life that were testing one man's faith. He turned to gospel music to strengthen his feelings, but he was slowly losing his determination as Act I ended. My husband and I had tears in our eyes when the lights came on for the intermission. We stood up to stretch our legs, and the couple in front of us did the same. Turning to us, the woman also had tears in her eyes and graciously said, "Oh my, you are truly enjoying our play."

"We are," I said.

"You are not from our city, are you?"

"No, we are visiting here for a few days," my husband answered.

Her husband shook my husband's hand and welcomed us to New Orleans. His wife went on to explain, "We apologize for the tensions in our city. It is usually not like this, and we hope the rest of your vacation goes well."

Three other couples around us shook our hands and welcomed us, too. Then the lights dimmed, and everyone returned to their seats. The second half of the play was inspiring, as the man steadily started winning his battles in life while keeping a firm foundation in the gospel. The music was fantastic, and we especially loved several old, spiritual hymns. As the play came to an end, the audience gave the cast a standing ovation when they took a final bow. Turning to leave, we waited to take our turn. Several individuals smiled at us, and one gentleman waved to us. Smiling and waving back, we were happy that we had chosen to attend.

The following three days flew by as we enjoyed another play at Tulane University, trolley rides through the Garden District, and jazz in the French Quarter. On the flight home, we reminisced about how we would never see the people who had attended the gospel play again, but, because they had reached out, we would never forget them. Although our trip had gotten off to an uneasy start, the people and businesses in New Orleans made the phrase "The Big Easy" come true for us.

— Brenda Cathcart-Kloke —

21

Friday Night Magic

Too often we underestimate the power of a touch,
a smile, a kind word, a listening ear, an honest
compliment, or the smallest act of caring, all of which
have the potential to turn a life around.
~Leo Buscaglia

I was single when my girls were young. As many single parents say, this was never my intention, but it was the way things turned out, and it would ultimately be for the best for all involved. The girls and I developed our own routine and adjusted as well as we could. We had many people around us who cared, we had things to do, and we had enough money in the bank to get by. But during that season of life, I remember so often feeling that I wasn't doing enough, that I couldn't give the girls enough time, that it was all so rushed as I juggled work and commuting with their activities and a semblance of family life. Work was a grind and not satisfying. Life for me lacked magic and excitement.

But Friday nights with my daughters were special. Every couple of months, I sent one of the two to their grandparents' house while the other daughter and I had a night out. As a single mom, this was my way of making sure they each had my time and my undivided attention. Our nights out typically consisted of dinner and a movie, or a trip to the mall for whatever little-girl trinkets were in the budget.

Eight-year-old Amanda and I arrived at one of her favorite chain restaurants on a cold night in November. The evening commute from work had been rough, so I was late to pick her up, and we were both hungry. We were seated in a booth next to a large, boisterous group at a long table, clearly celebrating something. Three generations of a family had gathered for a birthday or anniversary. I glanced over at them throughout our meal, half smiling at their cheerful banter and half longing for that same family scenario for myself, which I was unlikely to have as a single mom. As the banter continued, I caught the white-haired family patriarch watching me. He would look over and stare at me but then quickly look away.

Amanda happily chattered away throughout the meal, enjoying her chicken tenders and recounting the details of her spelling test that day. She hummed to herself as she drew on the back of the paper menu with the crayons provided by our server. My heart nearly burst as I witnessed her happiness and heard her perspective on school, life and food. I found myself beaming at her joy.

However, the man at the next table kept watching us. I was annoyed. I tried to focus on Amanda, the way her blond curls framed her face, her bright blue eyes, the slight lisp she spoke with. He still stared. What was he looking at? My handbag, a thrift-store find that had been in style when I bought it several years before? Or my hair, with mousy roots due for color? Was it my ringless finger that told the general public I was unmarried? Whatever he was looking at, it was annoying and started to make me nervous.

Amanda was oblivious to what was happening around her, and she continued with her story of what happened on the playground that day. She tried to talk me into dessert, not knowing that there were surprise brownies waiting for us at home. I told her I was watching our money, and there would be no dessert this time. "Next time," I said. As the words came out of my mouth, the man was staring again. I was truly uncomfortable. What did he want? Why was he watching a woman and her young daughter when his own family was with him? He had to be my father's age. Was he actually a kidnapper? Was he just nosy? I was concerned.

Amanda went to the restroom, and I watched the man like a hawk. That man would *not* follow my daughter if I had anything to say about it. Should I have asked to move to another table? What was going on?

As Amanda returned to the table, the man and his family got up and left. I held her hand across the table and glared at him as they walked by. When she asked why I was holding it, I said, "I'm just having such a good time with you, sweetie." Amanda went back to drawing as I waited for the check, relieved that the man had left but also hoping he would not be waiting in the lobby as we left.

The server came to the table and said, "I was waiting until the man at that table left to tell you that he is paying your check. He didn't want you to know until he left. You are free to leave."

I was dumbfounded. "What? Why would he pay for our dinner?" I asked the server.

She replied that he said he had grown up with a single mother and knew how hard she had worked. "He has been fortunate in his life and wanted to pay it forward." Her eyes were glassy, and she had a huge smile on her face. I believed her but was still amazed that a stranger would do this.

Amanda was thrilled. "Mom, that man is so nice! We should find him so we can say thank you! Can we get dessert now?"

The people at the tables around us had seen this unfold and cheered as we left. The man and his family were gone as we walked through the lobby. I would never know who he was. I choked up as we got to the car. A total stranger went out of his way to do something kind for me. He had had kind intentions and a story of his own behind them. I had been suspicious rather than believing in the goodness of others. Sometimes, magic does come into our lives when we least expect it. If we allow it.

That Friday will stay etched in my memory as a night that was magical and made my eyes shine almost as bright as my daughter's.

— Mary Eisenhauer —

22

Woe Is Me

What wisdom can you find that is greater
than kindness?
~Jean-Jacques Rousseau

It was Tuesday morning, but it was the Tuesday after Memorial Day weekend, so theoretically it was like a Monday — the start of a new week. Since my three-day weekend had been busier than a regular-length weekend, I was more tired than usual, and it was time to go to work. And it was raining.

I grumbled about my misfortune. *This day is terrible! What an awful morning! Things are so bad for me! This weather is miserable, and so am I!*

As I stepped out the front door, a gust of wind twisted my umbrella inside-out. I decided to run through the cold downpour to the car, but I didn't see the ankle-deep puddle until after I stepped into it. Time for more complaining.

Now I was damp and late for work. The car stalled twice before I could back out of the driveway, and I had forgotten to replace that worn-out wiper blade. More complaints.

The traffic on the expressway was bumper-to-bumper. A horn honked — someone thought I wasn't going fast enough. I would have listened to the traffic report on the radio, but it was broken. Woe was me.

Finally, after managing to navigate my route through the traffic on the exit ramp, I decided I would stop at that little coffee shop near work for a cup of coffee — make that a large cup of coffee. The line of cars at the drive-through was stretched around the parking lot, so

I figured it would be faster if I just got out and went inside.

I sighed impatiently as I waited in line until I reached the counter where I ignored the friendly greeting from the barista — I was too busy with my complaining — and ordered my favorite: a caramel hazelnut coffee, extra cream, no sugar. My order was served, and I moved to the register. That's when I realized I had left my wallet at home! More woe is me.

"Hey, no problem," said the man waiting in line behind me. He smiled and pulled out his wallet. "I'll pay for you. I'm already late for work — it'll be faster anyway if I pay for both our coffees." His hair and shoulders were damp from the rain, and his shoes were wet. "Add this gentleman's coffee to my order, please," he told the cashier.

Really? This man, who was damp — like me, and late — like me, but was not too busy complaining — unlike me, was reaching out and offering to buy my coffee.

"Thank you very much," I said gratefully. "I'm having one of those mornings."

"I know how that is," the man replied sincerely. "Enjoy your coffee and try to have a better day."

I've been back to that little coffee shop many times since then, and I've never seen that man again. But, thanks to the kindness of a guy with damp hair and wet shoes, I've learned to keep my internal complaining to a minimum and be grateful for kindness that can come in the most unexpected places.

— David Hull —

23

Held Your Whole Life

Gratitude is a powerful catalyst for happiness.
It's the spark that lights a fire of joy in your soul.
~Amy Collette

My life was unfolding according to plan. Meet a man while away at college: check. Fall in love: check. Get engaged: check. Buy a little, three-bedroom starter home. Get married. Enjoy married life and build thriving careers. Check, check, check.

First comes love. Then comes marriage. Then comes a little stick with two faint lines and life-changing ramifications.

Nearly three years after walking down the aisle, here comes the baby carriage.

We tossed names back and forth, shared pretzels in the middle of the night to ward off the queasiness, rejoiced when we saw our first child's heartbeat flickering on the screen, and talked about the places we'd go and the things we'd do.

Then the bleeding started.

It's fine, the nurse said over the phone. A lot of women experience some bleeding in pregnancy. Come in tomorrow, and we'll check on the little one.

In my first and last act of maternal intuition for that baby, I knew the nurse was wrong.

While the ultrasound tech futilely waved her wand over my swollen belly, the room was eerily silent. I finally offered the diagnosis myself.

There's no heartbeat, is there?

I'm sorry.

There's no emptiness like the emptiness of a mother without her child. Over the next week, as my body and Mother Nature took away my baby, I was plagued by questions. What if my body couldn't carry a baby to term? What if I wasn't meant to be a mom — the only thing I'd known that I wanted to be since the days of baby dolls? How could I go through this again?

Three months later, those two lines were back — along with a newfound fear. Every bit of red, every twinge, I was convinced it was the beginning of the end. My husband would come home from work to find me standing at the stove, crying over a pot of pasta that my baby was going to die.

I scoured books and websites, looking for any reason, any symptom, any indication that the first miscarriage was a mistake, a fluke. I became an expert on reading bloodwork numbers and ultrasounds.

Along the way, amidst my newfound career of Googling, a sad realization hit.

I was not alone.

Sitting at my computer, I discovered I was now part of the least cool club I'd ever joined: a very large, very sad, but unbelievably supportive community. One not-for-profit organization, Tiny Heartbeats, mailed me a home Doppler system so I could listen to my baby's heartbeat when doubt started to creep in. The founder of the organization, a bereaved mother herself, periodically checked up on me via e-mail, always signing off with the note that she was sending prayers our way.

Another organization, Held Your Whole Life, sent a hand-stamped necklace bearing the phrase "Held Your Whole Life" and an angel charm with the birthstone our first child would have had. Free of charge. The couple behind the organization began stamping jewelry for grieving parents in honor of their stillborn son. That precious boy and these other angels, the mission stated, "never had to experience suffering or sorrow, only love. It is such an inspiring gift to our babies to have held them their whole lives."

The trinket was and is a nice reminder of my baby.

But the mission changed my life.

My aching heart skipped a beat when I read that statement. My first baby had known that kind of love. My second baby knew fear, anxiety, and stress. If I were the only one to ever hold him or her, was this what I wanted my child to feel?

Right then and there, I made a promise. Regardless of the outcome, this baby was going to know how loved he or she was.

I sang to my belly. I rubbed my stomach in response to every flutter and kick. I took countless videos of limbs moving across my stomach. I prayed every night. I ate healthy and avoided any hazards. I held full-blown conversations with my unborn child on the way home from work.

If the only life that little one knew was in my belly, that life would be the happiest I could offer.

The pregnancy wasn't easy, but on his due date, our little boy entered the world with a hearty shriek and stole our hearts. Totally healthy, absolutely perfect, and utterly adorable.

Reilly won't meet his big brother or sister in this lifetime, but he was lucky to be born to parents who learned the hard way how precious life is and what a miracle a healthy, happy child is. Every messy, exhausting, frustrating moment is a blessing that can't be taken for granted. Just ask any woman who's lost a lifetime of those moments far too soon.

I am the mom of two babies. Two I hold in my heart. And one I hold in my arms every second I can.

— Caitlin Q. Bailey O'Neill —

Surprise Hospitality

*Hospitality is simply an opportunity
to show love and care.*
~Author Unknown

For as long as I could remember, I had wanted to travel into the Amazon jungle. It was so exotic and different from my home outside Toronto and it seemed to draw me like a magnet. During the last summer break at university, I decided to take the plunge and fly to South America.

I didn't have much money, so I found the least expensive flight to Lima, Peru. Once there, I planned on traveling to the frontier town of La Merced on the edge of the Amazon jungle. To get there, however, I had to cross the Andes Mountains through La Oroya, a rough mining city. Its elevation of 12,000 feet was higher than most peaks in the Rocky Mountains.

It was 4:00 A.M. when I arrived at the Lima dispatch station for *colectivos* (taxis) headed for La Merced. The back seat of my *colectivo* was already filled with three nursing mothers, so I ended up in the front seat for the next fourteen hours.

By the time I reached La Merced, I was so exhausted it was all I could do to find a hotel. I asked the man at the front desk if there were any roads into the jungle. His simple answer was "no." In fact, there was no way to go farther into the jungle except by hiring a boat to travel down the Amazon. As a student, I found that an impossible option.

At that point, I decided to get something to eat, so I set out in search of a restaurant. The sun had set, so I walked along the main street, which boasted five flickering streetlights. I had walked less than a minute from the hotel when the skies opened, and a torrential rainstorm swept across the town. I raced ahead to the closest restaurant to get out of the rain.

I took a table by myself and ordered a meal. I was hot, soaked to the skin and very tired. I was also feeling sorry for myself. I had flown down to Peru and then taken a fourteen-hour journey in a crowded *colectivo* over the back of the Andes only to discover there was no way to get into the jungle.

As I was finishing up my meal, I heard singing coming from the street in front of the restaurant. A minute later, a group of seven men came through the front door. One of them stood out from all the rest. He was blond and light-skinned, just as I was. As soon as they saw me, all the men headed over to my table.

"Hi, my name's Fritz," he said in English, extending his hand to shake mine.

I introduced myself and told him why I had come to La Merced. We ended up chatting for half an hour, and I basically told him my life story. He could see I was tired and frustrated, and his eyes softened as he listened.

"Come with me tonight and stay with me and my wife at our home in the jungle. We have a coffee plantation." Fritz smiled as he talked. "My children are away at school in Lima, and you can stay as long as you'd like." His friends all smiled and encouraged me to go.

I shook my head because the thought of traveling at night through the jungle rattled me.

"Alright, tomorrow morning. I'll take you on a trip into the jungle."

"Okay," I said slowly. "Six o'clock tomorrow morning." I honestly didn't expect he'd appear.

Lying in bed, I wasn't sure what I'd agreed to, but there was something about him I trusted, and I liked his friends. And, while I didn't know much about him, he didn't really know me either.

At 6:00 the next morning, I heard someone honking a horn outside my hotel. I looked out, and there he was in a brand-new Ford Bronco with 4-wheel drive. I dressed quickly and raced down the stairs to the front entrance. Fritz sat there in his Bronco with a big smile on his face.

I hopped into his truck, and we were off. Within minutes, we were out of La Merced and into the jungle. The paved road in the town quickly became a rough dirt trail as we reached the rainforest. Vines swept over the windshield, and startled macaws took flight as we drove through groves of some of the largest trees I'd ever seen. A few minutes later, we came to a small, shallow river. Fritz slowed down for a moment and then plowed through the water as if it was nothing. We talked en route, and it turned out Fritz had come from Germany to start his coffee plantation in Peru.

After a two-hour adventure on jungle trails, we emerged into a clearing with a ranch-style, wood-frame house and a large vegetable garden.

For the next five days, I was treated as a special guest in his home. His wife Helga had me select the vegetables I wanted every day from their garden, and then she prepared them for our meals together. Fritz was more than anxious to show me around his coffee plantation, which he had carved out of the jungle. He always carried a revolver in case he was attacked by a snake.

I had my own bedroom and bathroom powered with electricity from the generator behind the house. Each night, we visited different friends who had invited me to join them for dinner. One night, we traveled half an hour in an open vehicle to visit some of their German friends who lived in a Bavarian-style village in the jungle. Everyone welcomed me to their party "in the square" of that little village despite my broken German and limited Spanish.

A few nights, the three of us sat up late just talking. They told me about their two children at boarding school in Lima and their loneliness on the jungle frontier. Fritz shared his struggles to clear the jungle and plant coffee trees. The two of them also wanted to know about my life, from my education to my family. They took a genuine interest in me.

Every morning after waking, I'd open my window to the green jungle that blanketed the mountains and breathe the fresh, clean air. A sweet perfume wafted through my window from a nearby jasmine bush. Their home in the Montaña area of Peru is the closest I've ever been to a paradise on Earth.

When I first met Fritz, I thought he was eccentric and rather odd, but after five days I'd grown to like him and appreciate him and his wife. Their warmth and generosity imprinted on my heart. When it came time to return to Lima, Fritz drove me back to La Merced. As I said goodbye, I felt a wave of sadness wash over me. I realized I'd likely never see my two new friends again. But even after all these years, I've never forgotten the kindness of Fritz and Helga, and the amazing days I spent in their jungle home.

— Rob Harshman —

The Marriage Proposal

When we involve others in spontaneous acts of kindness,
we go from being strangers to becoming a united team
connected at the heart level
~Molly Friedenfeld,
The Book of Simple Human Truths

On February 28, 2019, I attended a fundraiser for a buddy named Jason who was kicking off his campaign for public office. After the event, a small group went to a nearby Irish pub, including a few of Jason's friends from his college days at the University of Florida. One of them was Lori.

Lori was beautiful, bright, and kindhearted. She had been Homecoming Queen at the University of Florida, got her MBA from Harvard, and ran a non-profit foundation focused on reducing poverty in Africa. She was also witty and had a positive energy about her. I was smitten. We started dating right away.

About two months later, I took Lori to see a Chicago tribute band concert near our hometown of Orlando. Our favorite Chicago song was called "Just You and Me." It was the first time we said "I love you" to each other.

Fast forward six months later. It was Lori's birthday. The date was October 19, 2019. As luck would have it, the real Chicago band was playing that night at the Clearwater Jazz Festival, which is only about an hour and a half away from where we live. I secretly got tickets and kept our destination a surprise until about an hour before the concert.

Now what I didn't tell Lori was that I had an engagement ring in my pocket and was going to propose to her at the Chicago concert. For sentimental reasons, my plan was to propose to her while slow dancing to "Just You and Me."

Oh, crap, I thought when we arrived at the venue, and I noticed the metal detectors at the entrance to this outdoor music festival. "Please remove everything from your pockets and put them in the tray," said the security guard. I didn't want her to see the ring. I said, "Hey, Lori, why don't you go through a different metal detector so we get through faster." And she did. Whew! Crisis averted.

We'd brought our lawn chairs but there was no space left to set them up. I had no idea how popular this event was. Apparently, thousands of people had been camped out since early that morning to get seats for this nighttime concert. We walked up and down looking for a space for about fifteen minutes without any success.

Luckily, a concertgoer named Terry noticed our dilemma and motioned for us to come over. Terry and his buddy had amazing seats near the front of the stage. They were Good Samaritans who could tell we needed help and had squeezed together to make room. Terry even moved his chair to the row just behind us so we could all fit — an incredibly kind gesture from a stranger.

Just before the concert started, Lori walked away for a moment to get a beverage. I took that opportunity to ask for Terry's help. I said, "I'm going to propose to her later in the concert, when they play the song 'Just You and Me.' If I give you my iPhone, would you do me a huge favor and record it on video?"

Terry replied, "Of course, man. Happy to do it."

About halfway through the concert, they still hadn't played the song. I felt a tap on my right shoulder. Terry leaned in and whispered, "Hey, man, is this thing still going down?"

I laughed and confirmed, "Yes, it's still going down. I think they play the song toward the end."

And then, a few songs later, I felt a chill as the familiar opening horns of "Just You and Me" began to play, and they sang the opening lyrics:

You are my love in my life
You are my inspiration
Just you and me
Simple and free

Up until that moment, I felt confident and relaxed. No more. Suddenly, I felt really nervous. Life comes down to a few special moments, and it hit me that this was one of them. I quietly slipped my iPhone behind my back to Terry.

Maybe my hand was shaking or something, but I think Terry could sense I was nervous. He put his hand on my right shoulder, leaned forward and whispered, "You got this, buddy. It's going to go great."

I asked Lori to slow dance to our song. About halfway through the song, I got down on one knee and put my hand in the front pocket of my pants to begin to pull out the ring box.

Lori didn't know what was going on and asked, "What are you doing?" as she got down on her knees with me. I opened the box, presented the engagement ring, and asked, "Will you marry me?

She said, "Yes! Yes! Yes!"

Unbeknownst to us, the crowd had figured out what was happening and erupted in applause after she said, "Yes." Like a seasoned Hollywood director, Terry captured everything on video: the slow dance, the band, a close-up of the ring, Lori's face the moment she said, "Yes," and the crowd cheering.

It was perfect. It felt like God had sent an angel to make everything go smoothly. Terry had been kind enough to make sure we had great seats near the stage, encourage me when I was nervous, and capture it all on video like a pro.

There was one thing I regret. In the excitement of it all, I forgot to ask Terry for his card, phone number or even last name.

Lori and I really want to give Terry a big gift certificate to a fancy local steakhouse as a way of saying, "Thank you."

Since we got married, Lori and I have been to about a half-dozen concerts near the area where we got engaged, including one additional Chicago concert. Every single time, Lori looks around the crowd and says, "I wonder if Terry is here."

We're still looking. I hope we find him someday. Maybe this little story will help.

— Ric Keller —

26

Hundred-Dollar Bill

The unthankful heart discovers no mercies;
but the thankful heart will find, in every hour,
some heavenly blessings.
~Henry Ward Beecher

My husband was working overtime. He did that a lot, but it still never seemed to be enough. I had stopped receiving child support for my oldest children from my ex-husband, and we were not even making enough to pay the bills. We were going to lose our rent-to-own home. My children had not had much stability, moving from place to place and even spending some time in a hotel for the homeless.

I was so broken. I struggled to hold myself together for my children but they knew something was wrong. And Daddy working and being gone a lot wasn't easy at all.

I took the kids with me to Walmart to buy groceries. I had a certain amount that I could spend. It was Christmastime, so I walked through the aisles carefully, making sure to stick to my list. That was key.

The kids were humbled at a very young age and understood what it was like to have nothing. They had to do without things, and they knew that we had no room for extras. But my youngest was only six, and he saw a cereal box with a Christmas theme and got so excited.. It broke me to have to tell him no. A four-dollar box of cereal, and we couldn't afford it. He was disappointed but understood. We left the aisle with me in tears.

In the next aisle, a woman in her sixties or seventies approached me. She said that she wanted to bless me today and handed me something as she smiled sweetly. Then she looked at my children, wished them a "Merry Christmas," and walked away. I was left holding a hundred-dollar bill. I cried again. I walked back to the cereal aisle and got that box of cereal for my children, finished my grocery shopping, and went home.

That day, I was not just blessed with a box of cereal for my children. That hundred-dollar bill also helped finish paying our electric bill. That sweet lady's kindness blessed us more than she will ever understand.

The world needs more people like that — those who help people just because. I am now in a position where I can help people, and I do — obviously, because they need it, but also to honor those who have helped me along the way. I don't know where my family would be without the kindness of others.

— Elizabeth Chenault —

27

The Long Flight Home

*Without a sense of caring, there can
be no sense of community.*
~Anthony J. D'Angelo

We'd had it all figured out. On discovering our family of five couldn't sit together on our flight home, my husband and I had gone back and forth, trying out different combinations. Who would sit where in the two-up-front, three-in-the-back seating we'd been allocated?

We considered how we'd board, carrying a tired toddler and five pieces of hand luggage between us. Juggling our two older children. Finally, we decided: my husband, up front with our older son; our daughter, younger son and myself in the rear. Three seats in row 29.

We boarded near to last due to our younger son's learning disabilities, thankful he wouldn't have to sit for longer than necessary in the cramped cabin. We settled our older son at the front and then slowly shuffled to the back of the plane. My husband searched through the already overstuffed overhead lockers, trying to find room for our bags. That's when he noticed. "There's a problem with those seats," he said. There weren't three seats in row 29 after all. There was one in row 28 and two in row 29. No matter.

Only, it *did* matter. Because it turned out that the seats were all singles. Fine for my daughter, but what about my son? He was to sit behind me. Diagonally across the aisle. Out of sight. Out of reach. My heart sank.

I called to the flight attendants.

"I'm sorry," I said, voice cracking. "I can't fly like this."

"Seats across the aisle are classed as next to each other," said one, as if that would help me.

"But they're not next to each other. One is behind the other, across the aisle. My son is only three. He is disabled. I can't leave him by himself. He has Down syndrome. He needs to be with me."

The aisle was a gaping chasm.

How could I possibly tend him when I couldn't even see him? How could he sit by himself for three and a half hours? My son was nothing like the average three-year-old. A non-speaker, he relies on his hands to do the talking for him. He needs a sign reader to interpret what his hands are saying, one who understands him. He gets rattled by unexpected, loud sounds. On the way out, the pilot's announcements reduced him to tears. We had to cover his ears and hold his gaze to help him through.

This would never do. Another mother looked over, recognition in her eyes. She had her own young brood with her. Perhaps she'd been in a similar situation herself and knew how it felt to be asked to put her children in peril.

The flight attendants glanced at each other. Murmured their understanding. Offered no solution. Panicking, I scanned the cabin, wondering where else we could sit. There were no spare seats. "The plane is preparing for take-off. Please sit down." I felt sick, felt impatient eyes bore into my back. But I couldn't fly like this. What to do? What to do? What to do? There was no way around, but I couldn't bring myself to strap my son into a far-off seat.

Before I resigned myself to putting him in the lonely seat, a good-hearted couple stood up. Unbidden. They simply stood. Wordlessly offered up their seats to me. I could've cried. I almost did.

I couldn't thank them enough. Slowly, my breathing returned

to normal. My mind and stomach stopped churning. I leaned over, helped my son get comfy in the seat next to me, and got ready for the long flight home.

— Angela Dawson —

28

Trapped

Saying thank you is more than good manners,
it is good spirituality.
~Alfred Painter

Sunlight streaming through the motel's window brought a smile to my face while I still snuggled deep in my pillow. We had escaped winter. Near dawn the previous day, my friend Jess and I had loaded our gear and my dog Bailey into my old Buick and headed southwest away from our snowbound, freezing home in Ottawa. We were Arizona-bound. Pushing the pedal hard to put the cold behind us, we arrived late afternoon to spring-like temperatures southwest of Columbus, Ohio.

Encouraged by that sunbeam, I made a quick bathroom stop, threw on my sweats, grabbed Bailey's leash, and set out for a morning walk to take care of her bodily needs and stretch my legs before another long day on the road. A little nip in the air sent me back for a jacket, but the lack of snow and the promise of a sun-filled day put a bounce in my step. Taking note of bursting buds and green grass, my spirits soared. Bailey, too, seemed to perk up. I looked to the heavens and gave a wee prayer of thanks.

An hour later, we were dressed, fed, packed and on our way. Proclaiming "Thelma and Louise" we high-fived as we pulled onto the freeway. The radio was playing lively tunes to match our mood. Bailey was queen of the back seat. Life was as good as it gets.

Several years ago, I had discovered a small town in Arizona that became my winter destination. Jess often joined me for a few weeks. It is near a well-known tourist area, Sedona, but more economical, with a small-town culture. I got a library card, volunteered at the local art gallery, and joined the community choir. My four-month stay was busy. I made friends and a home away from my life in Canada's frozen north.

With lots of miles behind us by noon, we pulled off somewhere in Kentucky at a rest stop that was like a glorious park. We would eat picnic-style and have a welcome break from the car. After a brisk walk, we enjoyed salads, crackers and cheese. The sun was beaming down on us, and we lounged in its warmth. However, the road beckoned, so reluctantly we headed for the car.

Once the food was stashed in the trunk, I opened the back door, tossing my keys onto the front seat, and settled Bailey before slamming the back door shut. For one last minute of pure ecstasy, we turned our faces to the sun to capture a few more rays before riding away. I pulled the handle of the driver's door.

"Oh, my god, Jess, the door is locked."

"What do you mean 'locked'? How did that happen?"

Full realization of what we were dealing with washed over me with dread. The remote must have triggered the lock when I tossed it onto the driver's seat.

"Everything is locked inside — our purses, the car keys and Bailey."

That is when I realized the danger. The temperatures had risen, and my trusting pet was sealed inside a hot box with no water.

Saying a quick prayer and practicing yoga breathing, I tried to calmly assess the problem. Surely, the Visitor's Center had an emergency phone. Running across the parking lot and into the building, I was relieved to see a pay phone. Posted above it was the local police number — the only free call. I dialed.

The call was answered by a soft-spoken voice with a masculine southern drawl. I needed a hero. Calmly, I explained the situation and asked for assistance.

"Sorry, lady. This is the local station. You are on the interstate, so you need to contact the state troopers."

"Wait, don't hang up. I can't call them. I don't have any money.

This is the only free number. My purse is locked in the car, too."

"But, lady, that is not our jurisdiction."

"You have to help. My dog is locked in the car and in danger of suffering heatstroke."

"Well, then, you better call a local towing service. I'm sure they can open the vehicle."

I sensed he was about to hang up.

"Please, you have to understand. I can't call anyone else but you." My tone was emphatic, frantic and loud. My breathing was becoming rapid. He was still on the line. I calmed my voice. "Could you please call the towing company on my behalf?"

He offered a half-hearted promise that he would see what he could do. At this point, it was the only hope I had.

Rushing back to Jess and Bailey, I explained what had transpired. Regardless of the officer's half-hearted promise, I was not convinced that help would be on the way before Bailey would start to feel the heat. She was looking out at us, happily wagging her big, bushy white tail. My anxiety levels were elevating again. I appealed to other motorists, but that brought no offers of how to resolve the predicament. In fact, I detected scorn leveled at my stupidity. They walked away, shaking their heads, and watched with curiosity from a safe distance.

"I'm sure the tow truck will arrive soon." My friend's words were meant to ease my desperation but were of little comfort. We waited for what seemed like forever before I heard a truck rattling into the parking lot. Expecting it might be the tow truck I sprinted toward the entrance and then slumped as the nose of a transport truck pulled into view. Then relief flooded over me when I saw that the decrepit transport was stacked high with wrecked autos. I returned to the car and waited for it to slip into a parking slot.

"Jess, if anyone knows how to break into a car, I'll bet those guys do."

"Molly, you are not going to ask them, are you?"

I was already walking in the direction of the truck across the lot and greeted the driver as he opened the door. I watched a broad, rugged, unkempt man in a soiled denim shirt and blue jeans climb down from the cab. I spilled out my dilemma. The passenger door opened, and the driver shouted across in a rough voice.

"Hal, did you bring the Slim Jim?"

"Nope. Why?"

"Looks like we could use it."

All the time, he was watching me, measuring me with deep blue eyes.

"Lady, we have to make a pit stop, and then we'll be right with you."

The passenger walked around the truck, and I was taken aback to find the most alarming character standing before me. He was a very tall, thin young man wearing black from head to toe, and he was grinning at me with a mouth full of gold capped teeth. At this point, I felt uneasy in their company and somewhat regretted my appeal for assistance.

They headed for the washrooms, and I returned to my car, expecting to find Bailey in some distress by this time. Although she seemed somewhat puzzled that I was on the outside of the car and she was on the inside, she was wagging her tail.

True to their word, my rescuers arrived and surveyed the situation.

"Yep, the Slim Jim would have been the answer. Hal, get that small crowbar and something to trip the lock. Now, lady, don't you worry. We are going to get that pretty pooch out of there in no time. By the way, Chuck's the name."

I shook his tobacco-stained, outreached hand. His soothing words had a calming effect. Hal arrived with the crowbar, a towel and a length of pipe. Jess and I watched two masters at work. Carefully protecting the car's surface with the towel, they eased the top edge of the door out about three inches. Chuck instructed Hal to "hold it there" as he slid a length of pipe down the side of the door and released the lock. It took less than two minutes.

My repeated "thank you" and offers of money were brushed aside. With beaming smiles, they roughed Bailey's coat and took their leave. We waved across the lot to each other, knowing our paths would never cross again but that we would always remember this day.

No sooner had they climbed into their cab when a tow truck

arrived. Hastily, I explained how the situation had been resolved and offered to pay for the service call. This was refused with words to the effect that he was happy that Bailey was safe. We watched both trucks exit the area.

"None of them looked it, Jess, but we just met three heaven-sent southern gentlemen," I said.

— Molly O'Connor —

The Right Words

29

Just a Few Words

Life is slippery. Here, take my hand.
~H. Jackson Brown, Jr.

I thought I had this nailed. After all, Mary wasn't my first baby, and I'd done this dozens of times before. So, as I dressed my two kids to go grocery shopping, I was a young mother full of confidence.

Matthew was two. Mary was three weeks. It was my first shopping trip since she'd come home from the hospital. But I'd nursed both my babies, changed their diapers, dressed them up, and piled them into the car.

Matthew had become traumatically brain-injured in a fall when he was one. I'd read that nutrients in mother's milk helped to build synapses in babies' brains and could help restore lost function in young children with brain injuries. So, I was tandem nursing both Matthew and Mary. It turned out to be a lovely arrangement for the three of us. Cuddling with a child on each side of me, my babies would nurse together. Matthew would often take breaks to hold his sister's hand or stroke her hair. And, even at her young age, she'd begun to respond to his caresses with genuine affection. So, I'd found that a quick nursing break before a task yielded contented children. Or so I thought.

When we pulled up to the store, I grabbed the nearest shopping cart and brought it to the car. I lined the shopping cart seat with my cart buddy — nicely padded with its own safety strap to secure Matthew into the seat — and then slipped on my carrier wrap and cuddled Mary up against my chest. And we were off.

As I walked through the produce section, I was feeling on top of the world. It had been a difficult birth, and Mary had spent a week in the NICU before I'd been allowed to bring her home. I, too, had spent several days in the hospital fighting an infection that she and I had gotten during the delivery. But now, at last, we were together, and this shopping trip felt like a victory lap in a long marathon run.

I grabbed some fruits and checked out the fresh spinach that I used to make the pea cakes that Matthew loved for snacks.

When I turned into the frozen section, both Matthew and Mary started to fuss. Rubbing his hands on his arms, Matthew began to whine, "Cold, Mommy! Cold, cold, Mommy!" Next, he allowed his teeth to chatter just so I wouldn't doubt the extent of his discomfort. Mary began to kick in her carrier, so I hurried through the aisle and just grabbed one or two things before I moved on.

Yet, as I walked, I was astonished at how big the grocery store began to feel — how foreign and overwhelming. Weeks of sleepless nights and postpartum brain fog suddenly made this simple task much more difficult and time-consuming.

Each aisle began to loom large as the kids fussed more and more.

Mary was wiggling and softly whimpering in her carrier, and Matthew, always the loving big brother, was becoming more and more agitated that I wasn't attending to his sister. "Bebe cry, Mommy! Bebe cry!"

No amount of distraction or soothing would ease my son's angst, and as he became more distraught, his sister's own distress increased. Back and forth, they set each other off, increasing the unhappiness and the volume as we inched our way through the maze of the store.

The more they cried, the less I could think. The less I could think, the longer I was taking. The longer I was taking, the more they cried.

Finally, I had no choice but to give up and go to the checkout stand. My victory lap had become a dismal farce and my screaming children a noisy spectacle.

As I stood at the checkout piling groceries onto the conveyor with one hand, patting my daughter with the other, and cooing to my distraught son, I felt my letdown response react to my children's cacophony of wails. Despite my nursing pads and an arm wedged against my chest, in an instant the front of my shirt was covered in a growing wet spot. The smell of my milk so close and yet so far away incensed Mary, who wailed even more. His sister's distress agitated Matthew, who wanted to open my shirt to help his sister find relief. As my children screamed and clawed, my hands fumbled, trying to unload the cart and move along with the line.

And, as my shirt got wet, so did my eyes. No matter how fast I blinked, I could not hold back the tears. I felt defeated, discouraged and totally inadequate to the task before me. I saw young moms grocery shop every day. Why couldn't I finish this seemingly simple task? My mind raced. My kids screamed. My milk and tears flowed. I was making a scene, and I knew it. I couldn't have been more demoralized.

"Honey?" The matronly woman behind me reached out and touched my arm.

Great! I thought to myself. *Now I'm going to get yelled at, too.* I couldn't turn to her. She'd see my shirt. She'd see my tears. It was all too embarrassing.

"Honey?" she tried again. I had no choice. I looked up at her.

"It's hard," she said. "No one really ever tells you that. But you're doing a good job, Mama. You'll do fine."

Despite myself, I burst into tears.

She softly laughed and handed me a tissue. "Hormones are funny things. It will get better."

Then she nodded, and I nodded back. I paid for my groceries and walked out the door. But I walked out buoyed, confident and determined.

They were just a few words, and yet they were the world.

— Susan Traugh —

30

Rocking COVID

The smallest act of kindness is worth more
than the greatest intention.
~Kahlil Gibran

hen the COVID pandemic hit in the spring of 2020, our son Thommy and his girlfriend Katie were both laid off from their jobs in the western part of our state. They quickly realized they would be unable to pay rent, so they moved back in with us in April. Fortunately, we had an empty apartment in our walk-out basement, so we had both the space and the means to help them.

The timing couldn't have been better because their presence in our lives at this time was also an amazing gift to us during what would have been a very lonely year.

Over the course of the first few months when everything was closed and jobs were scarce, Katie and I became walking buddies. We live right next to Nickerson State Park, where there are multiple walking trails that are never very busy. Those walks became my favorite part of the day.

At some point during our walks, we noticed that people began leaving kindness rocks along the trail. We were familiar with the concept because The Kindness Rocks Project began on Cape Cod where we live. It was started in 2015 by a woman named Megan Murphy who began leaving rocks with inspirational messages in public places.

The idea took off, and other people joined in, leaving their own messages of hope and encouragement for whoever found them.

The brightly painted rocks Katie and I found in the park ranged from surprisingly beautiful works of art to charming stones that were obviously painted by children. It became a fun scavenger hunt to find them, but we never took a rock home because we wanted to leave them for others to enjoy. If I saw a particularly inspiring one, I would take a photo of it and share it on Facebook.

After a few months of hunting for rocks that others had painted, we decided we needed to contribute to the project ourselves. We spent a memorably peaceful afternoon painting a pile of flat rocks collected from a nearby beach.

It was uplifting to think of words of hope, especially during what was a scary and dark time. Mostly, we just wrote the messages that we most needed to hear — messages of strength and endurance, of love and peace. During our next few walks, we dispersed them in the park to replace the ones that others had taken home.

At some point, all the kindness rocks on the walking trail disappeared except one that said "Love" that was perched too high up for most people to reach. The painted message on that rock was still readable, but it kept getting dimmer from the elements and time.

Over the winter, as the pandemic raged on, my anxiety about it grew. But, during that time, I discovered that my husband Steve is actually a kinder person than I am.

Before the pandemic, we did a lot of volunteer work together for non-profit organizations that provide meals for people who are food insecure. My husband is a chef, and I write a local recipe column, so it was the perfect way for us to give back by doing something we both enjoy and believe is important.

COVID canceled all volunteer opportunities at first, but it didn't take long for the people in charge of the non-profits to ask Steve to help prepare food. A new non-profit group had formed that wanted to give away drive-through meals to those in need.

This was before the vaccines were available, and COVID was still very much prevalent in our community. I was terrified for him to go back into restaurant kitchens to work. The fear he would bring COVID home almost paralyzed me, but no amount of arguing on my part would change his mind. He was determined to get back to cooking for those who needed a nutritious meal.

One night, I was telling my mother all my fears. I also told her how frustrated I was that I couldn't get Steve to see my point of view. Her words of advice were the first step in what became a healing process for me.

"You can't hate him for the exact same thing you love about him," she said.

I heard her, but the words didn't really sink in right away. Fear is mighty powerful, so it took a few more days and a big nudge to get me to start to think about things differently.

It is true that my husband's genuine compassion and generosity toward others (including me) is one of the things I love most about him. Despite my fears, I was very proud of him. For months on end, he volunteered to cook meals that fed up to 1,200 people a week. He also made 150 quarts of homemade soup every week during the winter for volunteers to hand out in a drive-through at one of the local senior centers.

A woman who works at the senior center told me how much that soup line meant for her clients. It not only provided nourishment for their stomachs, it also provided nourishment for their souls. She said it got them out of the house and socializing with friends they had missed. Many of them dressed up in nice clothes as if they were coming into the senior center in person, not just driving through the parking lot.

But even though I was proud of his service, I was still very frightened we would get sick. One day, not long after my talk with my mother, I was telling Katie about her advice as we were walking through the park. At the exact second that Mom's words came out of my mouth, I looked down and saw a bright yellow triangular-shaped stone nestled in the dead leaves.

"You've got this!" it said.

As I read that message, my mother's words finally sank in. I knew in that moment that I could not let my fear of getting sick prevent my husband from feeding those in need. But I also knew that I would need some reinforcement to keep steady, so I picked up that rock and put it in my pocket.

When we got home, I put the rock on the windowsill over my kitchen sink. Every time I felt myself get a little panicky, I would look at that rock to remind myself that it's important to let go and let God.

Coincidentally, one of the very first kindness rocks that Megan Murphy created had the exact same message that helped me: "You've got this."

—Laurie Higgins—

31

In Her Shoes

*I believe that kindness is the cure to violence
and hatred around the world.*
~Lady Gaga

"**W**hat do you think of these?" I picked up a pair of strappy sandals and offered them to my twenty-something daughter.

"Nah," she said. "Those are too low. I want real heels."

It was early spring, and we were in the shoe department of our local Target.

"Like these." Rachel held up a pair of platform wedges with three-inch heels.

She walked over to the plastic bench and sat down to try them on.

That's when I felt it. Someone was watching us. Not with a normal glance of recognition, or eyeing someone else's shoes and thinking, "Ooh, I like those." No, this was different. It felt focused and intense.

From the corner of my eye, I saw a woman about my age — maybe a tad younger — with shoulder-length hair and nondescript clothes. She wasn't anyone we knew. She definitely was watching us, in a trying-not-to-stare-but-not-quite-succeeding way.

My internal mom alarms began wailing. I went into full protective mode, positioning myself in front of Rachel, angling my body between her and the woman so my daughter wouldn't see this rude lady looking at her, so she wouldn't feel the uncomfortable eyes upon her. But my daughter didn't seem to notice as she chattered away about the shoes and how they would go with the new dress we had already picked out.

She stood up, tottered a bit, and began a slightly wobbly walk down the aisle.

"Those will take some getting used to," I said, trying to keep the worry out of my voice. I was still attempting to be a visible and physical block between Rachel and the staring woman, while at the same time being cheerful and lighthearted as one should on such an occasion: just a mom and her adult daughter out shopping in Target.

But this was not just an everyday shopping trip. It was our first as mother and daughter. It was the first time I would be buying her a dress and the first time I could buy her a cute pair of sandals.

Several months previously, my daughter had told me she was transgender, that the body she had been born into was at odds with who she was, that she was not a young man but a young woman.

The first thing I said when she told me was that I loved her and would support her. We talked for hours.

But I didn't sleep for three nights after that conversation. Not because I struggled with accepting her. There was no struggle. She is my child; gender doesn't matter.

No, it was because I knew that trans people are often harassed, discriminated against, and bullied. I knew they are more likely to be victims of violent crime. I knew that the simple human circumstance of walking down a sidewalk with a friend or needing to use a public restroom carried the potential for confrontation. I knew she would have to think about where she could travel, and what states or countries she would need to avoid, because people not only wouldn't accept her for who she was but would actively and angrily deny her the right to simply be herself.

I felt she wasn't safe anymore. That was what kept me awake.

I saw a hard and challenging road ahead of her. And, unlike when she was two or ten, I couldn't always be there to scout ahead for obstacles, to smooth the bumps, to clear the way.

In this journey, I followed my daughter's lead. I let her tell me when to start saying "she" and "her." When she shared her new name—Rachel

Mae, choosing one that honored both of her great-grandmothers — I was filled with joy and practiced saying it so I wouldn't accidentally use the old name, the one I had pronounced for more than two decades.

When I slipped up, I would apologize, correct myself, and move on, not making a big thing out of it. It helped when I realized she had always been Rachel; she had been born a girl, and I just didn't know.

While that thought helped me reset my language, it also made me want to turn back time and do all the mother/daughter things we didn't get to do when she was a young girl.

Less than a year after our initial conversation, Rachel announced she was going to come out publicly for her birthday. I offered to take her shopping and buy her a dress to celebrate — and she said yes.

I was thrilled that Rachel felt comfortable enough to be herself in public. And honored that Rachel would let me be part of that experience. But I knew the trip had to be just a mom and her daughter out shopping: no big deal. I let her decide where to go, and she chose our local suburban Target.

I was proud of her. But I was also terrified for her.

She was still transitioning, still learning how to be comfortable in her skin. She didn't have many women's clothes at the time, and I worried about what we might encounter in that store. Would people stare? Whisper? Comment out loud?

So, I walked into Target a mother tiger, claws ready to be unsheathed in a microsecond if I had so much as an inkling that someone would hurt my daughter when she was so vulnerable.

Which was why I kept my eyes on this woman who seemed to be watching her.

But then I was distracted by the sight of my daughter walking up and down the aisle, trying on different pairs of sandals. She was so happy. I was doing my best to hold back tears of joy. And I forgot about the woman.

Suddenly, it was too late. She was approaching us.

I braced myself, ready to whip out my verbal claws, when I saw the warm and welcoming smile on her face — and a pair of women's pumps in her hand.

She held them out to me. "Maybe she would like these?"

Rachel stopped walking for a moment, looked over at us, and grinned.

As I took the shoes from this angel of a woman, all my tension melted. I thanked her, trying to fit the enormous amount of gratitude I felt into my suddenly small voice while not losing it in the middle of the shoe department.

This woman had used the right pronoun.

Shown acceptance.

Demonstrated a touching act of kindness.

And did it all in a way that made it feel like nothing more than an everyday interaction among three women out shopping for shoes in their local Target.

That small act was thoughtful in intention. Powerful in its simplicity. And meaningful in its action.

It acknowledged Rachel as the woman she is. And gave me hope that my daughter could move through this world and encounter not just meanness and hate, but also the kindness and love of complete strangers.

We didn't buy the pumps that day; they weren't quite Rachel's style. But we left the store with two dresses, a pair of high-heeled sandals, and a little more faith in humanity than what we brought in with us.

— Rose Demarest —

32

Princess for a Day

Compliments land as soft and gentle
on my ears as a butterfly.
~Richelle E. Goodrich

I was wearing yoga pants and a tank top, staring at myself in my bedroom mirror. "Just go to class," I told myself. "Just get there, and everything will feel better again." What I really wanted to say was "Just stay home again today. It will feel good to get all sad and stay down in the dumps."

But I knew better than that. So, regardless of my feelings, I grabbed my yoga mat, and went to the studio.

While I loved yoga and looked forward to my weekly classes, getting there was a task that seemed insurmountable lately. It wasn't that I didn't want to go anymore, but I was feeling lackadaisical about it.

Truthfully, I was feeling lackadaisical about everything.

Like most folks, my life events seem to go in waves. Waves of good, waves of bad, and waves of change. I was going through the wave of change, and surfing that wave was proving to be difficult.

Everything was changing, from my kids' schools to my job and even my health. Everything I was used to — even the routine I was used to and the way I had my schedule set up — was changing.

I was fed up with change!

It wasn't that things were out of control, but they were so different. And as a caterpillar comfortable in my skin, I didn't feel like turning into a butterfly no matter how beautiful I could be. It was too hard, too painful, and felt like too much change for one person to handle.

But, as fate would have it, there would be more change to come.

Several of my good friends were moving. I mean, my *best* friends. And it was all happening within the year. One friend was moving to another part of town. While that wasn't awful, it still meant driving about an hour just to meet up with her. With our conflicting schedules, I already knew that would be troublesome.

The other two were moving away — *far* away — as in the opposite end of the state for one and across the country for the other. I never felt more alone in my life.

When you find friends who get you, love you, understand you and accept you, it's not easy to search out new friends. Now, I was in a quandary; I needed new friends. Finding replacements wasn't going to be easy. While being friendly wasn't hard, knowing how long it would take to find "my people" would be the problem.

Would I ever find friends again who liked me?

I grabbed my tote, signed into the studio, and hauled myself into the right yoga room. I laid down my mat and began stretching, watching the other students waltz in and put their mats down, pull their hair into a ponytail, get water, and do all the things yoga people do.

As class began, I remember thinking how ungrateful I had become. I knew that as I aged, it was easy to become complacent about the things in my life. Was complacency leading to my ungratefulness?

I'd assumed my best friends would be with me for a long time. I didn't think they'd move away from me. But, at the end of the day, I knew it wasn't about me; it was about them doing what they needed to do for their lives. And from experience, wasn't change the catalyst needed for more great things?

Even with this logical corroboration, I still felt alone and invisible.

I watched a girl come into class late and quickly get situated, moving into her yoga pose as though she'd been there the whole time. I smiled at her and, throughout the class, noticed she'd keep taking random looks at me. Perhaps she thought I was someone else. Perhaps she was wondering why I was in class since I felt so rundown, frumpy, and old. Did my feelings show that badly?

Class ended, and I picked up my mat. I smiled at the girl again and got ready to leave. But she walked toward me, held out her hand, and said, "I know this is a strange thing to say, but you look so much like Kate Middleton, the Duchess of Cambridge, and I just had to tell you."

Now, I don't follow the royal family as well as some folks do, but I did know who this was: the princess who could become queen!

"Gosh, thank you!" I said. I'd never been told I looked like her before, so not only was that a nice surprise but, in my opinion, Catherine was the most amazingly well-put-together and poised lady I'd ever seen. Here I was thinking I was looking dowdy and left-behind… and then this.

"Thank you," I said, reaching out to touch her hand. "To be honest, I was just thinking how old I looked today." Tears began to form in my eyes. She had no idea what I was going through, and yet all she did was tell me who she thought I looked like, and I was about to flood the floor with my tears.

"Oh, no, you look wonderful," she said.

I thanked her again. She smiled sweetly and off she went, leaving me to stand there awash in both embarrassment and elation. With a few simple words, she made me feel like someone new. With one kind sentence, she made me feel that I mattered.

Her kind words lifted me out of my self-induced despair, making me feel that things could be better again. I'll never forget how valuable compliments from a stranger can be. And, to this day, I strive to compliment others when I can.

I walked out of that studio like a new woman with a new friend who made me feel like a princess for a day.

— Heather Spiva —

33

Sundays at 7

*True friends aren't the ones that make your problems
disappear; they are the ones that won't disappear
when you're facing problems.*
~Author Unknown

Karen's chilling words echoed through the phone as I choked back tears and tried to hide my fear and disbelief. I struggled to find the right thing to say.

For the first time, I was speechless in a conversation with my best friend. When we moved to different states after college graduation, our constant phone conversations became a lifeline that sustained our connection. We reminisced about spring-break trips, sorority traditions and fraternity formals. Our frequent calls continued as we navigated our twenties together, exploring new careers and relationships, and planning bachelorette parties and weddings.

When she gave birth to her daughter a few months after my son was born, our bond strengthened as we tackled the challenges of colicky babies and curious toddlers. A few years later, it was exciting to be pregnant again at the same time, and we shared the woes of nausea and breast tenderness common in the first trimester.

A few days earlier, Karen had mentioned that, while clutching the side of her aching breast, she had discovered a pea-sized formation. While she waited for test results and started to worry, I reminded her that the doctor assured her it was likely nothing. She was thirty-two years old and in perfect health with no family history of cancer. When the phone rang, I was certain my advice would return to choosing preschools and researching the latest baby gear.

Instead, I was desperately searching for the perfect message of comfort as she shared her biopsy results. "It's breast cancer."

When no words seemed sufficient, I channeled my anger at the unfairness of it all into a photo album filled with positive quotes, funny memories and uplifting poems. I lived four states away, and if I couldn't be there beside my best friend at her stressful doctor appointments, this was the next best thing I could think of.

A cancer diagnosis at any age is awful, but to face this so young and while pregnant seemed exceptionally cruel. As I rushed to the post office to express-mail my token of support, it felt inadequate.

Over the next year, any gesture of encouragement seemed too small. Or too invasive. As I searched the Hallmark display, any card designed to cheer her up looked too funny. Or not funny enough.

As Karen met with oncologists and underwent a mastectomy during her pregnancy, I constantly looked for the right way to offer support in her greatest time of need. Was I calling too little? Or too much? I often felt paralyzed by indecision on how I could help.

Until Karen delivered her healthy baby girl and was in full remission from breast cancer, I floundered, wondering about the best way to be there for her.

Years later, when my dad received his own devastating cancer diagnosis, a small but significant gesture from his friend, Mike, taught me a simple yet powerful way to offer just the right amount of steady support. It can be applied to almost any difficult situation, no matter the distance. He gave my dad "Sundays at 7."

My father, Fred, and Mike became fast friends early on in their careers at Penn State University. When his position required him to relocate to Philadelphia 200 miles away, my dad stopped by Mike's office any time he returned to the college's main campus in central Pennsylvania.

In September 2014, instead of a routine visit for meetings with colleagues, my dad abruptly packed up his office. After a summer of sudden gastrointestinal symptoms and rapid weight loss, he was diagnosed with pancreatic cancer and forced to resign from his current duties to begin an aggressive treatment regimen near his home in Philadelphia.

The world's deadliest major cancer had a survival rate in the single digits. He was told he might not even live to enjoy one last Christmas or celebrate his sixtieth birthday.

Always thinking of others, my dad remained positive and strong with my mom, my brother, and me. He knew how distraught we were and didn't want to burden us with his own emotional turmoil. But in this visit with Mike, he broke down about the painful reality of a terminal diagnosis. He shared his fears about preparing his family for his death and his deep sadness about not being able to watch the four young grandchildren he adored grow up.

Mike listened and, at the end of their tearful visit, said, "Fred, can I call you this Sunday at 7?" My dad thanked him for the therapeutic talk but assured him he didn't need to go to any more trouble.

Mike called that Sunday, unsure whether my dad would answer. At the end of another emotional conversation, he said again, "Fred, can I call you next Sunday at 7?"

And so, each Sunday, Mike offered an outlet for my dad during a trying time. During a dark week, my dad knew he had a glimmer of light awaiting him in his weekly conversation. He found great comfort in a listening ear when he could be honest about the highs and lows of a cancer journey. Mike looked forward to this guaranteed time to catch up with his dear friend and cherished their talks. His wife, Suzy, says their ritual was just as helpful to Mike as it was to my dad.

Through fifty-two chemotherapy treatments, Mike called each Sunday at 7. Through the lows of learning the tumor would never be operable, Mike called Sunday at 7. Through the highs of our annual "last" family vacations, Mike called Sunday at 7. Through news that the cancer had spread to the liver, Mike called Sunday at 7. Through CAT scans that continued to show stable cancer, Mike called Sunday at 7.

It has now been seven years of Sundays at 7.

My dad's tumor miraculously remains stable. He jokes that he is superstitious that Mike's phone calls have brought him good luck, so they can't stop now. But, perhaps, there is true value in the therapeutic power of emotional support.

Too often, not knowing what to do when someone is going through a difficult situation leads us to the worst option possible: doing nothing at all.

Turns out we don't need to have the perfect words of comfort, create elaborate gifts or desperately search the aisles at Hallmark. The greatest support we can give a friend in their time of need is an offer of ourselves. A promise of a consistent call with a caring heart and a listening ear doesn't cost a thing but is a priceless gesture of just the right size. It's as simple as "Can I call you this Sunday at 7?"

— Jennifer Kennedy —

34

Chocolate Cake

Kind words do not cost much.
Yet they accomplish much.
~Blaise Pascal

am is autistic. Thus, dining out can be tricky. Though he loves to eat, he dislikes the loud noise inherent to restaurant dining. Ever resourceful, he has a solution: overpower all noise with a much louder noise of his own.

This begins what I like to think of as dueling tables: neighboring parties escalate their volume followed by Sam escalating his until some sort of crescendo is reached, making us quite unpopular with family, most friends and other diners.

Faced with a possible eternity of dining alone, I decided to work on dining skills at a trendy new spot early one Tuesday night.

To my delight, we arrived to an empty restaurant. So far, so good. Everything went well until two older women entered. Well-groomed and elegantly dressed in an understated way, they were seated two tables away from us. I felt a sense of impending doom.

The women began to chat, paying little notice to us. Sam happily took this as his cue to start talking and drown them out. I leaned into Sam and asked for a quiet voice, but unfortunately Sam had left that voice at home.

I glanced at the neighboring table, knowing we wouldn't go unnoticed much longer. I quickly resorted to Plan B: eat quickly and leave. Sam, who normally inhales food, suddenly embraced the concept of leisurely dining and refused to rush — all while chattering away endlessly.

"SHUSH!" I said, a little exasperated. Sam responded by giggling loudly. "Be quiet!"

I could see from my peripheral vision that the two women were now watching us. Finally, the older of the two women leaned over. *Here it comes*, I thought. She completely surprised me when she said, "Honey, stop shushing that boy. Clearly, he has something important to say." Smiling, she added, "I have friends that talk way more than he does, and they aren't nearly as interesting."

Addressing Sam, she said, "Now, what's your name? Sam? Don't you listen to your mom. You talk as much as you want. I want to hear everything you have to say." Turning to me, she added, "You have a delightful boy. Relax and enjoy your dinner — and don't let him skip the chocolate cake. It's divine."

Sam smiled. Finally, someone wanted him to do what he did best: make noise and eat chocolate cake. It turned out to be the perfect night. I met two wonderful women who were clearly heaven-sent. Sam found the chocolate cake to be heavenly, too.

I will always remember those two lovely ladies. Their kindness meant the world to a stressed-out mom. Wherever they are, we're sending them lots of love and hopes for chocolate cake. Sam and I will never forget them.

— Janet L. Amorello —

35

I've Been There

Kindness in words creates confidence.
Kindness in thinking creates profoundness.
Kindness in giving creates love.
~Lao Tzu

A s I stood in line waiting to cash out at my favorite retail store, I studied the customer in front of me who was perusing the magazines to our left. She was young, maybe early twenties, but she already had a stooped, tired look to her — as if life had beaten her down too many times.

Her eyes were red-rimmed, and her face looked drawn from exhaustion. Her thin, unbuttoned winter coat had seen better days, as had the threadbare scarf bunched around her throat that probably did little to protect it from the cold snap we were experiencing. Her hands, thumbing through a few pages, were chapped and red — possibly because the gardening gloves that dangled from a ripped pocket substituted for thicker winter ones. They would offer minimal respite from the below-zero temperature. When I looked down at her boots, I could see a small piece of a clear plastic bag peeking out through a hole where the leather had split from the sole. Everything about her screamed hardship and need.

The items in her cart included the cheapest cuts of meat and meal stretchers like pasta, rice, and potatoes. There were also lots of ramen noodles. Powdered milk, day-old bread, bargain soap, and inexpensive shampoo completed her purchases — well, almost. Carefully tucked in a far corner sat a little doll, some brightly colored unicorn stickers, and a pretty dress that was 50 percent off.

She continued to look at the magazines as we waited, and more people lined up behind us. She finally plucked one out and turned it over several times, trying to find a price before finally turning to me.

"I'm sorry to bother you," she began timidly. "But can you tell me how much this is? I forgot my glasses at home."

"Of course," I said, pulling out my own readers with a laugh.

When I finally found the small print and told her, she sighed quietly and put it back.

"They've become so expensive, haven't they?" I murmured sympathetically.

"Next!" The cashier called before she could answer, and she moved forward to begin her transaction.

When the store employee finally tallied up everything and told her the cost, the woman's face paled. She opened a frayed change purse and began counting small bills and change. It was obvious she didn't have enough, and she scanned her groceries to see what she could do without.

One by one, she removed things, but she still came up short. She continued to discard much-needed goods while the cashier patiently deducted things with a pleasant smile, setting them aside.

When she added the shampoo to the growing pile, I could almost read her thoughts — that dish detergent would do.

The child's items remained in the cart, however. In fact, the palm of her other hand lay protectively across them, as if she didn't want to be tempted to surrender them.

The man right behind me cursed loudly enough for all to hear, and the young woman's cheeks reddened with embarrassment. I wanted desperately to pay for her groceries outright, but I knew that would mortify her even more. Instead, I whirled around angrily and glared at the man.

"Be grateful you've never had to do that!" I hissed at him in a low voice. He had the decency to look ashamed as he backed up, slamming into the cart behind him before he changed checkout lanes.

"He probably drives the same way, too!" I commented, and both the clerk and woman giggled. "Take your time," I added soothingly as she tried to decide what other necessity she could return. "I'm in no hurry."

The woman finally whittled down her groceries, paid, and moved down to bag them. By then, I had rearranged my own purchases and tossed the magazine she had been eyeing into my cart.

When my turn came, I moved forward and placed several items with the magazine, motioned inconspicuously to the pile of items the woman had taken out, added all my meat and fresh milk, and whispered "Separate bags, same bill please" to the cashier. She nodded, winked, and quickly complied, even though it was a "pack your own" kind of store.

She continued ringing me up, and I moved next to the woman and got busy bundling my own supplies. I wondered how I could sneak the extra things into the old battered folding cart she'd brought without being caught. My co-conspirator clerk solved the problem by "accidentally" rolling several oranges hard enough on the conveyer belt so that they flew past the lady and onto the floor.

"I'll get those," the woman offered kindly and ran to pick up the runaway fruit. I quickly tucked the two extra bags into her cart while she retrieved the last orange from under the next cashier's station. Just as I put the second one in, I noticed a twenty-dollar bill peeking out that I had not placed in there. Not missing a beat, I rammed it in further, ensuring it would not fall out. I rushed back and pretended to still be intent on my order just as she returned with my fruit.

"Thank you so much," I gushed.

"Thank *you* for your patience," she replied before pushing her cart toward the door.

"You put that money in there, didn't you?" I accused the clerk with a laugh when I went to pay my bill. I was surprised when she shook her head.

"Nope, it was her," she replied, pointing to a grinning woman who had taken the belligerent man's place behind us.

"I stuck my twenty at the bottom," she added.

"That was so nice of both of you!" I exclaimed.

"I have a feeling all three of us have been there at one time or another — maybe even more than once," the other customer murmured.

"Yes," the cashier and I replied in unison.

I left that store and stepped out into the wintry day, thankful for my warm clothes. I didn't know that woman's or the other two people's stories, but I knew mine and my husband's. We had walked many a mile in similar leaky boots and had rolled pennies to buy precious formula for our baby boy, now a grown man. We once also refused to surrender the one cheap outfit or toy we could ill afford. We were by no means rich now, but we had enough to get by.

I was home an entire hour before I realized I'd never replaced the groceries I meant to bring home. That night, as we ate macaroni and cheese, I told my husband, Don, about how my small, insignificant gesture had rippled to become a larger kindness than I ever could have imagined. As Don and I reminisced about past difficult times, my thoughts strayed to the young lady who I hoped was enjoying a hearty beef stew with her little girl, and I sent a silent prayer her way that her life would take an easier turn soon.

— Marya Morin —

Chapter 5

Friends & Neighbors

Unknown Gifts

*At times our own light goes out and is rekindled
by a spark from another person.*
~Albert Schweitzer

My husband and I had our first child during the COVID-19 pandemic. We had been planning on having children for years, but it never quite seemed like the right time. When COVID happened, so did a death in our friend circle, and it seemed like waiting was no longer an option.

We still lived in the same apartment we rented when we first began graduate school seven years earlier. We loved this apartment, mainly because it was always so quiet. The bulk of the residents were retired and kept to themselves. Since my husband and I were teaching at the local university, this atmosphere was ideal. We didn't want to be around parties or student life anymore. When we first moved in, the residents in our complex were kind when we ran into them, and they seemed interested in having more youthful faces in the building.

Throughout my pregnancy, I maintained my exercise routine. It was nothing rigourous, merely walking while listening to audiobooks. Since many of these residents also had dogs, I often saw them when I went out for my own walks. We only exchanged hellos, but as my pregnancy progressed, it became obvious that my husband and I, once graduate students, were now becoming parents. The older residents reached out to us more. They said hello more often, asked when the baby was due, and if we had names picked out.

Then I gave birth. It was in the middle of winter, and we were getting a mold situation in our apartment fixed. Days before I went into labour, the super had finally realized that the growing spot we'd been pointing out for the past few months was not merely a lack of cleaning or stained tiles. There was a bad situation underneath the floorboards. We needed our dishwasher and kitchen floor replaced, and we needed it done fast.

The super worked harder than I have ever seen to get this done. Still, she was unable to get the task completed by the time our son was born. The broken dishwasher — the cause of the mold — had been removed, and we had been assured of the safety of the apartment, but it was still demoralizing to come home and see a gaping hole in our kitchen and dark tiles that we now knew were moldy. It wasn't exactly the homecoming we wanted for our new son, but we had assurance from the super that it would get done. It was just taking a while due to COVID-19.

We understood and tried to go on with our new lives as parents.

One day just after Easter, when our son was six weeks old, I found a note slipped under our apartment door. It was not uncommon for the staff to do this when announcing new changes in management or garbage days, but this was handwritten. It simply said, "Gift outside."

I opened my door to find a green package hanging on the handle. I looked around but saw no one in the hallway. I took the package inside and quickly unwrapped an Easter present: a golden yellow duck holding Easter eggs, plus a card that congratulated us on the baby. It was unsigned. I had no idea who'd sent it, but I was overwhelmed with the kindness of the act. After so much struggle and heartache over our kitchen, and a few post-labour difficulties, this small present brought me much joy. I immediately wanted to thank the person but had no idea how.

Then, I remembered my Polaroid camera. My husband had bought me a bright pink Instax camera for Christmas. I grabbed it, positioned the duck with my six-week-old son, and took a photo. He smiled and beamed — he was always such a happy baby, even as his parents were grumpy from lack of sleep or needing to do all the dishes by hand — and the photo was great. I wrote on the edge of the image THANK YOU! and taped it on our door.

It was gone within the hour, but I still had no idea who to thank.

Eventually, I figured out that it was one of the many residents who had come up to us during the last few weeks of my pregnancy — a girlfriend of the man who lived next door. She'd been thrilled to see a young boy, since he reminded her of her son. She kept the photo of the baby on her fridge like we kept her card on ours.

What was so wonderful about this act of kindness was the mystery behind it. Not knowing who sent us the gift made me go back through all the people who had suddenly shown us interest and curiosity as we reached the end of our pregnancy. It allowed me to focus on the goodness inside our apartment complex while in the middle of a tug of war with the management to get our floor fixed. That floor would be fixed, the dishwasher replaced, and our lives back on a more even keel, but we would be even more friendly with all the neighbours. They know our names now, as well as our son's, and we do more than just greet each other in passing.

We are part of one another's lives, not just because of COVID, or my son, or even mold or anything else, but because I finally opened my eyes to the kindness that was already there.

— Eve Morton —

Closed Doors, Open Hearts

We rise by lifting others.
~Robert Ingersoll

I am prone to locking myself out. I leave my keys in the door, forget to turn off the stove, and rarely remember to close the windows before a thunderstorm. So, when I moved into a studio apartment for my final year of graduate school, I knew it would be wise to get acquainted with my neighbors.

The first time I met Ali, my across-the-hall neighbor, we were rushing off to our separate activities. Him, a law student with a full course load, and me, a frazzled journalist working remotely during the COVID-19 pandemic.

Though I am generally shy, I fought the urge to return his quick wave and hurry off. Instead, I introduced myself.

"I'm Sophie. I just moved in. It's nice to meet you," I said. "Do you think we could exchange phone numbers in case one of us gets locked out?"

He agreed. A few days later, my phone vibrated with a new message. *Hey, it's Ali! I left a batch of vegan brownies by your door.*

Another few days passed, and I received another message *Hey, it's Ali! I'm at the store. Is there anything you need?*

These acts of kindness continued throughout the year—through the highs and lows of graduate school, the bitter Midwestern winter, and the heaviness of an ongoing global pandemic. Sometimes, he knocked and I could see the shadow of a smile behind his mask, but mostly we exchanged small gifts— stickers, baked goods, once even a pocket-sized Constitution—asynchronously.

Inspired by Ali's unexpected generosity, I decided to pass on the kindness. I dropped a loaf of homemade bread—and, later, spicy Doritos—outside Ali's door, fresh banana bread and my favorite vinyl pin to a neighbor down the hall, and a batch of soup to a friend on the fourth floor. In turn, these neighbors slid kind notes under my door, borrowed each other's pots, pans and ingredients, and exchanged warm greetings in the hallways.

This small, informal network of helping, borrowing, and looking out for one another was a highlight in an otherwise dark, isolating year. Though the pandemic prevented us from gathering close, sharing a meal or handshake, and even revealing the bottom halves of our faces, we were able to find community in an unexpected place.

I'm in a new apartment now and have roommates to let me in when I lose my keys, but I will always remember the difference that a small act of kindness can make in a stranger's life.

—Sophie Bolich—

38

Grumpy Old Mr. Roberts

No act of kindness, no matter how small,
is ever wasted.
~Aesop

Looking out of the window of our new house, I was impressed with the colorful leaves that had dropped onto our lawn from the neighbor's gigantic, ancient beech tree. I noticed an older gentleman raking in his yard that morning while my son and I were having a quiet and lazy breakfast. Feeling energized by the coolness of the fall, I called my son to come outside with me. We grabbed our jackets and looked for our rakes among the boxes that were freshly unpacked and piled in the garage. We both loved having a yard of our own and cheerfully started to rake.

I saw the old man leave his house and get into his car. I waved happily at him, smiling, while he simply glared before turning his back.

"Hmm, that seems unfriendly," my ten-year-old stated. I threw some leaves at him, and he gleefully retaliated.

Two boys stopped by, introducing themselves to my son as our neighbors. They were brothers. The boys hit it off immediately and took turns with our rakes, making a gloriously large pile of leaves on our side of our property line. They warned us that "Grumpy Old Mr. Roberts" hated children, and they were careful to stay away from his yard. The boys told us that they were walking to the school bus one day, and, on a whim, they jumped into the pile of leaves that Grumpy Old Mr. Roberts had raked into a sweet mountain next to the bus pickup. The old man had hidden some dog poo in the leaves, and they spotted him chortling behind a curtain in the window as he watched them discover the surprise. The boys had to go home and change, making them miss their ride.

"I guess he doesn't want anyone to jump into his leaves, eh?" I observed.

With a roll of their eyes, they said, "He doesn't want anyone in his life."

After some hot chocolate and donuts, the boys said their goodbyes and promised to show my son around the neighborhood soon.

The next day, the boys' mother, Carole, came over bearing a gift basket filled with goodies and more hot chocolate. The subject of Mr. Roberts came up, and she gave me a bit of neighborhood history concerning him. Everyone just left him alone, she told me, considering him surly and unpleasant. She warned me that I should just ignore him and not look for trouble.

After she was gone, I wondered how I would feel knowing I was getting old and being so alone. My son and I decided to try and befriend him. We put some goodies from the welcome basket on a plate to take over to him. We knocked twice and put smiles on our faces. Grumpy Old Mr. Roberts answered with "What do you want?" as if we were selling him something. We introduced ourselves to him and offered him the plate of goodies. He gave a little growl and slammed the door in our faces. My son was very indignant, but by the time we reached our front door, we both decided he was sad and angry for some reason that had nothing to do with us.

A few days later, it was time to do more raking. The neighbor's beech tree had dropped so many leaves that we could not tell whose yard belonged to whom. We finished our yard, but our pile could have been bigger, so on a whim I walked firmly over to Grumpy Old Mr. Roberts' door and knocked. When he came to the door this time, I did not give him a chance to growl but blurted out my question, "May we rake *your* yard?" He looked quite surprised but said, "I suppose so, but I will not be paying you anything." I assured him we would never ask for money.

The neighbor boys came over just as we were starting to rake, and they ran home to get more rakes. The four of us finished Grumpy Old Mr. Roberts' yard in record time, with only a little leaf-throwing fight but much laughter and chatter. I told the boys to rake it all into our yard to add to our leaf pile, creating the largest mountain of orange, red, brown, and yellow leaves we ever saw. The boys were exhausted and promised to come back the next day when we were going to have a "pile in" and play in the leaves.

The next day was a beautiful Saturday with clear skies; it was warm enough to leave our jackets inside. My son took his time finishing breakfast and doing his chores, and we were just sitting down to lunch when we heard the scariest sound, like growling, and then screams just outside. We looked at each other in shock and both raced out to the porch to see what catastrophe had happened.

Well, there in our huge mountain of leaves floundered the two neighborhood boys, squealing in delight. Then up popped a third head. A grizzled, gray-haired head. There was our old neighbor pretending to swim in the leaves, laughing so hard he could not speak. That was the day we said goodbye to Grumpy Old Mr. Roberts and hello to our neighbor Mr. Roberts.

—Sheree Negus—

39

Porch Fairies

Fairies are invisible and inaudible like angels
but their magic sparkles in nature.
~Lynn Holland

"Who can that be at this hour of the night?" I asked my husband Harold as car headlights shined through our kitchen window. It was close to midnight, and we couldn't imagine who would be pulling into our driveway that late. I peeked through the window to see who it was just in time to see someone running back to their car. Seconds later, the car drove off. I slowly navigated back to the kitchen table in darkness only lit by a candle.

"Who was it?" Harold asked.

I shrugged my shoulders and told him I had no idea. I didn't recognize the car, and the person who came to our door ran off too quickly. I could only see their back. We both thought it was odd but came to the conclusion that they had been lost and come to the wrong house. We had more important problems to think about that night. Our power was once again shut off for non-payment, and we needed to figure out our next plan. We didn't want to ask family members to tide us over until things got better.

We had four small children and Harold had been out of work for two months with no job prospects in sight. I worked part-time in a church daycare. My paycheck was just enough to buy a modest amount of groceries. We had fallen behind on our bills and mortgage.

This particular month was proving to be the hardest. It was our second day without power, and that afternoon our phone was cut off. We were determined to get through this by ourselves without help, but we didn't know how.

We planned to head to the grocery store in the morning to purchase ice to keep whatever food we had from spoiling. We had just enough money for a little gas for our car and the ice.

In the daylight the next morning, we discovered the box on our porch. It was filled with staples. Canned goods, pasta, peanut butter and cereal were just a few of the items that filled the box to the brim. Farther down in the box was a bag that had three adorable stuffed bears, two yellow and the other pink. One for each of our daughters. There was also a small rubber toy truck appropriate for our son. The person who dropped off the box had to know our family. Digging deeper into the box, we found a sealed envelope. We were hoping there'd be a card to reveal who had delivered the box.

"Thinking of You" was printed on the top in a delicate, flowing script. We were astonished to find fifteen gift cards inside, some for our local grocery store and some general gift cards that could be used anywhere. Harold and I stood there too stunned to say anything. I was embarrassed that someone knew what we were going through and felt ashamed that we needed the help. We had wanted to keep our situation private.

In perfect penmanship, the sender wrote, "During tough times, we come together as a community to help our neighbors in times of need." The card was signed, "With Love, from your neighborhood Fairies."

I blurted out, "That's it! Now the whole neighborhood knows what we're going through!"

Harold stopped me before I could say another word. "These people from our community came together to help us. They did it because they care," he said calmly.

I pondered those words for a while. I knew he was right, but I couldn't get past being ashamed. I was always there when others needed a helping hand. I regularly donated to food banks and gave clothing to the church. So, why did I find it so hard to accept help from others?

That evening, while sitting in my kitchen, I felt relieved that we were able to restore our power because of the kindness of our community. I sat there replaying the day's events and realized I felt a sense of comfort. I was humbled that our community and friends got together to help us because they truly did care. Sometimes, pride should take a back seat to need, and I realized that. I shouldn't feel ashamed, I told myself. I should be grateful.

We never did find out who all our neighborhood fairies were, but we had some ideas. We learned a lot from our experience. Nowadays, it warms our hearts to sprinkle our own fairy dust on those who may be going through similar hardships.

—Dorann Weber—

40

A Helping Hand

A kind gesture can reach a wound that only
compassion can heal.
~Steve Maraboli

The words every parent dreads hearing were spoken to me at my son's bedside in our local hospital early last year. "Ma'am, your son is very sick."

What began as stomach pains had turned into a loss of blood that landed him in the emergency room the night before. After testing, it was confirmed that my previously healthy and vibrant son now had a colon that was attacking itself. It would have to be removed.

Of course, money wasn't the first thing on our minds. His survival was front and center. But over the next few days, as we waited out the lengthy process to get him transferred to a university hospital for surgery, it suddenly began to dawn on me: How would we pay for this? We had insurance, but it was the bare minimum that we could afford. This was happening at the beginning of the year, so our first and most terrifying hurdle was meeting the staggering $7,500 deductible.

To some families, this might not seem like much. But we are just an average-income family and coming up with that amount of money at once was next to impossible.

I tried to put it out of my mind and keep all my focus on my son and his health. We had a long road ahead of us and stressing over something beyond my control was not going to help the situation at hand.

But, still, it was there.

On one of those endless hospital nights waiting for his transfer, I was texting my good friend Vanessa and let that figure slip: $7,500. I knew there'd be many bills to come, but that first seemingly unattainable number kept floating around in my mind. She sympathized and let me get out my fear and frustrations like the great friend she is. Then we said good night, and I tried to get some sleep on the cot the hospital had provided for me.

The next morning, everything would change.

It started with a message from Vanessa. "I want to do this, but I want your permission." She went on to say that she wanted to start a GoFundMe for us.

Ironically, just the previous year, I had my first experience with GoFundMe when I raised funds to help my children's disabled father get a vehicle that would haul his power chair. It was successful, and I learned so much about the process.

But this would be different. A GoFundMe for me? Would my pride allow that?

"It's not for you. It's for him." With those wise words from my all-knowing friend, I gave her the go-ahead.

Within days, we had almost the entire amount to pay our deductible.

I could not believe the outpouring of love and support that came from such unexpected places. So many people that I didn't even realize knew my name were suddenly throwing generous sums our way. The collective love coming through that computer screen was a feeling I had never known. Strangers were helping us through the hardest thing we'd ever been through.

Complete strangers!

After that first deductible hurdle was overcome, things started looking up financially. My son was approved for a state-based insurance plan that covered most of his treatments and medications. Instinctually, I had known that that first amount was what we needed to achieve, and things would be okay from there. I just never dreamed that we'd get there so quickly.

My son is still fighting his health battle. And there have been countless moments of kindness that have been extended to us both over these past two years. But that first hand reached out to us by my friend Vanessa, and then by the countless others who followed her example, made all the difference to us. They eased our burdens.

Their kindness changed our lives.

—Melissa Edmondson—

41

Clever Kindness

*Through the kindness we bestow on others and through
the kindness others bestow upon us — we help keep
each other afloat in the stormy seas of life.*
~Orly Wahba, Kindness Boomerang

I'd just returned from a beautiful fall early-morning walk with my dog. At the front door, I dug around in my pockets for the keys. When I discovered I didn't have them, I decided to return to the paths we'd taken. I would surely spot them in plain sight.

My little dog ran in circles of excitement that we would do a repeat of our just-finished outing. I spent an hour looking, brushing aside tall grasses, but the keys remained lost. I was beginning to get upset as I thought of the consequences of losing them, so I continued to retrace our steps, to no avail.

At home again, I pulled the backup key from its hiding place, let myself in the house, and fell on the couch in exhaustion. At my age, one excursion is usually plenty! I began to take key inventory. The house key wasn't that important as I had an extra. The mail key was a big deal because getting a new one takes a lot of time. I had a spare car key, but it was temperamental, and the key fob would be expensive to replace. But the iron heart made by my grandson was precious beyond measure. For some reason, thinking of it being gone forever made tears come to my eyes. I admonished myself for losing the keys and not being more careful. In my head, I retraced my steps again and again but finally gave up. Life is too short to agonize over these things, I reminded myself.

For some reason I will never understand, I didn't begin the various tasks involved in getting replacements. Instead, I continued with the day, perhaps in some kind of denial that anything was amiss.

That night, it turned colder and we had a snow flurry. I enjoyed a comfort-food dinner, played soft music, and settled into a peaceful evening.

It was peaceful until I heard the horrific screech of my car alarm blasting from the garage. I rushed to the car, inserted the temperamental key in the door and finally opened it, and then wiggled it in the ignition until the alarm stopped. I felt red-faced as I imagined my next-door neighbors being startled and annoyed.

I went back in the house but it started again. I turned it off, went back inside, and the alarm blasted again. I repeated the process.

Back in the house, I waited, but the next sound was the front doorbell. Assuming it was a neighbor ready to fuss at me, I opened the door slowly and turned on the light with apologies ready.

In the light snow stood three neighbors from several streets away. One of them held out her gloved hand, with my keys hanging from her pointer finger and a giant smile on her face! I wanted to hug her, to express my deepest gratitude, but in a COVID world, all I could do was say, "Oh, my goodness! Thank you!"

She said, "Sorry about all the racket, but your key fob has the alarm button, and we kept pressing it until we found your home!" I took the keys in my grateful hands and gushed, "How can I ever thank you? What a brilliant idea! You are so very kind!"

I was dazzled by her cleverness and didn't think to ask where she had found them. Before she and the other neighbors waved goodbye and disappeared into the evening snow, she said, "It's not a big deal. Happy to help. You would have done the same thing!"

I don't think I would have done the same thing! Pressing the alarm until I heard a car alarm would not have occurred to me. I was astonished by her clever kindness and wished I could have hugged her. Instead, I hugged the keys.

— Caroline S. McKinney —

42

My Christmas Story

A good deed is never lost; he who sows courtesy reaps friendship,
and he who plants kindness gathers love.
~Rock Bankole, How to Be Happy

n Christmas Eve nearly fifty years ago, I was a cub reporter at a small-town Kansas newspaper. Still wet behind the ears, I would soon discover that an act of kindness, whether large or small, is sometimes found in the most unlikely of places and at the most needed of times.

On this special day, the boss had made a deal with us employees. If we all met early deadlines, he would put the newspaper to bed a few hours ahead of schedule.

Since I covered the "cop shop," my main task was to check in there to learn whether there had been a bank robbery, jail break or some other major crime.

"Nope," the officer at the front desk said, anticipating my question. He added with a chuckle, "Too cold for the local criminals."

As he did every morning, he handed me the blotter — the police department's handwritten list of the telephone calls it had received. With my pointer finger, I went down the list. Mostly piddly. There was one entry, however, that caught my attention. A woman named Sheila from the north side — the poor part of town — had called to report that all her clothes had been stolen.

The very next entry was written about two hours later. Sheila called again, this time reporting that all her clothes had been found.

"You know the scoop?"

"Nope," the officer replied. "In that neighborhood, you never know."

I had a hunch there might be a story there. Besides, I had not yet come up with a local human-interest story for the front page. I tried to have one daily, one that would make my readers smile.

I drove my Volkswagen Beetle to Sheila's house in search of the crime scene. With notebook and pencil in hand, I knocked on her door and explained I was hoping to write a story about her "incident." She was holding a baby in her arms, and two little boys were hiding behind her skirt.

"Don't mind them," she said, patting them on the head. "We've never had a visitor before; they don't know what to make of you."

She explained that this had not been a good time for her family. Her husband had been ill and lost his job. He was asleep in the next room. Preparing for Christmas, she washed all their clothes. The dryer was on the fritz again, and the landlord hadn't gotten around to fixing it. She could have taken the wet clothes to the laundromat on the other side of town. "But," she whispered, "that costs money." Instead, she hung them all on the clothesline behind the house. When she checked a short time later, she discovered that all the clothes were gone. Stolen! That was when she called the police for the first time. A couple of hours later, there was a knock at her door. By the time she got there, no one was there. Instead, there was a large cardboard box at the front door. In it were all the clothes: dried, pressed and folded. And there was a note: "Wish we could do more. Merry Christmas."

Back at the newsroom, I hollered out for the first and only time in my journalism career, "Hold the presses!"

"This better be good," the boss grumbled.

With the story ready to explode in my head, it took only minutes for me to type it up. I rushed it down the line to the proofreader. It was with the layout person that I hit a snag. "You forget our early deadline?" she asked. "Today's paper is already laid out. Best I can do is try to squeeze it onto Page 7."

"Page 7," I shrieked. "The obituary page? No way. This goes on Page 1. And put it above the fold."

The press was warming up with its usual hum. The carrier boys had arrived. Each would be given a hundred newspapers to fold and tuck into a canvas bag slung over one shoulder. On a shiny new Schwinn or worn-out hand-me-down, they would deliver the newspapers all across town, flinging one onto each awaiting front porch. The hum became a roar as the press started. When the printed newspapers began coming out on the conveyor belt, the boss handed me the first one for both of us to read. There it was: my Christmas story. Page 1. Above the fold.

"Good job," the boss said with a rare smile and even rarer pat on the back. "Because of your story, our town will have a better Christmas. So will I."

Back at Sheila's, I gave her a couple of extra copies. She read one with a tear in her eye. "Your story is beautiful," she said. "Will you read it to my family?"

"Of course," I told her. "But this isn't my story; it is *your* story."

With her family seated at my feet, I began to read. That was when I noticed they all were wearing clothes that were freshly dried, pressed and folded, looking almost brand-new.

— Don Lambert —

43

Grace for the Moment

*Imagine what our real neighborhoods would be like if
each of us offered, as a matter of course,
just one kind word to another person.*

~Mr. Rogers

"**M**ommy!" I called over my shoulder. "Grace is here!" Our neighbor, Grace, stood on our front porch holding a medium-sized cardboard box. She wore a pretty, green housedress and lots of red lipstick, and she smelled of cigarettes and beer. Her brown and gray hair was curled in a fashionable 1960s bob.

It took Mom a few minutes to get to the front door. At forty-two, her health wasn't good, and her hair had gone prematurely gray. She had an odd, flat-footed gait when she walked that her doctor called "drop foot," an aftereffect she suffered when she was pregnant with my younger sister. She wore her only outfit: a sleeveless housedress covered by a bib apron. She was a bit younger than Grace, but she looked decades older. On this particular day, her face was swollen, and her eyes were puffy. Still, she smiled at our next-door neighbor.

"Come in and have a cup of coffee."

"I can't stay, Kassie," Grace answered in her raspy, southern drawl. "I just thought you all might be able to use some of this food. We get more at those giveaways than we can use."

I felt relieved that Grace couldn't stay. She was friendly enough, but she and her husband drank a lot — at least that's what my parents told me — and they were given to loud arguments late at night. Sometimes, the police had to come and break up the fights. I was a little frightened of them. Our aunt and uncle, who lived in the other half of our house, warned us to stay away from Grace and her family.

"You hear them fighting," my uncle would say, "plug your ears. Kids shouldn't hear words like that." This from a man who could hold his own in any swearing match!

Grace placed the box on the yellow Formica kitchen table. Mom, who was not the sentimental type, got tears in her eyes.

"Grace! We can't take this."

Dad wandered in from the bedroom where he had been napping. He wore a dingy undershirt and trousers, and he needed a shave. He wasn't dealing very well with the layoff at the steel mill, and he spent most of his time sleeping or watching TV. I studied him carefully, afraid of his reaction to Grace's box of food.

"We don't accept charity," he said.

"Now, Jim," said Grace, "this is no time for your pride. You have two little girls and a sick wife to think of. This isn't charity. It's one neighbor helping another. You'd do the same for me, I know it."

I stood a little distance from the grownups, looking into each of their faces, wondering what was going to happen next. My little sister had come in from her nap. She leaned into my mother's leg. Mom pulled her close.

"I thank you kindly," Dad said at last. He looked embarrassed. Ever the gentleman, he hated to hurt anyone's feelings. In that moment, I knew he wouldn't refuse the box of food. "We'll put it to good use."

"Now, Kassie, if there's anything else you need, don't be afraid to ask," Grace said on her way out the door.

When she was gone, we examined the contents of the box. It contained instant milk, powdered eggs, half a brick of yellow cheese, and miscellaneous canned items including Spam, salmon, and sardines. It wasn't what we were used to.

Mom smiled and said, "This will get us through for a couple of weeks." Her cheerfulness was a stark contrast to Dad's morose, beaten-down expression.

Mom had a talent for creating meals from what we had in the pantry. She made spoon bread with the canned salmon, accompanied by whatever was on sale at the corner grocer's that week. We had powdered eggs and Spam for breakfast — and sometimes dinner — more times than I care to count. She made grilled-cheese sandwiches with the cheese and days-old bread that the corner grocery store gave away. Dad was the only one who liked the sardines, and he was welcome to them as far as I was concerned.

The gesture from Grace confused me because she wasn't family, and she wasn't even close friends with us. According to the neighborhood gossips, she wasn't a nice woman. Even though I didn't like most of the food in that box — especially the sardines — I knew there was something significant about this woman's generosity. I could sense it in the gentle way my parents spoke to her, how they invited her into our home, how she graciously refused the offer of a cup of coffee. It wasn't until I was older that I understood her refusal didn't mean she was being rude. She understood that even in our poor neighborhood, there were boundaries one didn't cross.

A few weeks later, she was out on her porch smoking a cigarette.

"Hi, Grace!" I yelled across the cement block wall that separated our properties.

"Is your daddy back to work?"

"Yes, ma'am! That food you gave us was sure delicious." It wasn't what I was thinking, but for some reason I needed to say it.

After that, I didn't care what my aunt and uncle or anyone else said about Grace. When I saw her outside, I spoke to her. She didn't have much to give, but she gave what she had at a time when our family needed help. Of all the people in our town who could have reached out to us that summer, including people from our own church, the only one who ever did was Grace.

— Elizabeth A. Dreier —

44

Neighbor Helping Neighbor

Kindness and compassion are powerful forces to help inspire,
heal, and transform the world.
~Germany Kent

It sounds like a riddle. What can simultaneously tear a community apart and knit it together? My husband and I returned from a week of vacationing with family at the beach and inadvertently found our answer.

We couldn't believe the destruction. While we were away, a tropical storm had brought flash flooding to our neighborhood and ravaged our town. We peered into our basement at personal belongings floating atop five feet of water and were grateful that it was only our basement. Nearby, neighbors lost their cars and even their homes.

As we pulled old photo albums, school yearbooks, childhood stuffed animals, furniture patiently awaiting a larger home, and years' worth of memories out of the floodwaters and piled them into trash bags, we could save very little. But I noticed a pattern.

"I forgot we had this!" I found myself exclaiming to my husband again and again.

The message was clear. It was only stuff. In a year or two, I wouldn't be able to keep track of the items that were lost to the flood versus the things that were salvaged. I envisioned myself rummaging through our basement five years from now and once again exclaiming in surprise, "I forgot we had this!"

But there are some things I won't forget. I'll remember the faces of the dozen neighbors who were standing outside our door with masks, gloves, shovels, buckets and supplies ready to help us clean out our basement. They stayed all day until it was finished. There was the high-school football team that shoveled inches of mud from the floor in record time as if they were, well, a team of high-school football players.

There were phone-charging stations that dotted the neighborhood as kind strangers made sure everyone without electricity could still talk to their loved ones. And there was the local electrician who gave up his day off to spend six hours at our house making sure we had power as soon as possible.

I won't forget the coolers full of water, cold beverages and sandwiches that neighbors set outside for anyone in need, or the local restaurants that offered free food and drinks for those too tired to make dinner after hauling waterlogged items from their homes.

I'll always remember the look of joy on the face of one passerby as he said, "My mother's keys! Someone found my mother's keys! She was going to have to pay seventy-five dollars to replace them!"

They washed up on our sidewalk, and our neighbor returned them to this man. Everyone lost so much in the flood; I watched as this simple act of kindness lit up his whole face.

Friends wrote us letters, sent gift cards, and offered nights at hotels while our electricity was out. They invited us to their homes for hot meals and hot showers until our boiler could be replaced. They delivered food and much-appreciated bottles of wine and empathetic conversation. Local businesses left cleaning products on front doorsteps; neighbors lent time, money and equipment; and no one thought twice about extending a helping hand to someone else in crisis. Even a simple "I understand what you're going through" went a long way. We were all in it together.

In fact, nearly the entire community gathered in the library parking lot for beer, burgers and a few laughs at the end of a very long weekend of cleanup. I looked around, feeling as though we had lost so much but gained so much more thanks to the kindness of friends and strangers alike. That memory will always stay.

There's a bench in one of our parks that sports a plaque saying our town "is about neighbor helping neighbor." I pass it sometimes on my morning walks. But it's taken on a different meaning since I watched members of our community hang a large sign over the most devastated part of town that reads "Together, we will rebuild."

With time, hard work and perseverance, I know we will. In hope, spirit and togetherness, it's clear we already have.

— Elizabeth Blosfield —

45

Christmas Friends

*Christmas is the season for kindling the fire
of hospitality in the hall, the genial flame
of charity in the heart.*
~Washington Irving

Christmas of 1997 was a huge hurdle for our family, but we managed to chop down a tree and decorate the house in preparation, as usual. Our two daughters and our son were as excited as ever, but the struggle surfaced for them as much as for my husband, Andy, and me as we were all trying to make the best of the new shape of our family.

"Can I hang Noah's ornament, Mom?" Hannah asked, pulling her brother's Baby's First Christmas ornament out of the box. It had been three months since Noah died at age fifteen months, leaving a gaping wound in our family.

"Sure, honey," I answered, wishing I could add, "but hang it up high where Noah can't grab it." Seven months old the previous Christmas, Noah had been mostly interested in lying under the tree and swatting at the ornaments, longing to stuff them all in his mouth along with any wrapping paper he could get his chubby fists on. This year, I imagined he would have discovered the art of unwrapping gifts, delighting in what he'd find inside.

Christiana and Micah helped Hannah hang the remaining ornaments, and then we all walked next door to Noah's new home — the cemetery. There, we'd planted a sweet gum tree on top of his ashes.

The granite bench we'd ordered had recently been placed underneath, and the kids took turns standing on the armrest, hanging a Noah's ark ornament on a lower branch along with others that seemed weather-proof enough to withstand the elements. Solar lights not being readily available in those days, I'd wanted to run a long extension cord from our house and wrap his leafless tree in twinkling lights, but that, of course, proved to be impossible. Like my baby boy, his tree was simply too far away from us for a warm embrace.

And yet, there was some magic in the air that season. On the first day of Christmas, I opened the front door in the morning to find a wrapped gift on our doorstep along with a note. I read it aloud to the kids: "For the Kittel family, on the first day of Christmas. There are no words that can bring comfort to you this first Christmas without your little son and brother, but we want you to know we care. Each night as we make our visit, we will be praying for you."

"Who's it from, Mommy?" Christiana asked.

"It says, 'From Your Christmas Friends.' And there's one more thing. It's a Bible verse from 2 Thessalonians 3:16 (NASB): Now may the Lord of peace Himself continually grant you peace in every circumstance."

"Who could they be?" Hannah asked.

"I wonder," I mused, genuinely perplexed myself but feeling a little more peaceful given the reminder.

"They must be elves! I'll open it!" Micah offered, always ready to help.

I don't recall what Micah unwrapped that morning, nor do I remember even one of the gifts that were to follow, as our Christmas Friends left us something every night for the twelve days of Christmas. We never caught them in the act or discovered who these thoughtful folks were, making elves seem like a distinct possibility, but their kindness soothed us all in our time of great struggle.

The kids went to bed each night with anticipation and awoke each day with excitement. And it was maybe even more affirming for Andy and me, as we both needed something greater than our worldly sorrow to focus on. Each of those twelve dark, winter days began with a sparkle of light, giving us all the encouragement we needed to get out of bed with a little more lightness in our steps and a sense of wonder in our hearts.

— Kelly Kittel —

One Good Turn Deserves Another

46

Cash, Credit and Kindness

Appreciation is a wonderful thing. It makes what is
excellent in others belong to us as well.
~Voltaire

The post office is not my favorite hangout, but that day I barreled through the heavy glass door with a huge smile and an elated heart. My story had been accepted for publication in a *Chicken Soup for the Soul* book. I had read the e-mail three times before I actually believed it. After months of slogging through a string of stressful life events, I had a spring in my step and a lightness in my heart.

Grasped firmly in my hand was the form giving permission to print my story. No faxing for me — I had decided to send it back through the mail just to be sure it reached its destination. I was taking no chances.

I riffled through the array of mysterious forms. Did anyone know the difference between certified and registered? I chose the certified form and filled it out.

My favorite clerk had the uncanny skill of making the post-office experience pleasant. Luck seemed to be flowing my way, and she looked up with a smile and called, "Next!"

Bubbling over with excitement, I told her about my good news as she stuck the form to my envelope.

"Wow, look at you go!" she said. "That will be ten dollars."

The cost was nothing compared to the peace of mind already wrapping itself around me. I reached for my credit card.

"Our system is on the blink today, so we can only accept cash or check," said my friend.

I pawed through my purse in dismay. Before the pandemic, I carried cash. Now, I rarely did, shuddering to think of bills and coins passing through scores of germy fingers.

Tears clouded my vision. I just wanted to get this done before I met my friend for lunch. Why was everything so difficult?

Then a deep voice behind me said, "I'll take care of it."

I hadn't noticed the man behind me, who was keeping a respectful social distance. I turned to meet his sympathetic gaze as he held out a ten-dollar bill.

"Congrats on your story," he said. "Just pay it forward."

As I left the post office, that often-overused phrase sent a zing of joy down through my toes.

With my rose-colored glasses firmly back in place, I drove to the seaside restaurant to meet Tina. We hadn't seen each other in months, and we laughed and talked our way through the meal. Waves gently splashed against the seawall, and a flock of pelicans soared overhead. I inhaled the bracing, salt-tinged air, and reflected on the kindness of the man at the post office.

As Tina and I walked back toward our cars, I noticed something on the sidewalk, glimmering in the sun's reflective rays. I picked up a credit card and thought, *This can't be good.*

"How are we ever going to find the person who dropped this?" Tina asked in dismay.

I was in a hopeful space, determined to roll with it. "First, let's try to spot someone who seems to be searching frantically," I said. Tina looked doubtful.

We continued to walk, our gazes swiveling between the beach and the cars diagonally parked nose-in to the curb. The sun-loungers and Frisbee players seemed carefree. After we played detective for several more blocks, I checked my phone, thinking of my fast-approaching Zoom meeting.

One Good Turn Deserves Another |

"I'll bet that's her!" Tina exclaimed. A young mother was wrangling three children into a silver SUV. She had a baby propped on her hip as she dug through some bags in the back.

A toddler bounced around in the front seat, and a little girl peered under the vehicle.

I approached the woman. "Are you Jessica Slate?" I asked.

Her eyes got round. "Yes!"

"I believe this is yours," I said, handing her the card.

"Thank you, thank you! I had no idea where I dropped this." She wiped away a solitary tear. "During normal times, I'd give you a hug."

We laughed and bumped elbows instead. She tucked in her shirt, grabbed the pen her baby was about to stick in his mouth, and tucked the card into her small purse.

"You saved my day," she told me. "Truly."

During my drive home, I mused that being on both the receiving and the giving end of kind gestures felt equally good. I had experienced a literal interpretation of paying it forward—first with cash, then with credit.

When it comes to acts of kindness, all forms of payment are acceptable.

—Kim Johnson McGuire—

47

An Artist in Nepal

Wherever there is a human being,
there is an opportunity for a kindness.
~Lucius Annaeus Seneca

I always thought I was a kind person. I teach English in developing countries, and I make very little money. I figured that earned me some karma points. My job was helping people, so I didn't need to do anything on top of that.

One day, while I was traveling alone in Kathmandu, I saw a teenager selling paintings on the street. He called out to me, saying that he made all the pictures himself, and he was saving up money for school. The pictures were beautiful, brightly colored landscapes of mountains and traditional houses. In a different city, I might have bought one, but I figured that he could be some sort of scam artist, so I thanked him and kept walking. As I left, he asked if I had just a bit of change to spare. I did, but I told him no.

After a few hours of shopping and roaming, I found myself back on the same street. Somehow, I had wandered into the middle of what seemed like a political rally. Everyone was shouting in Nepalese, so I couldn't figure out what was happening, but I saw these big black flags, and everyone looked really angry.

I made a quick U-turn and tried to leave down a side alley, but it was full of people shoving each other. A group of at least six policemen was walking right toward me. They were clearly trying to break up the demonstration, and I had walked right into the middle of it.

Before I knew it, I heard a voice shout at me from a half-opened door. "Hey, American!" I didn't know who it was, but I knew right away that this was someone trying to help me. I rushed toward the door and saw the face of that teenaged artist looking through the crack. "You shouldn't be there," he said.

I had to choose between trusting him or staying in the midst of what could very easily turn into a riot. He opened the door enough for me to enter, and I did. I saw that I'd made it inside a sort of art studio. The teen and a bunch of others about his age were inside, and the walls were covered with their pieces.

I really didn't know what was going on, but I knew that I was in a safe place. He introduced himself and said that he'd recognized me from before. I asked him why he wanted to help me, and he just shrugged, like it was the dumbest question anyone could ask.

As we waited for the commotion outside to die down, he gave me a tour of the place. He showed me his favorite painting — a beautifully intricate Nepalese design that seemed to have a hidden meaning behind each curving line. It was truly beautiful.

It took about twenty minutes for the demonstration to break up. Looking back, I probably was never in any real danger, but I will forever be thankful for the kindness this young man had shown me. He didn't try to sell me anything or demand any sort of payment for his help. He just gave me a tour and kept me occupied before it was safe to go back outside.

When he finally told me it was a good time to leave, I asked if I could buy one of his multicolored landscapes. It was a small way to pay back his kindness, but it was also a way to have something to remember him by.

I still have that landscape up on my wall. When I look at it, I think about my time in Kathmandu and that young artist's kindness toward me. I don't know what happened to him, but I hope that he was able to save enough to go to school.

— Evan Purcell —

48

The Submarine Sandwich

Carry out a random act of kindness, with no
expectation of reward, safe in the knowledge that
one day someone might do the same for you.
~Princess Diana

About a month ago, my husband and I found kindness in an unlikely place: standing in line at a Subway sandwich shop to pick up a quick dinner. It was extremely busy on this particular night, and I noticed a dad behind us with his little girl, who looked to be around four. The man seemed as exhausted as my husband, but the little girl was chirpy and excited as she waited for her sub and cookie.

I watched as the man behind us got closer to the front of the line. He started to look worried. Right before we checked out, I heard the man say to the woman who had made his subs that he was sorry but didn't have enough money to pay for them all and to just leave his out. He looked very embarrassed. His little girl continued jabbering and jumping around excitedly.

I quietly asked the cashier to add the man's whole order to ours. I paid the $87.73, and we got out of there before the man behind us knew what had happened.

Like many others since COVID-19 hit, our family of five was living on one income. I was holding our debit card and knew that we only had $90.16 in our account. That was all we would have until payday three days later. But still, it felt great to be able to help that family, even though we would be out of money for a few days.

What happened next was amazing. My husband went back to that Subway the next week to pick up five subs that I thought would cost $44.58. There was $47 in our account.

But it turned out the dinner cost more than we had on the card. My husband told them to put his sub back because he couldn't afford it. Then he paid for the four subs and headed to our van. As he opened the door, one of the workers ran out to catch him and handed him his sub. She ran back into the building before he could ask any questions. With a grateful heart, he assumed that the ladies had just given it to him since they had already made it anyway.

About two minutes later, he was getting ready to back out when he saw that same man and little girl from a week earlier. Now my husband knew what had happened. The two men nodded at one another and went on their way, making sure for the second time that they both left the store with dinner for their families.

In a world where face masks, standing six feet apart, and hand sanitizer have become our new normal, it's refreshing and soul-lifting when someone does something kind for you, even if it's only at a local Subway. Helping one another in kindness is about all we have left.

— Danielle Stauber —

49

What Goes Around, Comes Around

*The act of giving and receiving is where the real magic
of human connection occurs.*
~Leon Logothesis, The Kindness Diaries

One day as I drove toward my home in a small Colorado town, I passed the local bus depot. Several passengers had already exited a bus and were making their way to parked cars or setting off on foot to their various destinations.

I pulled up as a group of people crossed the road in front of me. As I watched, I noticed a thin, shabbily dressed older lady struggling with a preposterously large suitcase.

She managed to carry it for a few yards before setting it down on the ground. After resting for a few moments, she picked it up with the other hand and pressed on, stopping periodically to rest and change hands. When the traffic started to move again, I saw the same elderly lady still struggling with the overweight suitcase. (This was before the days when suitcases were fitted with little wheels that enabled travelers to pull their luggage behind them with the least amount of effort.)

Now, witnessing this lady and remembering similar struggles I had experienced in the past when traveling, I pulled up alongside her and leaned over to call out through the open passenger window, "Excuse me. Would you like a lift?"

She stopped and stared at me suspiciously without answering. I repeated, "Do you want a lift?" She still hesitated and then started to walk slowly toward me, dragging her suitcase along the ground. "I'm going right into the town," I said. "If you want to tell me where you are going, I'll drop you off. That suitcase looks awfully heavy."

"Well, all right," she answered in an almost hostile voice. And after we had both lifted her luggage into the back of my pickup, she settled herself without a word on the front seat beside me. My attempts at conversation were a failure, so I settled for an uneasy silence except for directions to her destination. When we got there, I helped her down with the suitcase. Standing on the sidewalk, she dug her hand into a pocket.

Abruptly, she said, "What do I owe you? I don't have much."

Surprised, I said, "You don't owe me anything. I was glad to be able to help."

Her expression changed immediately, and she stared at me unbelievingly.

"Well, God bless you, lady. No one has ever done me a kindness like that before. I hope someone will do a good turn for you one day." Then she disappeared down an alley without waiting for any further help from me.

Shortly after the encounter with the suitcase lady, I decided to spend a day in the mountains. My husband was visiting his parents in another state, and I looked forward to spending some time in the high country alone. I had several dogs at that time, all rescues, and I decided to take one with me for company. I chose Blue, a huge Old English Sheepdog with strikingly beautiful blue eyes. Blue was advanced in age but excited about going for a ride. Ensuring that I was properly equipped for mountain travel, I set off in my pickup, which was also elderly but serviceable.

After driving for nearly two hours, I found myself on an overgrown track that in the past had probably been an old logging road. Having been in the area several times before, I was not concerned about getting lost but decided to retrace my steps and take an easier route. I was not prepared for the next turn of events. There was a sudden loud noise, and with a jerk and a shudder my truck came to a full stop. I found that, as I turned around on the narrow, overgrown track, I had hit a boulder half concealed in the heavy undergrowth.

Now, in a remote area, with no hope of finding another person, I knew I was in big trouble. I could tell by the lack of tire tracks or hoofprints that no one had traveled in this deserted area for a long time.

Cell phones or other means of contacting civilization were yet unknown, and it would take many hours on foot to reach a highway of any kind. I doubted if Blue could make it, even if I could. Over and over, I blamed my own stupidity for being in a deserted area with no possible chance of help. I hoped that no wandering bear would come to investigate. Or a hungry mountain lion — with babies. My imagination ran riot.

I thought I should start walking but didn't want to leave Blue. It would take many hours to reach any kind of help and return to the scene of the accident. Even locked in the truck, he could be in danger from large wild animals. I tried to plan, but when I came up with nothing, I started to quietly panic.

Then faintly, in the distance, came the roar of motorbikes. Peering down the mountainside, I could see a string of perhaps twenty bikes far below, coming in my direction. As they drew nearer, I could see by their leather jackets and the logo on the back that they were a dreaded motorcycle gang.

Back then, these kind of motorcycle gangs were feared by law-abiding citizens as rough, tough, violent men, capable of any deed. And here was I, helpless, with a string of outlaws approaching. I looked for somewhere to hide, but there was nowhere. To my horror, the leader pulled up beside me, and everyone stopped.

"Do you need help, ma'am?" I heard a concerned voice say. I almost fainted with relief. The first few bikers propped up their Harleys, or whatever they happened to be riding, and formed a group around the truck. A couple of them crawled underneath it.

"You have a broken axle, ma'am. You'll have to be towed," came a muffled voice from under the pickup. Another said, "I'd take you back to town on the back of my bike, but I can't take the dog. He's too big."

The whole adventure ended with a volunteer making the long trip back to town. He waved to the leader as he sped off, shouting, "You all go on. I'll meet you there."

I never knew where "there" was, but they all cranked up their bikes and waved farewell as they roared away. In due time, a tow truck appeared, and my pickup, Blue, and I were all transported back to safety. I shall never forget the kindness of the motorcycle riders who stopped.

Some people will say it was all just a happy coincidence, but personally I like to believe the old proverb, "What goes around, comes around."

— Monica Agnew-Kinnaman —

The Right Thing

There seems to be a trend that I have noticed.
It seems the more peace and love I wish on
others the more peace and love come to me.
~Germany Kent

I hadn't worn jewelry for the entire pandemic year. What for? I barely got out of my mix-and-match sweatpants and pajamas. But one morning, trying to organize my space, shuffling things from one side of the room to the other, I picked up a gold bracelet with a tiny diamond chip in a blue velvet bag that I had bought at a flea market years before. I put it on to admire it, and then rushed out to get lunch and completely forgot that I was wearing it.

"Somebody must have lost this," a soft female voice announced from behind me in the bagel shop. A hand passed the sparkling gold bracelet to the person behind the cash register.

Shocked, I yelled out, "It's mine."

As the clerk gave it to me, I noticed that the safety latch was loose. I turned around to thank the person who had found and returned it, but she had disappeared quickly. I was overcome with gratitude for her kindness. The bracelet obviously had some value, and she could easily have walked out with it. But she didn't.

Looking at it, I remembered the day that I had bought it. "Why are you selling such a lovely bracelet?" I recall asking the young woman at the flea market.

Clearly, not the best approach for a bargaining position. In gam-

One Good Turn Deserves Another |

bling, it's called "showing your hand."

The bracelet had stood out because everything else on her display table was pottery. I looked at the small white tag with the price attached to the bracelet.

"I'd rather not sell it," she replied. "I had this made for me. But my car broke down, and I need the money to fix it. I live in another state, and I have no other means of transportation. I don't know what I'm going to do."

I'm a native New Yorker and, quite honestly, I've heard it all. But this felt different. Her forlorn expression was very telling, and the bracelet was certainly worth what she was asking for it.

She looked at her watch, realizing that the flea market was closing in an hour. "Would you be interested if I took off," she hesitated, "twenty more dollars or thirty?"

How could I morally negotiate a price with someone in such a position? I paid her the original asking price, and she came from behind her stand and hugged me.

"Thanks so much," she whispered.

"No, thank you," I replied. "The bracelet is beautiful, and I'm grateful to be able to have it. But I must admit I feel as though I'm a pawnbroker taking advantage of the situation."

"Oh, please, you are doing me the biggest favor." She hugged me again. "You're paying me a fair price, and now I can get home."

I thought of this encounter last year during COVID. As I was walking down a local street, I saw money lying on the ground. It was fifteen dollars, a ten and a five. I stood there waiting for someone to come back to retrieve it. Maybe it would be a frantic child or a senior having dropped it. I waited a while, but no one came.

When I got home, I put a notice on our community e-mail site. "Found money on Henry Street. Please contact me if it is yours." Shortly, a notice was posted beneath it. It read, "Boy, you must really be rich to be able to give the money back." I must admit, I was flabbergasted. How could anyone respond in such a way? How do you measure decency? Or respect for another person's misfortune?

Later that morning, there was another notice from a woman who wrote that she had lost fifteen dollars, a ten and a five-dollar bill. Bingo. I called her.

"I'd be so happy to return it to you," I said.

"Thank you, but please donate it to an organization that takes care of cats," she replied.

Apparently, she was also paying it forward.

—Linda Holland Rathkopf—

The Traveling Ice Scraper

*No one is useless in this world who lightens
the burdens of another.*
~Charles Dickens

My windshield wipers pushed the icy slush across my windshield as I pulled into a parking spot at the far end of the lot. I glanced at my dashboard clock. Despite the bad weather, I was only a few minutes late for work. From the look of the half-empty parking lot, however, it seemed I was not the only one who had trouble negotiating the slick roads. I would have loved to remain at home a bit longer that morning, nursing my cup of coffee until the road crews finished clearing the roads. But when you work in a health-care facility, you're expected to arrive at your designated start time regardless of circumstance.

With that in mind, I snapped off the ignition and then gingerly stepped from my car. As I shielded my eyes from the blowing snow, I spotted several night-shift staff struggling to remove the layer of ice that covered their car windows. One staff member was poking and prodding at her windshield with nothing more than a gloved hand. Instinctively, I reached for the ice scraper I had hastily thrown in my tote bag. It was my favorite, made of sturdy royal blue plastic with an unusual hot pink stripe down the handle. That didn't matter — she needed it. And, as someone who lives by the Boy Scout's motto to "be prepared," I knew I had at least one more ice scraper in the trunk of my car.

I approached the woman and handed her the ice scraper. "Here," I said. "Use this."

"Why, thank you," she answered, looking a bit taken aback and extremely grateful. "But how will I get it back to you?"

I waved my hand. "Just keep it," I said with a smile. "It's going to be a long winter." Then I forgot about it.

But here's the funny thing. Later that week, I saw that same ice scraper in the hands of one of our nurses. After another particularly bitter storm, I spied the scraper's distinctive handle in the palm of one of our van drivers as he cleared ice from around the edges of his vehicle's door. And, in the midst of an unexpected spring snow, I spied a sturdy royal blue ice scraper with an unusual hot pink stripe down the handle peeking out of the tote bag of one of our administrative assistants.

"I'm just curious," I remarked. "Where did you get that cool-looking ice scraper?"

"Someone lent it to me last night since I'd left mine at home."

I took a close look at the royal blue plastic. It looked a bit worn but still useful. I don't know how many grateful sets of hands that implement has traveled through since I first let it go that one cold winter morning, but I certainly never imagined the series of kindness created by my one small act.

— Monica A. Andermann —

52

A Little Extra

Thankfulness is the beginning of gratitude. Gratitude
is the completion of thankfulness. Thankfulness may
consist merely of words. Gratitude is shown in acts.
~Henri Frederic Amiel

"**D**id you recognize the boy who delivered it?"

Tom shook his head, running a rag across the bar. "Never saw him before. But he was young. Maybe eleven or twelve."

I eyed the name on the front of the envelope, written neatly in blue ink.

Then I slipped a finger under the corner edge and tore it open.

My breath caught.

"What is it?"

I took out the bills and counted them in my hands. "Oh, my goodness," I whispered. I checked the envelope again, thinking I had missed a note, but found none.

An anonymous gift.

I stuffed all the twenty-dollar bills back inside the envelope and flipped it over to study my name once more. My first name. That's all.

Who sent this?

I scrunched my eyebrows, focusing and thinking, trying hard to identify the script. But I couldn't.

It could be anyone.

But who would send me money?

What made me so special?

I'd been waitressing for about six months. It was a local place. A hangout for all types. Professors and students from the university. Business owners from all over town. Farmers who drove in for a bite to eat and some local gossip.

I'd moved to Kansas, several states from home, and settled in a small, sterile apartment in student housing. The graduate school had given me a teaching assistantship, and with my part-time job at the restaurant, I got by. I didn't complain.

But there was always something, of course. And one of my professors had enlisted me to help her organize a student trip to Italy that summer. I'd get a discount for my work, but I still had a lot to pay just to get over there. Never mind meals or the possible souvenir.

So, I picked up as many lunch and dinner shifts as I could. I'd be able to pay my bills, buy my books, and get myself to Europe. I would make it work.

The days blurred with so much busyness. Teaching freshmen classes and grading papers. Attending my own classes and writing essays. It felt like a loop on the treadmill, constantly in motion, forcing me forward, never slowing.

Until I left campus.

When I flew down that hill, the graduate school fading behind me, tension fell away. Opening the back door to the restaurant, tying my half-apron around my waist, I was free. For a few hours, I could just be me.

Red plastic baskets of food. Tall lemonades. Pop music, retro leather bar stools, framed portraits scattered above the booths lining the wall. The giant jack hanging from the ceiling. It was a space where most everyone came to take a break from the world.

I enjoyed waiting tables because, really, it didn't seem like work getting to know people. I found that if one had a sense of humor and took life a little less seriously, people warmed up pretty fast. And a lot of people in this college town liked to chat. Ask how I was doing. Lament about the football team or joke about the inch of snow that crippled traffic.

Some folks asked about my personal life, what I was studying or if I had a boyfriend. Some wanted to gush about their own lives. Sometimes, chitchat simply passed the time. Often, it provided comfort. But it always felt good to connect with people. It made me feel like a part of the community and not just a transient college student. The restaurant put everyone on equal terms.

So, if someone casually asked, "Don't you ever get time off?" I probably laughed and explained I had the trip of a lifetime coming up.

Who could blame me for being excited? Spilling too many details?

Maybe someone from town felt generous or took pity on me — or both. Maybe they wanted me to have a nice meal in Venice and Florence. Perhaps someone just wanted me to return home with no debt.

My academic advisor, also a regular at the restaurant, knew about my trip, but we didn't discuss it at meetings. Still, he was a kind man, and perhaps he thought I could use some help. Who knew?

Maybe I had an admirer? But an admirer would send a note, I reasoned, so that couldn't be.

The possibilities extended like a vine, winding every which way. But they were flimsy at best, with no strong leads.

The bartender stopped cleaning the counter and settled his gaze on me. "How much is in there?"

I leaned toward Tom, out of earshot of our lunchtime customers, and whispered, "Two hundred and forty dollars."

He whistled. "You know who it's from?"

I shook my head. "No idea."

The bell over the door chimed, and three undergrads walked in. I gave Tom a look that said, "I got this," and quickly buried the money in the pocket of my black apron before calling out a welcome.

Three boys, none of them my students thankfully, smiled their hellos while the one in front took my hand. He flipped it over and, much to my surprise, planted a kiss in my palm.

His friends laughed. I was more embarrassed for him than myself. I grabbed three menus and turned to lead them past the bar.

Tom raised his eyebrows. *Are they bothering you?*

I shook my head. *Harmless.*

They ordered and ate, but despite the strange overture, nothing else extraordinary happened. They left an ordinary tip.

The huge tip in my apron, however, still burned with questions. *People do strange things,* I thought. *It could be anyone.*

I had hoped someone might come to the restaurant that afternoon and confess. Tell me why I was chosen.

But my shift ended four hours later the same way it began: with no answers.

A couple of months later, I sat on a plane over the Atlantic. I had my passport and some cash from that mysterious envelope in a pouch around my waist. How lucky was I? I still couldn't believe someone would give me so much and not even want to be named. I told myself that when I landed in Italy, I would light candles in every church I passed, asking God to bless this unnamed person.

After my trip to Italy, I worked at the restaurant another full year before graduating. Every time I tied my apron, I wondered if it would happen again. Or if someone might saunter in, take a seat at the bar, and I'd just know.

But no such luck.

Twenty years have passed. In my mind, my trip to Italy and the gift money are linked. I wish I could have thanked the person who helped me, but I've found another way.

Nowadays, when I go to a restaurant with my husband and two kids, I leave a little extra for the server. You never know how much they need it. A few bucks here and there. It means something.

And I want to pass it on. Appreciation. Thanks. Because someone gave me a little extra a long time ago. And more than the money, it's the feeling that lingers.

— Mary Jo Wyse —

53

Three Cheery Lemons

Kindness is love in action.

~*Tara Cousineau, Ph.D., The Kindness Cure*

I didn't know her, but I saw her often around town with her two small children. She appeared to be shy, always looking down, trying not to make eye contact. She often wore the same clothes, as did her children. I felt her discomfort when I saw her at the grocery-store checkout. She reminded me of myself from years ago during a tough time we had gone through.

Back then, I couldn't afford a new winter coat for my daughter, and I didn't know what I was going to do. Luckily, my three younger children could wear hand-me-downs. That night, I said a prayer for the first time since my husband's unemployment.

The next morning a parishioner came in to the church nursery where I worked. "I don't know why, but while praying I had an overwhelming feeling you needed this," she whispered. She pressed twenty dollars into my hand. My eyes started to tear as she continued, "I also have a box of clothes in my car that I was going to donate. Please take what you need." Was this the beginning of my prayer being answered?

Going through the large box of clothes, I found several winter items for my children, including a dark purple jacket that looked like it would fit my daughter. Although grateful, I felt embarrassed. The woman must have sensed my discomfort. She raised my chin so I could look at her. "We all need help at one time or another," she assured me. "One day, you'll be the one helping someone in need." I thanked her and promised I would always try to pay it forward.

I felt relieved and lighter. Maybe it was the comfort in knowing my daughter now had a warm coat. Or perhaps I realized it was okay to accept help and not be embarrassed. Although the coat was slightly big, my daughter loved it. It would fit her the following year as well.

That afternoon, my daughter draped the coat over the dinette chair as we got ready to do some crafts. I found some acrylic paints that were slightly dried out, so I watered them down a bit, perfect for splatter paintings. We dipped our brushes in the brightly colored paint and started to fling the paint onto paper lining the dinette table. While splattering the paint, we were giggling so hard and having so much fun that we didn't notice we were also splattering paint everywhere, including on ourselves. Our polka-dotted faces made us laugh even harder. I hadn't laughed like that in a long time, and it felt good.

After we finished our masterpieces, reality hit. We had used acrylic paint, which is permanent. We hurriedly washed our arms and faces. The girls each took a shower to get the paint out of their hair before it completely dried as I wiped down the table and walls.

Later in the evening, when I went to hang up my daughter's new coat, I discovered to my horror that there were three bright yellow paint splotches right on the chest area. I tried desperately to spot-clean the stain. No amount of soap and water could remove it. I was worried that my daughter would be upset.

Then the phrase "When life gives you lemons, make lemonade!" came to mind. I had an idea! I took out my paints and made the yellow paint blotches into three cheery lemons. I added stems and green leaves as well. I was pretty satisfied with the outcome and hoped my daughter would be, too. To my delight, when she saw the lemons, she excitedly screamed, "It's prettier than before. I love it!"

My daughter wore the coat the following winter, too, although my husband was back at work and we could afford a new one. My two younger girls also wanted to wear the coat when they were able to fit into it. By the time the coat was ready to retire, I didn't have the heart to donate it. I tucked it away as a bittersweet memory of what we went through. It was a reminder of how we made the best of a hard situation and prevailed as a family.

The coat hung in my closet for over twenty years until I decided it was time to let it go to someone who might need it. It was still in good condition considering it was loved so many times. I packed the coat in a bag with other donations and headed to the grocery store before going to Goodwill. Standing in the grocery checkout, looking at the woman who was so similar to my former self, I felt compelled to say, "Hi." She smiled. Without hesitation, I repeated words similar to what the kind woman had said to me many years ago at the church. "I have a bag of clothes in my car that I was going to donate. Would you like to take a look?"

To my surprise, she said, "Yes."

Back at my car, she went through the clothes. She picked up the purple coat with three brightly painted lemons. "My daughter will love this coat. Thank you." She smiled as her eyes glistened. My heart was full as I thought about what a blessing that coat had been. And how it would now make another little girl happy.

— Dorann Weber —

54

A Simple Sign

*Share your kindness with the world,
and see what happens!*
~Barb Walters, Kindness Grows

I had moved across the country to take a job. After less than a year, the company did a ten-percent reduction in force, an across-the-board layoff, firing the most recently hired people in every department. I had worked so hard for that company, giving them my all. Now I had nothing, and my roommate had told me that he wanted to move away, too.

I wanted to stay. I lived on a lovely mountain in an octagon-shaped house by a wonderful swimming pond. But I had no money. As I parked in the grocery store's parking lot, I counted the few dollars in my wallet. I could get eggs, milk, and maybe some salad greens, but what about next week?

I looked up at the sky and thought fiercely, *Lord, nothing makes any sense anymore. Why am I here? Why am I anywhere? If you want me to stay here on this Earth, you need to give me a sign because I am at the end of my rope here. Lord, do you hear me? Please, give me a simple sign.*

The only sound I heard was the whisper of the wind through the trees. I wiped my eyes on the back of my hand and squared my shoulders.

I gathered my groceries together. They had a sale on sweet potatoes, so I added one to my basket, plus a couple of lemons. *I definitely have enough lemons for some good lemonade,* I thought ruefully.

In the checkout line, the woman ahead of me turned suddenly and gave me a big smile. I did not feel like smiling, but I managed a small sliver of one.

"You don't know me, but I need to pay for your groceries," she said.

"What?" I replied.

"It doesn't matter who you are," she said. "If you were a millionaire and I lived on food stamps, I still would need to pay for your groceries. Please. I have to do this."

"Why?" I asked.

"The Lord told me that you need a sign, and you need it right now. Everything is going the way it ought to go, and it will be all right," she said. "I'm your sign. Me paying for your groceries, that's your sign."

"How did you know?" I gasped in surprise.

I hadn't spoken aloud in that car. It had been a private conversation, but somehow this stranger knew.

"You will know when to pay it forward," she said. "He'll let you know. It's simple."

We left that grocery store, both of us smiling big. I enjoyed that simple meal so much that night, and I got a new job the very next day that helped me keep going, one I enjoyed much more than the old one.

Months passed, and then a year. I got in line at a different grocery store behind a man and his young son. Something tugged deep down inside me.

"Sir, please excuse me, but I need to pay for your groceries," I said. "I know you don't need the money. The Lord says you need a sign, and me paying for your groceries, that's your sign. You will know when to pay it forward."

The man simply nodded and quietly said, "Thank you."

— Kiesa Kay —

| One Good Turn Deserves Another

55

A Gift from the Heart

Blessed is the season which engages the
whole world in a conspiracy of love.
~Hamilton Wright Mabie

Salvation Army bells were ringing at the entrance to the supermarket. "Winter Wonderland" was playing over the P.A. system inside the store, and everywhere I looked I saw smiling faces.

That was the atmosphere when I went to pick up some last-minute items for dinner, planning to pay cash for the few things I needed.

After filling my cart, I stood in the checkout line, humming along with "Rockin' Around the Christmas Tree."

When I got to the front of the line, I watched the cashier ring up my purchases.

"Oh," I said to her when the total appeared, "I don't seem to have enough cash with me. Just give me a moment to see if I have some extra bills somewhere."

I rummaged through a few compartments in my purse, but when I realized how long the line was behind me, I stopped my search and said, "I'll pay by credit card instead."

I took out my Visa card and was about to put it into the chip reader when the cashier said, "Wait, don't put the card in yet." I stood there holding my credit card in my hand, ready to insert it when given the okay.

"Wait a minute," the cashier said again. She beckoned to a manager to come over. After a short conversation, the manager approached me and asked for my credit card.

Puzzled, I gave the card to her.

"What's going on?" I asked. I wondered if the card had expired, but I hadn't even put it into the machine for it to be rejected. I wondered if they thought I stole something or if someone pointed me out as being a suspect in something or other.

"Come with me out of the line," the manager said. "Everything's okay. Nothing to be worried about." She got behind me and guided me out of the line.

I looked back to see my purchases being bagged.

"I need my credit card to pay for my groceries," I said. "Can you tell me what's going on? Did I do something wrong?"

"No, I told you everything's okay. You'll see in a minute."

I was more bewildered than ever, especially when I saw that all my groceries were now in bags in my cart, and the cashier was pushing the cart out of the checkout line.

The manager escorted me to the Exit door. "Stay right here," she told me. She handed my credit card back to me, walked over to my filled wagon and brought it to me. She put her arm around my shoulder and guided both the wagon and me to the outer lobby of the store. She gave my shoulder a gentle squeeze and said that one of the women in line behind me had handed her credit card to the cashier and requested that it be used to pay for my groceries.

I was stunned. Why would someone pay for my groceries? Then I realized that since it was obvious that I didn't have enough cash with me to pay for my items, someone had assumed I needed the help.

I remembered seeing a movie called *Pay It Forward* and how I thought at the time how admirable the concept was and wondered if an opportunity would ever present itself so that I could do just that.

That concept presented itself that evening at the grocery store, but I was the recipient.

I asked the manager to stay with my wagon so that I could find the woman and thank her for her kindness.

"No, acknowledging her would take away the spirit of her generosity," she replied. "And please don't go back into the store to look for her."

Warmth flooded my whole body, and I hugged the manager. "I hope you'll tell her that the feeling I'm experiencing by being the recipient of her goodwill is indescribable."

As I left the store, Judy Garland was singing "Have Yourself a Merry Little Christmas."

In the Salvation Army area, the bells were still ringing.

"Why not!" I said aloud, as a big smile spread across my face.

I took out all the cash in my wallet that I had originally intended to use for my groceries, walked over to the bellringer, and paid it forward.

—Linda J. Cooper—

Compassion & Understanding

56

Sympathy Flowers

Flowers always make people better, happier,
and more helpful; they are sunshine,
food and medicine for the soul.
~Luther Burbank

The first morning after the fog of grief rolled in, my friends dropped by and surprised me, bringing gifts to my door. They brought me candy, hot-chocolate mix, a card, and, most curiously, a gift box filled with white flowers.

I didn't know what to make of it all at first, other than offering a distant thank-you for stopping by. It was a forty-minute drive for a two-minute conversation, with me standing awkwardly on the front step in ugly, loose sweatpants and a white button-up. I had been staring blankly at my computer screen for hours, trying to write something vaguely coherent for my senior capstone paper without much success. When they asked me how I was, I made some half-hearted, self-deprecating joke about my outfit, something about the shirt feeling put-together but tight and the pants feeling depressing but comfortable.

The joke did not land, settling with a sad chill in the cold and quiet January air.

"Be gentle with yourself," one friend told me. Some bitter part of myself raised its hackles, telling me I didn't know how to do that, but I told her I would anyway. At least, I thought, I could try.

Thinking back, those were probably the most important things they could have given me. Candy was a gentle reminder to eat. Hot chocolate was for the heavy moments of silence, to have something warm to hold onto. The card, of course, was obvious: a reminder that they were there and loved me, that this was real and happening. That sometimes words are wholly inadequate, but they're all we have.

For the longest time, I got stuck on the flowers. They sat in their little, open-air gift box with the wrapping that obscured their base, staring back at me.

I thought they were a bouquet at first. Yet another thing I would have to watch wither and die. Having just put down my dog, I was certain of one thing: the idea of letting something die is horrifying because we feel we are responsible for killing it. When there is nothing we can do, the first place that blame turns is the mirror. Even if it is not true, even if it is horribly unkind, it is the only place we know we can turn to and take control over. I was already overwhelmed, not ready to accept even that meager responsibility.

I didn't mention the flowers for the longest time. I tried hard to ignore them and got angry when I couldn't. Then I felt stupid for feeling angry about it, asking myself why I couldn't just be grateful, why I had to stew over something that felt so inconsequential. They hadn't done anything wrong. They hadn't done anything, really, except look nice while I dressed myself yet again in sweatpants and barely brushed my hair.

Be gentle with yourself, my friend had reminded me. *Take a step back and be gentle with yourself.*

Eventually, I realized that the gift box didn't actually contain a cut bouquet at all. It was a perennial ready for planting, sitting patiently in that box with its dirt obscured by the wrapping. It was not dying, not plastic, yet living and breathing all the same.

Still, it confused me. I wracked my brain for why they could have brought it. In my grief, I was tired of trying to make everything beautiful, of trying to make pain poetic and consumable. I wanted to just feel it.

I sat at the dining-room table and stared at the plant, hearing the clock tick away the seconds. I became increasingly frustrated with my inability to string together words like I used to. With the dog dying, the time passing, the semester coming to a close, and my inability to sit down to write about existentialism in postmodern literature only worsening, I couldn't pretend that time moved as it normally did.

After a while, I gave up trying to think it through. I scurried to my room with my card and chocolates. I cried knowing they had thought of me long enough to buy these things, long enough to make the forty-minute drive up and back. I think what hit me hardest was that they had thought about me longer than *I* had thought about me.

The plant was a staple on the dining room table. My mother would tell me when she watered it, how nice it was, how it needed more sunlight. The white buds greeted me through the days, reminding me to eat, reminding me to take my time, reminding me I was loved. Slowly, setting the plant by the front window in the sunspot, seeing how it looked brighter than it had the morning they brought it, I finally figured it out.

Even in the harsh and desperate ticking of time moving forward, perennials are always in a state of growing. The flowers may wither and turn brown, crunch and die, but there's the promise that, should they be tended to, they will return next spring. They endure the cold and the dark for each thin beam of light, roots stretching carefully under the surface. And should they be granted the care they need, they will grow beautiful once again, exhaling fresh air with the new beginnings that spring provides.

— Casey McMullin —

57

A Shared Struggle

*Kindness begins with the understanding
that we all struggle.*
~Charles Glassman

ushing into the IGA that fall afternoon, I did not know I would get to be a part of something beautiful. In all honesty, I can't even remember why I was in this grocery store. I never shopped here. It was out of my way and out of the circle that I lived my life within. But it was meant for me to be there at this particular time.

I can't remember what was in my cart or what I went in for except that they have the best fresh candy selection in town. That was probably what I was checking out with! I do remember that it was close to Thanksgiving. That is the important part of this story — the when, not the what.

After selecting my items, I proceeded to the checkout line. I noticed a young woman in the line in front of me. Her clothes were raggedy, and she looked so tired. She had a toddler who could not have been more than three and a newborn who was just a few weeks old. Frazzled is how I would describe her. Bless her heart, the toddler was running and jumping around just like toddlers do. The baby was crying. My heart went out to her. I had been in her shoes with my own two sons.

She managed to get her groceries on the conveyor belt amidst all the chaos of her kids, and the clerk started checking out her items. As I stood behind her, I noticed that she was losing patience with her kids but didn't know what to do. She was trying to balance both tasks without causing a huge disruption. I began to whisper a prayer of peace and strength over this woman. The line behind me continued to snake its way into an aisle. The pressure was growing.

As I watched her, I remembered a time that I had been in a grocery store with a toddler who was running around and a screaming baby. I remembered the grumpy, old man behind me and the inappropriate comment he made to me as I checked out. That memory took me away from the IGA line for a moment. When I came back to the present, I realized that the young woman was looking at a few items and trying to decide what she needed to put back. The people in line behind me were getting impatient and frustrated that she was holding them up even more now. The dancing toddler and screaming baby just added to the stress of her situation.

I touched her on the arm and asked her a simple question, "Honey, do you need these items for your children?"

"Yes, ma'am, but I don't have enough on my EBT card to pay for them. I need them for Thanksgiving."

My heart broke for this mama. It wasn't my place to judge her, but it was my place to offer her what I could. The groceries that were lying there were certainly not luxuries but pantry staples.

"Ring up those groceries for her," I said to the clerk.

"What?" the clerk asked.

"Ring up the rest of her groceries. I will pay for them. She needs them for her children."

The young mama turned, looked at me and said, "No, it's okay. I will put them back."

"Are you a single mom?" I asked.

"Yes, ma'am, I am," she replied hesitantly, almost embarrassed to admit it.

"Honey, I'm a single mom, too. Get those groceries. I'm happy to pay for them. I've been in your shoes. I know what it's like." To the clerk I said again, "Ring up the rest of her groceries." With a wink, I said to the young mother, "Us single moms have to look out for each other." The woman was moved to tears and grew silent.

The clerk did as I said but with a huge smile on her face. She said, "I have never seen anyone do something like this before!"

The man who was standing in line right behind me heard the whole conversation. He piped up and said to the clerk, "Whatever the total is, I will pay for half of it."

I turned to him and said, "That is not necessary."

He said, "I know it's not, but what you have just done for this young woman has touched me. I've never gotten to be a part of something like this." Then he turned to the young woman and wished her well.

She was seriously crying by this point and said, "I don't know how to repay you."

He said to her, "I'll take a hug!" Instantly, she wiped her tears and hugged both of us. The clerk wiped her tears, too!

I gladly accepted my hug as payment for these groceries. I also said to her, "You can pay me back by remembering this. One day in your future, you will be in a place where you can do this for another single mom. Pay it forward. That is how you can pay me back besides the hug!"

She beamed. "Yes, ma'am. Thank you." She happily pushed her groceries to the car. The dancing toddler was still dancing, and the baby was still crying, but now no one seemed to mind.

The total cost for the rest of the groceries was less than thirty dollars. The man behind me and I split that total and left the IGA with full hearts that danced like the toddler. It was worth every dime. Wherever she is today, I hope that young woman does remember what it's like when she sees a struggling mama, and will pay it forward. Kindness can be given and received everywhere — even in the checkout line!

— Amy Mewborn —

58

First Came the Apology

You can cultivate mercy when you extend acts
of compassion and kindness.
~Bree Miller

The jolt came hard and fast, stunning me into silence. My seat belt did its job, but my body still vibrated from the impact of the Buick Rendezvous smashing into my back end. I stopped myself from bolting out of the car to size up the driver who clearly did not see the four-car line-up at the red light.

"Are you okay?" His first words. Young, maybe my son's age, twenty-five. He began to apologize, and I nodded, telling him I needed a minute. Was I okay? Could I drive? Was the car drivable?

"It hasn't been going well for me. This is my second accident in a month." His voice trembled.

We drove to a parking lot, and I wondered why he was telling me this. Did he want me to feel sorry for him? Was he intoxicated or high? Who has two accidents in one month?

I exited my car and walked to the back to see the damage on my car and then his. Had it been a bar fight, the tally would have been two broken noses, cracked teeth, dislocated collarbone, a broken leg and blood spatter. No clear winner.

No one was hurt so no need to call the police. Plus, they don't prioritize accident scenes when there are no injuries. I pulled out the dusty joint-accident report from the bottom of my glove compartment. The young man paced around the car, taking hauls from his cigarette and clutching his mobile phone like it was life support.

"I'll fill out the report. I need your licence, insurance and registration," I told him. He handed them over in a flash and apologized again. His apologies started to annoy me.

I replayed the accident in my mind. I had missed the exit going home and had looped around the highway so I could do it all over again. I wouldn't have been there if I hadn't missed the exit. I had just dropped off my son after he got his wisdom teeth pulled. He had moved out only two months ago and needed a lift to the dentist and back because he wasn't supposed to drive. I was adjusting to this new phase of our relationship. My bear cub had vacated the den, and we were trying to figure out how to stay connected. He had thanked me for chauffeuring him, and it felt good to be there for him.

"I'm really sorry, madam. Really sorry."

I waved him off with the back of my hand. I just wanted to do what needed to be done and go home. I didn't want to say it was okay. He was shaken up, but I had to focus on keeping the papers from flying off the hood of the car while I tried to put the right information in the small boxes.

"Okay, here, have a look." I showed him the diagram of the accident I had drawn and read out the description: Car A waiting behind three cars at a full stop. Car B hits Car A from behind.

"If you agree, sign at the bottom."

"It's exactly that. Yes, exactly."

I ripped off a copy of the report and gave it to him. Now that we had exchanged information, I took a step back to examine the driver more carefully. His driver's license put him at thirty. He looked barely twenty. He had reddish hair, crooked teeth and a skinny build.

I wanted to ask him what had happened, if he was texting, to yell at him for being so stupid and reckless. This was his second accident in one month. Had the lesson of the first one worn off already?

"Tell me what happened. Were you distracted by something?"

His words flowed like water, and his pain bubbled to the surface.

He spoke as if he needed to get the words out of his head and into the air.

"I broke up with my girlfriend. We were together for ten years. Now she's saying all these things about me that aren't true. I smashed our other car and, today, this. I don't know what to do anymore."

Then, as if he remembered my question, he added, "Maybe I was looking at the radio too long."

His eyes were red-rimmed, and he was jittery like he was trying to escape his thoughts. Maybe if he kept moving, they wouldn't land so hard on his heart.

I had planned on giving him a solid warning and chastising, but I didn't. He was as smashed up as our cars. I didn't want to know if he had kids because that might worry me more and make me change my mind about what I was going to say.

"I'm going to tell you something, and I want you to listen carefully. It's going to sound hard to believe, but here it is: You are not always going to feel this way. What you are feeling right now will pass. You will be okay again. I promise. You have to trust me on this one."

The tears flowed from his eyes like waterfalls, and his face turned toward me as if wanting to hear more. "I'll say it one more time. You are not always going to feel like this. The accidents mean something. They are signals for you to pay attention. It's time to take care of you now. You will not hurt forever."

I almost expected him to apologize again. Instead, he said, "Thank you."

And I replied, "It's okay."

— Voula Plagakis —

59

The Gift of Hope

Compassion isn't about solutions.
It's about giving all the love that you've got.
~Cheryl Strayed

I looked down at the two lines on the pregnancy test, and my heart stopped. I had only recently graduated from college. I was married, but we were newlyweds, and my husband had just lost his job. I was working in a temporary position, struggling to find permanent, full-time employment. Having a child was a "someday plan" — and that day was supposed to be many years in the future.

A few weeks later, I had a bad day at work. My bus ran late, my report didn't save, I jammed the copier, and I accidentally left my lunch at home. On a typical day, these things would have been minor annoyances at best. Since my thoughts were already consumed by the possibility of being responsible for another life while struggling to take care of myself, they seemed completely overwhelming.

I started to tear up at my desk and made a dash for the women's restroom. Soon, I was in the middle of what could only be described as a nervous breakdown — loud, anguished, hormonal sobs complete with mascara running down my face. I hid in the stall, but the sound was impossible to disguise.

A handful of people entered the room, heard me crying, and left without saying a word. I didn't blame them. We've all been told that crying at work is unprofessional — even if it seems like your world is falling apart and you have no idea what to do next.

Then, one older woman to whom I'd only spoken a few times knocked on the door to the stall and handed me a tissue. Nobody I worked with knew I was pregnant at the time, but I told her everything between attempts to make myself look somewhat presentable.

I fully expected her to imply that I was careless and irresponsible for getting myself into such a predicament. It's the story I was telling myself, and women of her generation didn't seem to have such bad luck.

Instead, she gave me a hug and told me that everything would work out. She said that even if I didn't think I could handle the responsibility of an unplanned pregnancy, I was smarter and stronger than I gave myself credit for. She told me that if it was what I wanted, I would be a wonderful mother, and my baby would be the light of my life.

Later that day, I found an envelope on my desk. She had written a note wishing me well and enclosed what I suspect was all the cash from her purse. I cried again when I found it — only this time it was because I was relieved that someone believed I'd find a way to make things okay.

One of the things I bought with that money was a small Winnie-the-Pooh baby rattle. My son's a teenager now, but that rattle is one of my most prized possessions. Whenever I look at it, I'm reminded that hope is the most precious gift of all.

— Dana Hinders —

He Will Be Okay

When words are both true and kind,
they can change the world.
~Buddha

He moved quickly around the room, touching everything that could be touched. I followed him, trying to head him off before he ran down the hallway. He went to the front desk and knocked all the papers off the table. I firmly helped him pick them up. I could feel the eyes staring at me, judging me for not having better control of my child.

I silently admonished myself. I should have known not to come so early. The waiting was too much for him. I dug around in my bag. Maybe a candy would help. I came up with used tissues and pennies but no quarters. I kept searching my bag for something to distract him and came up with a bouncy ball. I called him over and showed him how to bounce it off the floor onto the wall and catch it. He began to play earnestly, laughing hysterically as it bounced off down the hall.

A father and mother sat together waiting for their child. They stared at me and my son, and I heard the words "out of control." I could feel my face flush red. I wanted to tell them that he has a disability, that he's not being bad; he's just having trouble waiting. Another part of me wanted to punch them and ask if that helped to give them good manners. I did neither. I sat down and watched him play with the ball, and I tried hard not to cry.

The instructor called the group together, and my son went off to play sports with the other five-year-olds. I prayed that this time he would follow the rules. That he would keep his hands to himself. That this time the instructor wouldn't need to have a "quiet word" with me at the end to tell me my son was not ready to take this kind of class. I closed my eyes and willed him to be okay.

"He'll be fine."

I opened my eyes and looked beside me. I must have had a confused look on my face.

"He'll do great. *You* are doing great. You are a great mom. I can see it in all that you do for him," a petite stranger to my right said. Before I could respond, she added, "My brother was like that as a kid. It gets better. You will have to do a lot for him, but in the end he will be okay."

We sat and talked, and I felt the tension leave my body. I forgot to keep watching the clock, and I felt no anxiety about him getting kicked out. She told me about her brother and her parents and all that her mom did for her brother over the years. She told me about how he turned out great, got a job and lived on his own now. Before I knew it, the doors opened, and all the kids ran out, including my own, beaming with excitement and pride. "I did it!" he exclaimed. I picked him up. I turned to thank the lady, but she was gone.

If I could find her, I would tell her, "Yes, it took a lot of work, but he's okay. And so am I."

— Tina Szymczak —

A Change in Perspective

A purposeful act or extension of kindness to another
is never wasted, for it always resides in the hearts
of all involved in a chain of love.
~Molly Friedenfeld,
The Book of Simple Human Truths

I have been a nurse for over ten years, mostly in emergency and trauma. I liked the fast pace and quick turnover of patients but I was headhunted by a recruiter for an entirely different position a while ago.

The position was as a nurse in the prison services. For children. When I say children, their ages were twelve to eighteen.

I hemmed and hawed for a while, but the money was excellent, the working hours sweet, and it was a government job, so the benefits and pension scheme were fantastic. I took on the job with reservations and a completely judgmental attitude. After all, these kids were juvenile delinquents. Some were violent offenders, murderers, drug dealers — with absolutely no respect for society or civilised living.

My first day on the job, I was shadowed by my line manager who explained the routine, the medications, rounds, etc. We had to go to each unit where the youths lived, eight to a unit, and dispense medication where needed. One kid, let's call him Daniel, fourteen years old, was to have a multivitamin each day because of a vitamin deficiency caused by drug-taking and fast living. My line manager had explained earlier that we needed to check that the kids actually swallowed their medications since some liked to hide them in their cheeks and then give them to other youths in the unit for a "high." After all, we were dispensing ADHD medications, anti-psychotics, and more.

I gave Daniel his vitamin tablet and asked to check his mouth. That started four months of him verbally mocking me, shouting through the open school windows, mimicking my accent, and being insolent, rude, and disrespectful.

I hated going to his particular unit every day to the point where I would bribe the other nurses with donuts just so they would go for me. I was beyond delighted when he served his sentence and was released from the detention centre. No more annoying comments. No more bullying from a mere child. Not even reading his case file could make me feel empathy for this child. He had had every opportunity to rectify and try to change his ways, but he just didn't want to.

Fast forward a year. I had changed my views dramatically. I realised that these kids, for the most part, had never stood a chance from the day they were born. The families they were born into enabled and facilitated criminal activities from an early age. Sometimes, poverty had forced them to steal food. Gangs in the local area had groomed them from early ages into addiction and then debts. And to pay the debts, of course, one must deal drugs.

So, I was reformed. I started to see these kids in a different light. I talked to them and understood them more. I felt I had judged them way too harshly.

And then guess who came back? Daniel. I groaned out loud when I saw his name on the whiteboard the next day when I came into work. The other nurses were laughing and shaking their heads. It was inevitable, they said. He was in and out of the detention centre like a revolving door. He had many years to go before he was out of the juvenile system.

I took a deep breath and psyched myself up. But I comforted myself with the fact that I only had four weeks to put up with his behaviour as I had handed in my notice for work overseas.

I went to his unit that evening and exchanged pleasantries. He had grown a good couple of inches, but he was still the same cheeky, mocking teenager who had left just months ago.

On my last day at work, my colleagues bought me a present. We'd had donuts, and it had been a fairly pleasant day. I could have left early, but I wanted to see the day out. I'd made some good friends. I had good connections with some of the kids, and I wanted to make my rounds and say my goodbyes at the end of my shift. The whole Centre knew I was leaving, including the kids, so it was no secret.

During the lunchtime medication round, Daniel casually asked what time I would be in his unit. I was vague and said something like after 8:00 P.M. He was insistent that I come to his unit earlier than that. He had a problem and needed me there before that time. Reluctantly, I agreed and carried on with my duties.

At 7:30 P.M., I went into his unit. I went to the office and asked the staff where he was. They were smiling and nudging each other. *Weird,* I thought.

"He's in the kitchen waiting for you," I was told.

I got to the kitchen, and Daniel was there with a homemade chocolate cake that he had made especially for me after his school hours. He said, "Tammy, this is for you. For your leaving present. I couldn't get you a present or a card, so I made you this cake instead."

I stood there with a lump in my throat. This teenager had made my job difficult during his stay with us, constantly taunted and scoffed at me, and yet here he was with this cake. Tears welled up in my eyes. Throughout my nursing career, I had never felt so touched or humbled that somebody with so little to give financially and emotionally could give me so much in the way of a cake to show that he cared and was thankful for the care I had given him.

This act of kindness warmed me like nothing had ever done before. Here was a boy whose family had neglected him from an early age. He had been in and out of juvenile-detention services his whole young life and had very little respect for authority figures. But he had made me a cake to say thank you and good luck.

My faith in humanity was restored. It showed me that we don't need money, status, reputation, or other materialistic things to show kindness. I had been given thank-you cards and chocolates from previous patients in hospitals, but this was different.

I will never forget Daniel. Even to this day, I still have a lump in my throat when I think of his beautiful homemade cake.

— Tammy Thornton —

62

A Special Blend

Having friends who are accepting, supportive,
available, and loving are key to feeling safe.
~Tara Bianca, The Flower of Heaven

I got married right out of high school. It wasn't one of those rare success stories.

My husband was in the military, and we moved around. Our second location was less than desirable. We had moved over 1,700 miles away from family and friends. We lived in a trailer park twenty-five yards from a busy railroad track and one block from a strip joint. Going out, even in daylight, was always a bit sketchy. But that wasn't the worst of it. He and I weren't getting along.

Unfortunately, I was stubborn. Family and friends had said it wouldn't work. So, instead of swallowing my pride, admitting things weren't working out, and calling for support, I tried to muddle through. One evening, things got pretty heated, and my husband went off on a tirade.

He stormed out that night and took off to the base. I was stranded in a trailer park on the wrong side of the tracks with no phone, vehicle, money, or family and friends nearby. The cupboards were bare except for a box of Hamburger Helper and there was no meat to mix with it.

The next morning, I debated whether to waste quarters on laundry or venture up to the pay phone near the strip club to call home. My pride won out. As I hauled laundry back to our trailer, the neighbor across from us came outside. She invited me to come inside and share some pineapple upside-down cake that she'd just baked.

I followed her inside. The kitchen table was at the front of her trailer. She motioned me toward a chair in front of where a coffee mug and newspaper sat. She scooped up the items and put them on the other side of the table.

I couldn't help but notice the large gap in the curtains from where I could clearly see the front entryway of our trailer. A wash of humiliation coursed through me, praying she hadn't seen the previous evening's events. She served the cake and sat with me. I'd never had a cake so delicious before; it filled my stomach and my heart.

She never directly told me what she saw or heard, but she really didn't have to. She talked about her marriage (which was nearing fifty years) and friendships that had come and gone in her life. She peppered little bits of insight throughout the conversation: It's okay to regret a choice. Every day is a chance to start anew. Some things aren't meant to be. Learn the lesson and move on. She didn't preach or pry. She seemed to have a life story filled with wisdom that I needed to hear that day.

Back in our trailer, my pride began to weaken. I felt like calling home with a couple of those quarters. It took a year and a half before I finally left my husband. But that visit was when I began to realize it wasn't meant to be. It was okay to make a poor choice, learn from it, and move on.

Whenever life overwhelms me, I have a yearning for pineapple upside-down cake. I've bought a few and I've made a few over the years. Oddly, they have never tasted as fabulous as hers. They've never filled my heart and soul as deeply as hers did. There's just no replicating the special blend of love, kindness, and warmth that I got that day from my neighbor.

— Diane DeMasi Johnson —

63

Compassion from a Stranger

In compassion, when we feel with the other,
we dethrone ourselves from the center of
our world and we put another person there.
~Karen Armstrong

It was a sunny afternoon when I decided to head out for some retail therapy. I packed up my infant and toddler and headed to a local department store for what I thought would be a normal day of shopping.

When I arrived, I grabbed a cart on my way in, buckled my infant in the seat and placed my toddler in the lower portion of the cart. Though placing my toddler in the cart, unbuckled, wasn't safe, I could see her at all times this way and was hoping to avoid chasing her around the store.

At least, that's what I thought.

Soon after I began shopping, I turned the cart around the corner of the aisle while my three-year-old daughter stood up in the cart as it was moving. She toppled out of the side of the cart, and her head hit the tile floor.

She was knocked unconscious.

Though it was only for a few seconds, it felt like forever. I immediately dropped to my knees in the middle of the department store. I scooped her in my arms, screaming her name and urging her to wake up. My one-year-old son was crying while still buckled in the cart.

Soon after she fell, my daughter opened her eyes as I sat on the floor holding her.

A woman approached us, a complete stranger. She asked if my daughter had fallen out of the cart and if we needed help. She proceeded to locate an ice pack from an employee. During the chaos, my son continued to cry. She held him while I calmed my daughter and myself.

We elected to go to our pediatrician nearby to have the lump on her head checked out. I composed myself, calmed my children down, and proceeded to the exit. As I reached the parking lot, the woman followed me to my car. She helped me buckle my children in their car seats as I wiped tears from my face, trying to see clearly enough to drive.

I was terrified that I had unintentionally caused long-term damage to my daughter's brain. I was disappointed in myself for placing her in the cart. I didn't know what to do in that moment, and I was scared.

The kind stranger continued to calm me down.

She then got in her own car and followed me to our pediatrician's office. She walked in with our little family and sat quietly in the waiting room until after our pediatrician gave my daughter the green light.

It was just a bump. A big bump, but she was going to be okay.

We were lucky that day. A stranger showed us compassion. She put her own errands on hold and helped a young, fearful mother who needed assistance. She offered kind words without judgment, and I will forever be grateful to have met her.

— Kori Sciandra —

Sharing Lunch and a Lifetime

You give but little when you give of your possessions.
It is when you give of yourself that you truly give.
~Kahlil Gibran

My husband Buck and I divorced in 1995—and not exactly amicably. Even though we shared our lives for a quarter of a century, the relationship was doomed from the start of our four-month courtship.

I was responsible, reliable and, I am sure, more than a little boring. He was outgoing, exuberant, and never met a stranger. Someone told me that living with Buck must have been "an adventure." That was putting it mildly—especially for straitlaced, shy, and soft-spoken me.

After our divorce, Buck lived on the outskirts of our small town in a mobile home, and I lived a couple of blocks away in the house we once shared. Only on occasion did we run into each other in the local grocery story or the convenience mart, which was about halfway between us.

As he got older, Buck suffered complications of diabetes. His eyesight began to fail, and he could no longer drive. He had partial amputations of both feet and had to use a cane.

I was suffering my own woes. I had a painful back condition and had been born with deformities in my legs, which eventually required a knee replacement.

After several days in the hospital following the knee surgery, I returned home to find walking difficult. The first morning home, the trek from my bedroom to the kitchen took almost forty-five minutes. By the time I reached the fridge, I was too tired to do more than slap together a few pieces of bread with a glob of peanut butter.

On my second day home, I was ravenous but dreaded the trip to the kitchen. About noon, my doorbell rang, and I hoisted myself to my feet, hoping whoever it was would just go away. They probably would, I thought, as slow as I was getting to the door. The bell pealed again, and with a hint of aggravation, I swung open the door to find my ex-husband. Buck's face was pasty; he was pale and sweating. He leaned unsteadily on a cane, but a big smile covered his face.

"Here," he said, offering me a Styrofoam object. "I brought your lunch."

He brushed through the door and collapsed into a chair. I opened the meal on my lap and found roasted turkey, potatoes with gravy, and a side of sweet corn.

"My goodness," I said, amazed. "Where did you get this?"

His smile broadened. "At the deli," he said. "I imagine you're hungry. You always were."

I ignored his comment about my ever-present appetite as I tried to get to my feet.

"What do you need?" he asked. "I'll get it."

"Something to drink. And another plate. I'll share this with you."

He shook his head. He wouldn't have a bite, but he watched me eat. After I had polished off the last bite of the homemade roll, he leaned heavily on his cane to get out of the chair and started his tedious walk back to his own home. He had already walked about six blocks to bring me lunch, and now he was ready to hobble home to rest.

He wished me a quick recovery. I wished him better health. And for the first time in many years, I saw why I had married this man. No words of "I'm sorry" were spoken, but an air of forgiveness seemed to melt away the years of resentment that had built up between us. I stood at the door and watched Buck walk tediously up the sidewalk. Then I climbed back in bed. I had not only had a knee replacement but an attitude adjustment as well. Both were much needed and appreciated.

—Shirley Nordeck Short—

65

A Healer in Every Respect

Wherever the art of medicine is loved,
there is also a love of humanity.
~Hippocrates

My daughter Wendy was born healthy but had an infection that shut down the small blood vessels of her body. She spent more than 180 days in the hospital. At the time, we were living in a small Vermont town, but we had to move down to the Boston area to be closer to Massachusetts General Hospital, especially once we knew that Wendy needed a kidney transplant.

At the end of an appointment, Wendy's doctor asked how we as a family were doing with the move and how Wendy was adjusting. I answered that our apartment was fine, and transportation to and from the hospital was good, but I was worried because Wendy had no friends. She couldn't go to preschool because she was medically fragile, and she had been in and out of the hospital for so long that she really didn't have any interaction with other kids. I was worried that though she was safe by being closer to the hospital, she wasn't having all the fun a four-year-old should be having.

The doctor was silent for a moment and then said, "I have a daughter. She's only a few years older than Wendy. Let's have them meet." A few days later, we met at the playground by the frog pond in Boston Common, and Wendy began to play with Ashley. They ran around, swung on the swings and slid down the slide.

We met once a week, every week, until Wendy's kidney transplant. She had a friend she could look forward to meeting, and her mom also happened to be her nephrologist.

Wendy's doctor was a healer in every aspect.

— Darcy Daniels —

Chapter 8

Ever Grateful

Christmas Kindness

*Sometimes it takes only one act of kindness
and caring to change a person's life.*
~Jackie Chan

I knew there wouldn't be any presents under the tree. I was twelve and the oldest. My sisters Angie and Susan didn't understand that our parents had no money but I saw the nearly empty pantry. I knew Dad had been laid off.

Grandma Margaret, our neighbor across the street, was a good friend to my mom when she so desperately needed one. My momma's family all lived in Eastern Kentucky, and we were lucky if we saw them once a year. We couldn't afford the gas. So, Margaret became someone in whom my momma could confide, and either Momma told Margaret about the financial struggles that holiday season, or Margaret saw there were no presents under the tree.

One day near Christmas, we heard a knock on the door, and in walked Grandma Margaret with a huge bag of something and a wrapped, very heavy present. I knew it was heavy as she was struggling to carry it. She walked over to the tree and placed that gift under its branches. "For your mommy and daddy," she said with a wink and a giggle. Then she opened the garbage bag and began calling our names. Each time she handed one of us girls a gift, she would say, "Not 'til Christmas morning!" Seven times she called my name, seven times she called Angie's name, and seven times she called Susan's name. Twenty-one gifts where there once were none, and they were all from our beloved

Grandma Margaret. We were ecstatic!

After she left, we rushed to the tree and started shaking the packages, trying to figure out what was in each brightly wrapped package. I walked over to inspect my mom and dad's gift. I picked it up because I, of course, was a strong, little girl, and when I did, I realized just how heavy the present was, especially compared to the smaller packages for us girls. I tried to imagine what might be inside. New work boots for my dad? No, the gift was for my mom, too, and she didn't need work boots. New plates for the dinner table? No, our dinner plates were fine. What in the world was in that package? I called my little sisters over, and they could barely budge it. "What do you think it is, sissy?" they both asked with wide-eyed wonder, almost at the same time.

Fast forward to Christmas morning. We girls raced downstairs to wake up our parents. "Hurry up, Mom and Dad! It's Christmas!" They sluggishly rolled out of bed, and we sprinted to the living room. The night before, we'd placed all our gifts in separate piles. Now we plopped down beside our stacks. Finally, after what seemed like an eternity to three excited, impatient girls, our parents entered the living room, coffee cups in hand.

My dad prayed and thanked Baby Jesus for this special day and for Grandma Margaret's kind generosity. Then we girls opened one gift at a time until all our gifts surrounded us. I don't really remember what those gifts were. I suspect Grandma Margaret had gone to the nickel-and-dime store in our town and picked out twenty-one inexpensive gifts, things like jump ropes, jacks, and simple games. While those gifts were precious, the real act of kindness — and hilarity, I might add — was what she had given my parents.

You see, my dad was a proud man who had trouble asking for help, especially when it came to finances. In fact, he rarely accepted gifts of money for his struggling family. Food and clothing for his little girls and wife were gratefully accepted, but money was not.

Mom and Dad sat together as Mom lifted the heavy package onto her lap. We girls wanted her to rip into that present, but she carefully unwrapped it as if savoring the wonder. With the paper off, we found a simple cardboard box, taped shut. Our impatience was mounting.

What was in that box that was so heavy we could barely pick it up? Mom removed the tape from the outside and peered in. Her look of puzzlement and bewilderment was obvious. "Bobby?" she asked in confusion. Then she lifted out a big, dirty ROCK! I'm sure it had come from the rock landscaping that surrounded Grandma's house.

We sisters were equally confused. Why would Grandma give our parents a dirty rock?

Mom, who was trying to be diplomatic and grateful for the gift, turned it around for us to see. In the process, she must have felt something strange on the bottom, so she flipped over the rock and found an envelope taped to the bottom. Our eyes widened! She removed the envelope, and inside she found a $100 bill! I don't think I had ever in my life seen that much money!

Instantly, Mom's eyes teared up as she looked hopefully at my dad. Normally, he would have been too proud to accept a gift of money, but his eyes danced in amusement at the clever way Grandma Margaret had given the gift. He simply nodded his head and grinned at Mom, as if to say, "It's okay. You can keep it."

Over the years, I remember lots of other acts of kindness by this dear woman. Once, at just the right time, Mom went to the mailbox and found another envelope that simply said, "Bobby and Barbara." It, too, had a hundred-dollar bill inside. (We were fairly certain that envelope came from Grandma's son and his wife.) However, no act of kindness has ever equaled her Christmas gifts the year I was twelve.

— Sherry Furnish —

67

Two Acts of Kindness

Kind people are the best kind of people.
~Author Unknown

I was the recipient of two acts of kindness from strangers and near-strangers after my husband died. The first happened when I went to the neighborhood Walgreens to have a photo printed for the memorial flier. Choosing the self-service kiosk was the only way I felt able to interact or, in this case, *not* interact with others. Enveloped in grief, I was unable and unwilling to have a discussion with anyone or pretend to be cheerful. Just driving to the store had taken more effort than I expected. This was supposed to be one of the easier tasks for the funeral, but it felt overwhelming as I walked into the building.

I had often used their print service and was normally in and out within ten minutes. But, on this particular day, nothing went right. First, my USB wouldn't load properly. When it finally did, I couldn't seem to locate the proper menu to size and crop the photo. Overcome with helplessness, I broke into tears. People came and went around me, seemingly oblivious to my distress. I was crying so much I couldn't see well enough to find my USB on the screen. When I did find it, it wouldn't eject. I had never felt so helpless or hopeless.

Then a tall young man approached me. He quietly asked if he could help before he went on lunch break. I sobbed that I was unable to get the machine to work. He pulled up a stool and, with a few quick taps on the keyboard, brought up the photo. He moved as if to leave, but instead he sat back and waited. When I didn't move, he asked if this was what I would like printed. Still crying, I shook my head and said it needed to be cropped. He put it into crop mode and again sat quietly next to me. I pointed out what to cut. He obligingly cropped the photo and then waited again.

Through tears, I told him what size I wanted and the number of copies. He put it all into the system and waited. I thanked him for his help as he handed me the USB. He acknowledged my thanks and sat waiting quietly with me until I was composed enough to walk out. I knew my eyes and nose were red from crying. Tears were still running down my cheeks and onto my T-shirt but his silent support made all the difference to me. By sitting silently, he permitted me to cry without judgment or the need for apologies. He didn't ask what was wrong or offer well-meaning but unhelpful comments. Silent and supportive, he allowed me to connect with my grief in a safe, cared-for space. Somewhere in that brief exchange of time, I felt some of the hopelessness lift.

A few weeks later, I was waiting for the pharmacy to fill a prescription when someone passed the aisle. He stopped, backed up, looked at me, and gently asked if I was okay. I looked up and saw it was the young man who had helped me with the photo. I smiled and said, "Yes, thank you." He nodded and went on his way. I never saw him at the store again. My heart healed a little more knowing someone cared enough to ask a simple question.

A month or so later, I ordered a dump-truck load of rock. I needed to do something physical to distract myself. Planning out a rock garden and a labyrinth seemed an ideal solution. The areas were marked off, and I looked forward to many hours of hot, sweaty work where my thoughts would be on the task at hand, not on the hole in my heart.

Focusing on shoveling and moving the rock was satisfying. Once a load was dumped, I would rake it smooth and then return to fill the wheelbarrow and repeat the dumping and raking. I was in the middle of raking the third load when I looked up and saw three men enter the back yard, each pushing a full wheelbarrow of rock. They were neighbors I barely knew. I would wave as I drove past their homes, but I couldn't recall ever having a real conversation with them.

They greeted me with a grin and asked where I would like the rock. I pointed to the outlined area. As one neighbor upturned his wheelbarrow, he remarked he couldn't let me do all this work myself and had called the others to help. A fourth neighbor showed up and took my wheelbarrow, leaving me to rake. In less than half an hour, the rock garden was completed. Although I had wanted to move rock until I was exhausted and empty, my neighbors had filled me with gratitude and a sense of peace. I thanked them for their help and felt the hole in my heart close a little more.

Nine years have passed, but I still feel deep gratitude to those five men who gave me a sense of peace and healing.

— TG Gilliam —

Mr. Petrucci's Handkerchiefs

Extend yourself in kindness to other
human beings wherever you can.
~Oprah Winfrey

Fresh out of college, I had a job as a receptionist at an optical store. As in any retail environment, we had both nice and nasty customers — people we dreaded seeing walk in the door and others who saved the day with their cheer or charm.

One lovely elderly couple would come in often for one thing or another. The woman was very sweet, often had questions, and liked to chat. There were days when it was so busy that taking the extra time with her was challenging, but she was so very likeable and undemanding that I let her go at her own pace. In truth, I really liked the woman and her husband and imagined it would be lovely to have them as neighbors.

One day, Mr. Petrucci came in and walked up to my desk rather than taking a seat in the waiting area. It was unusual for him to come in without his wife, but that didn't register with me at first. I greeted him and asked what he needed. He told me that he didn't need anything; he had just come in to see me. When he haltingly told me that his wife had died, I was crestfallen. My heart ached for this man losing a woman he clearly loved and had been with for most of his life. Then he handed me a package and said it was a gift for me. He said he wanted to give me something to remember her by because I had always been so nice to her.

Thinking about that moment still brings tears to my eyes. Here was a man who had just lost his wife of probably fifty years, still grieving, and he made a special trip to thank me for being nice to her. I opened the box, and it contained a wonderful, old-fashioned set of Irish linen embroidered hankies. I told him how fond I was of her and how very touched I was by his thoughtful gesture.

I never saw him after that. That was over forty years ago, and I still can picture him standing there telling me how much it meant to him that I had been kind to his wife. I still have one of those lovely hankies — I have kept it in my scrapbook all these years. It always serves as a reminder of how the smallest of gestures can be so important to someone. Just as I had no idea that I was making a difference to him and his wife, he could never imagine how much his gift meant to me or how much it taught me. We touch each other's lives in ways we often never know about — for good or for ill. The smallest amount of kindness has lasting repercussions. I try to remember that every day.

— Geri Moran —

69

The Purple Coat

Generosity is the most natural outward expression of
an inner attitude of compassion and loving kindness.
~14th Dalai Lama

I could already picture myself wearing it on a winter's eve, with snow falling softly around me. The cape-like royal purple coat didn't fit everyone's style, but it certainly fit mine! I gazed dreamily at it. It was full-length, with deep pockets, perfect for blustery winter days. The colour was a real showstopper! And the best part? It was crowned with a plush, faux-fur collar and cuffs, all in that glorious shade of shimmery eggplant.

It was bold and unapologetic, everything my twenty-year-old heart wanted to express to the world.

The coat wasn't even in a fancy store window. It was simply hanging against the gym wall in our church basement. Our annual rummage sale was underway, with shoppers and volunteers vying for space in the ancient hallways. It was a red-letter day for bargain hunters, with the added benefit of supporting the church's charitable outreach programs.

I'd been there all week, setting up tables and moving boxes. Truth was, that church was my second home. It was a respite from the pressures and busyness of university life. In this building, I was loved and accepted — not based on grades or popularity or accomplishments — but just for who I was. Most days found me prowling the halls in some attempt to be useful, whether by assisting in the office, singing in the choir, or just getting to know our diverse community.

Outside of Christmas and Easter, the rummage sale was the busiest day of the church year. The most serious treasure hunters had lined up at sunrise to get first pick of the bounty. I'd arrived just as early to welcome shoppers and make coffee for the volunteers. By late morning, when I finally got my shopping break, most of the good stuff was long gone.

So why was this incredibly striking coat still hanging on the wall?

I looked at the paper tag pinned to its cuff. I did a double take. It's general knowledge that rummage sales are places to find bargains. Even high-end items go for pennies on the dollar. Well, not this coat. For some reason, the handwritten tag had the coat listed for full price. Full designer price! At a rummage sale!

I turned to the volunteer. "Is this correct?"

"Yes," she said, giving me the side eye. "Isn't it ridiculous?"

"Why would you price it so high?" I asked.

"Oh, it isn't us," she explained. "Mrs. Sharp said she'd only donate it if it could bring in a very large donation for the church. She's the one who named the price."

I couldn't believe it. That wasn't the spirit of the rummage sale! Yes, we wanted to raise funds for the outreach programs, but this was also a chance to gently benefit the less fortunate in our area. Most of our shoppers needed a good bargain. These were single moms trying to outfit growing children. Seniors on a fixed income dreaming of a new dress for this year's Christmas party. Out-of-work adults seeking something respectable for next week's job interview. And students like me — young people with big dreams and small budgets, using their creativity to make ends meet.

I sighed when I looked at the coat. There was no way I could afford it. My spirit was bold, but my wallet was weak.

Suddenly, I felt myself getting angry. I knew Mrs. Sharp. She was a regular fixture at the church, and she wasn't just comfortable — she was wealthy. If she really wanted the church to have a large donation, she could easily give it herself.

"I'm sorry," I said to the volunteer. "I just can't afford it."

"Don't worry, dear," she said. "You're not the only one. I have a feeling it's not going to sell today."

And she was right. All day long, the purple coat stayed on its hanger. Starry-eyed ladies of all ages gazed lovingly upon its plush collar and soft furry cuffs, but one look at the price tag and they walked away.

As the day came to a close, I gathered with the late-shift volunteers to pack up the unsold clothes and tidy the room. Suddenly, the volunteer from the coat table came over to me with a large garment bag draped over her arms.

"For you," she stated with a smile.

I looked at her with curiosity and zipped open the bag. It was the purple coat!

"What do you mean 'for me'?" I asked.

"It's for you, a gift," she stated excitedly. "When Mrs. Sharp came to the table, we had to explain to her that we couldn't sell her coat because of the price. She asked if anyone had even been interested in it. We said yes, lots of people, but that you were particularly fond of it. She reached up and stroked that plush collar like it was the most precious thing in the world. She said, 'You know, I remember the day I got this coat. I was just a young woman back then. Draped in that purple splendour, I felt like a queen, like I could take on the world! This coat and I have made a lot of memories together.' Then, she opened her wallet and gave us the amount on the price tag. The full amount! For a moment, we didn't understand what she was doing. Then she said, 'This needs to be worn by someone who will truly appreciate it, someone who will create lots of extraordinary memories wearing it. Please, give her the coat.'"

I couldn't believe what she was saying! Not only had Mrs. Sharp paid for her own coat, but now she wanted me to have it! I was overwhelmed.

Suddenly, my stomach twisted into a knot. I'd made a horrible assumption! Here, in this place where I'd received so much love and acceptance, I'd been so quick to judge someone else.

And yet, in this same moment, I was given not just a coat but overflowing grace and generosity.

I gathered the soft purple folds into my arms. It was heavy and lush. I knew it would keep me warm in the winter. It would be a joyful flash of colour on a grey day. I knew we'd create lots of memories together.

And I also knew it would remind me of a powerful lesson: People aren't always who you think they are. Be slow to anger. Be slow to judge.

And when, given the chance, be outrageously generous. Be boldly, unapologetically kind. Surprise others with your compassion and goodness. You never know who you might bless in the process.

— Allison Lynn —

70

Respect

The things you do for yourself are gone when you are gone,
but the things you do for others remain as your legacy.
~Kalu Ndukwe Kalu

Even after twenty years, I immediately recognized him across the mall corridor. We smiled as we walked toward each other, not saying a word, and wrapped each other in an embrace. Our hug was almost embarrassingly long until we stepped apart, and he said to me with a tear in his eye, "You always respected me, man." I had no idea what he was talking about.

He was an old friend from my days in the maintenance department. On the day we met in the mall, we had both been retired more than fifteen years and hadn't seen each other for at least twenty.

When we first met, I was a newly graduated engineer, trying to figure out how to supervise a skilled-trades crew, and he was a trainee assigned to me. He was "Scamp," short for "Scamper" — a nickname acquired from his days of running with a football in high school.

It was in the early 1960s, and he was one of the first Black candidates admitted into our company's skilled-trades training program. He knew what he was facing. Some people in management and his union felt there was no place in skilled trades for people of color. They looked forward to his failure.

But I wasn't one of them. He had greater skills than many seasoned journeymen already working for me. I did my best to encourage him — but not for any noble reason. I encouraged him because he was a highly skilled asset I wanted to keep on my crew.

On a few occasions, he talked to me about being discouraged and giving up, but I never commiserated with him. Instead, I assigned him increasingly more difficult projects that he did himself without guidance. The projects relied on his ability to figure things out for himself, and he couldn't resist challenges like that.

He went on to a successful career as a journeyman millwright, and I moved on to other departments and plants. But I did what I could to maintain contact. Whenever I was near his workplace, I looked him up, and we would reminisce about the old days.

He had a well-deserved sports reputation from his high-school days but was also well-known as more than a sports hero. He was active and influential in civic projects, where he enjoyed the respect of both the Black and white communities. That was evidenced on the night Plant Security paged me to escort Scamp to the main gate because the cops were there to pick him up.

I was dismayed that Scamp had done something to cause him to be arrested but was later ashamed I had had that thought. It turned out that a few years before, Scamp had organized a group of local Black leaders and sports heroes, who met with police to create a response team in the event there was racial unrest in the city. The police came to the plant that night because they needed his help. It was 1968, and a hundred cities around the country were being torn apart on that night. However, the one raging in his own city got stopped early — in part because Scamp and others he recruited were on platforms with bullhorns asking for restraint.

That memory and others flashed through my mind as we wrapped ourselves in a hug that day in the mall, and I felt an affection for this man I hadn't seen in so long.

I didn't understand when he said, "You always respected me, man!" I said to him, "Scamp, what do you mean? Of course, I respected you, but I never did anything special that would call for you to thank me!"

That's when his big grin appeared, the one I remembered. And with a few remaining tears, he said, "That's the beauty of it, man. You never knew it was special."

— Lynn Gilliland —

The Gift of Life

Heroes come in all types and sizes.
~Author Unknown

I have only given blood once. It was during one of those annual drives at the high school where I taught. The Red Cross trailer pulled into the bus parking lot and welcomed students over the age of eighteen to donate. Truth be told, most were lured by the promise of free cookies and juice. Missing math class was a bonus, too.

The faculty was encouraged to pop in during planning periods to participate. After watching the heart-tugging video at the most recent staff meeting, many of us volunteered to donate, myself included.

What I hadn't anticipated was the backup as kids lined up for their turn in one of the three reclining chairs. Several teenagers giggled and whispered to each other as they mentally calculated how much time they had been out of the classroom, figuring they had pulled one over on the unsuspecting administration. A couple of names were tossed around as the stories of friends who had passed out at the sight of the needle were repeated. The next day, the embellished versions would be told over slices of pizza in the cafeteria. Such is the stuff of high school legends.

I was graciously ushered to the front of the line by the Student Council member who carried a clipboard and tried to be as efficient as possible, all the while sporting a deer-in-the-headlights look. So much responsibility rested on her young shoulders, and things were quickly unraveling.

I slid into the chair and took a deep breath. The process was painless but time-consuming, and the nurse had just removed the needle from my arm when the bell rang for the next period to begin. I grabbed my cookies and juice and climbed the three flights of stairs to my classroom. By the time I opened the door for my students, I was lightheaded and dizzy, with a queasy feeling in the pit of my stomach. I don't know how much learning took place for the rest of that afternoon, but I made a mental note to reserve such adventures for after-school hours. High-school teachers need to be firing on all cylinders.

In subsequent years, the few times when I tried to donate, I was deemed unfit, either too anemic or too soon after a strong antibiotic regimen. And then, quite frankly, the idea fell off my radar as I grew busy with the other responsibilities of life. That might be true for many of us.

But perception always changes with experience. Early in my cancer treatment, I walked through the infusion center one morning and noticed the bright red and yellow bags hanging from random IV poles. I had quite the epiphany: For each blood product donated, there is a living, breathing recipient. And, most recently, I was one of them. When this newest medication, meant to keep the malignant cells at bay, attacked my platelets, I found myself weak, fuzzy-brained, and covered in tiny bruises. My doctor's chemo nurse, who called with the news, told me to cloak myself in bubble wrap and go to bed. I was to get a transfusion early the next morning.

There is something sacred about the process. Unlike chemotherapy, which is mixed by the resident pharmacist, this comes from the hospital blood bank, sent through a special tube and marked to be handled with care. There is a tag attached, and before the transfusion begins, the nurses cross-reference the typing for both the donor and the patient. As they call out the information to each other, I whisper a prayer for the kind soul who has given me this precious gift, one which I can never repay. The bag is hung and attached to the tube that leads to my port. While I watch the liquid enter my veins, I am fascinated by the fact that platelets are bright yellow, like the sun, the yolk of an egg or a tart lemon.

I have needed two of these transfusions in as many weeks, and I have thought a lot about how we are wonderfully made. It is nothing short of a miracle that a part of one person can save the life of another. We were designed to be interdependent, to understand that each of us can indeed be our brother's keeper. That's nothing short of remarkable, and, I suppose, something we often forget in a society that salutes individualism.

I am grateful for many things: friends, family and, of course, the heroic medical folks. I treasure moments that someday will simply be memories. I still appreciate chocolate and a good red wine. I am also indebted to the generous stranger whose kindness has allowed me to rebuild my weakened body and live to fight another day.

The Greeks have several words to define love. The most powerful is *agape*, which means "love with action," particularly when it is concerned with the greater good of another. And to so many, myself included, that's exactly what blood donation has been.

— Paula W. Millet —

72

The Letter

*Kindness is the golden chain by which society
is bound together.*
~Johann Wolfgang von Goethe

That afternoon, I had a bazillion errands to run before I returned home, made dinner, and got myself ready for the night shift. First stop I needed to make was my mobile-phone store. That infuriating contraption had no buttons, and I couldn't figure out how to download apps or find music. Luckily, Carlos (the nice, young man who sold me the device) stood behind the counter, assisting a gentleman. Carlos was quick and efficient, so I knew the wait wouldn't be long.

Within seconds, an elderly lady hoisted her walker onto the sidewalk out front. Without saying anything, Carlos hopped over the counter, dashed across the store, opened the door, and helped her inside. The lady sat next to me as Carlos returned to his first customer. Apparently, the poor guy had missed a lot of work because his wife had been hospitalized with cancer. I don't know how he did it, but Carlos made a call and got his late fees dropped and a forty-five-day extension on his payment. I sat there feeling grateful and pretending I couldn't hear everything that was going on. As the man thanked Carlos with a tear trickling from his eye, Carlos consoled him with kind words and a pat on the shoulder. A few seconds later, that poor guy walked out of the store visibly renewed.

Carlos initiated my download and then went about chatting with the lady in the walker. Surprisingly, she was there to bring Carlos some cookies for being so nice to her the previous day. Just then, an entire family entered the store followed by an impatient, young man in an NFL jersey. Carlos welcomed them inside, invited them to check out the displays, and assured them it wouldn't be a long wait. The young man broke into a chuckle when Carlos referenced a popular trope about his beloved team.

I was in the store only ten minutes; I'm sure of it. I checked the time when I parked, and I checked the time when I drove off. And in that small amount of time, I'd seen so much humility, consideration, and charm. That night at work, I kept thinking about Carlos, how he called each customer by name, and how he made everyone feel like family. Carlos was a salesman, but he wasn't pushing a financial agenda as much as making us feel valued. I couldn't get over his kindness.

The next day, I positioned myself in front of my keyboard and drafted a nice letter to Carlos's boss. I thought his boss would be interested to know how Carlos treats people and how it represents their store. Since I took my time and did a pretty good job, I decided to mail copies to their local headquarters, their state headquarters, and — why the heck not — the CEO who ran the whole shebang.

A couple of months later, I zigged when I should have zagged. While at the gym, I attempted to open my music app and deleted the darn thing instead. I was mad at myself and my fumbling, fat fingers. No worry, though. I figured I'd pop by the phone store and see if kind Carlos would reinstall the app. But when I entered the store, there was a mile-long line and no Carlos. I waited an eternity as the overworked woman behind the counter assisted customers. When it was my turn, I explained my problem. She shook her head and scowled. "Sorry, that's really not my job," she stated, "but I'll do it this once because you waited so long."

"I don't see Carlos," I mentioned as she turned on my phone. "Is he off today?"

"Carlos don't work here anymore."

"Why?" My heart skipped. "Did something happen?"

"Some woman wrote a letter and…"

"What?" I gasped. I shrank two sizes as my intestines slithered into my gym shoes. Had I said something that got Carlos fired?

"Corporate liked the letter, so they promoted him and gave him his own store. Can you believe it? His. Own. Store. Lucky brat. I've been here five years, and they haven't given me anything."

She handed me my phone.

"Thank you very much," I said, and then I turned to walk out.

"Good for him, I guess," she called to me, "because his wife just had their first baby."

"Yeah," I nodded as I floated toward the door. "Good for him."

— January Joyce —

73

Easing Trauma with Kindness

There is no duty more obligatory than
the repayment of kindness.
~Cicero

When I was a young girl, my mother told us she was going out to do some school shopping for us, which wasn't unusual. At least, it didn't seem so at the time. I'm the middle child in my family, and my two older brothers and I were past the age of needing a sitter. We were just three years apart, and we were also responsible enough to care for our two sisters for short periods. They were ages five and two back then.

Our mother had been gone for several hours when we started to worry. Surely the stores were closed. Where was she? My brothers and I decided to call our father at the grocery store where he was working the second shift. He asked us to call him in another hour if she still wasn't back, and we did. Suspecting something was up, he hurried home.

Shortly after he walked through the door, his suspicions quickly turned into a reality check. He discovered two notes in their bedroom — one for him and one for us. The one for us said that she needed to get away from us before she had a nervous breakdown and that she loved us very much. I never read the one that was for my father, but I assume it said that she'd left him to be with his best friend because he cried when he read it. That is, the guy who had been his best friend before that day, and who later became my stepfather.

Shortly after, our father packed up all five of us and we moved in with his sister's family. With my aunt, uncle, and their four kids, there were twelve of us living in a modest home. Tight as the living quarters were, they fed us and housed us during an intensely sad and uncertain time. Many years later, I learned that our father had considered placing us in an orphanage at the time and ultimately decided against it. Despite everything, our father had to find a way to move forward.

Someone my father knew rented a house to us at a reasonable rate. The kind acts seemed to multiply from there. As a grocery man, our father was well acquainted with the truck drivers. Two of them also made deliveries at a little market in our new neighborhood. Both made the little market the second-to-the-last stop on their route. They made our house their final stop, and we got whatever was left on the truck for the week. We got sodas on Thursday and pizzas on Friday. I never knew their names or anything about them, but they were kind enough to think of five motherless kids and a single, struggling dad every week.

Around the same time, our father told us he was taking us to see a friend of his. It was a customer who came into the grocery store and stopped to chat with him every week. After hearing about what had happened to him and us kids, he invited all of us to his home.

I don't remember a lot about that day, but I do remember that he was an African American gentleman, and his wife fed us lunch that day. Before we hopped in the car to go home, the man had a heart-to-heart conversation with our father. He handed our father a camera and an envelope with money in it. Our father tried to refuse it, but the man wouldn't take no for an answer. While his name and face escape me today, I remember the feeling of compassion that radiated from him as we drove away in our old Chevy station wagon.

In retrospect, it wasn't only the acts that each of these men performed to help our family in such a great time of need that made such an impression on me. It was what they, and so many others like them, did collectively that helped us survive that difficult time.

After I started a family of my own, my husband and I decided to become foster parents. Going through the process of becoming foster and adoptive parents triggered my own traumatic childhood, and I almost backed out. After getting acquainted with a few foster children, I realized that I was exactly the kind of mother that parentless children needed.

We eventually adopted two boys from the foster-care system who needed a family. As someone who nearly became a foster child, I found that I could connect with them because I could identify with their fear and pain. I'm aware that the love and kindness that I've shown them over the years can never take away their own traumatic memories. Yet, as I think back to how fearful and anxious I was over losing the only family I'd ever known, I know that it takes only a bit of kindness to carry us through the worst times in life. It feels even better when it comes from those from whom you least expect it.

— Toni Hoy —

74

Hello, Human Kindness

When you are kind to others, it not only
changes you, it changes the world.
~Harold Kushner

I'm all about sentiment. To my husband's chagrin, I've held onto myriad mementos over the past thirty-three years of our marriage that I've only begun to sift through. Many have faded with age; others have withstood the test of time. I stumbled upon the latter the hard way when my wedding ring—a simple, ten-karat gold band—went missing. And one person's kindness changed my tiny corner of the world.

I only know her as Tricia—an OR nurse sporting black Converse shoes on her feet and angel wings beneath her hospital scrubs.

Six days after a hiking accident, medical staff prepared me for surgery to repair a broken bone in my left wrist. Unfortunately, prior to anesthesia, my wedding band refused to budge.

With a heavy heart, I granted permission to medical staff to cut off the ring if necessary.

Approximately ninety minutes later, I stirred from a deep sleep, struggling to adjust to the dim lighting and unfamiliar sounds. One of the first things I registered upon waking was a woman's voice—Tricia's. "They were able to remove your ring without cutting it off," she said, eyes twinkling.

A tear rolled down my cheek. "Really?"

While I no doubt asked the same question over and over, Tricia assured me each time that she'd given the ring to my husband, Bob.

Once I was dressed with Tricia's help, she pushed me in a wheelchair to the main entrance where Bob would be waiting at the curb.

But just as we entered the hospital lobby, I saw him enter through the double doors, his lips drawn tight.

"Bob... Bob!" I called, drawing his attention toward Tricia and me. "They saved my ring!" I blurted as our eyes met.

Instead of sharing my enthusiasm, however, the color seemed to drain from his face. "I lost it," he responded.

"What?" I wanted to blame my confusion on the lingering effects of the anesthesia, but the sadness in his voice spoke otherwise.

"I lost your ring."

Comprehension set in, and the next several minutes proved a whirlwind as the three of us — Tricia pushing my wheelchair behind Bob — retraced his steps. First, we boarded the elevator, and then we combed the hallway where he'd waited during my surgery and Trisha had given him my ring.

The next thing I remember was Tricia assisting me, empty-handed, into the passenger seat of our vehicle, with her well wishes and Bob's apologies ringing in my ears.

Yet even while sadness accompanied my husband and me during our ride home, I could not be angry. Neither of us had slept well the previous night, and it wasn't until after my surgery and Bob had gone to retrieve his car that he remembered my ring.

Midway to the parking ramp, he'd stopped in the valet area to check his pockets and backpack, but the ring was nowhere to be found.

Later that day, as I rested on our living room sofa, I heard Bob on the phone filing a report with Lost and Found at the hospital.

But when close to a week passed with no updates, I accepted the inevitable. That was one memento I would never see again.

And then one afternoon, my husband's ringtone chimed. "It's the hospital," he said, handing me his cellphone.

"This is Chris," I said, assuming it was a post-surgery follow-up call.

"Hi, this is Tricia. I took care of you in the recovery room."

I pictured the young Converse-sporting grandma — the OR nurse who worked twelve-hour shifts and whose granddaughter called her Gigi.

After exchanging pleasantries, she continued, "Remember the ring your husband lost?"

Until Tricia's call, I had forgotten the role she played in those precious minutes in which the three of us searched for my missing band.

"Yes?" My voice sounded small to my ears.

"We found it."

With those three words, my vision clouded once more.

"You're kidding!"

"Nope, the valet found it and brought it to me." Tricia gushed with happiness as she recounted the time she'd spent scouring the pickup and drop-off areas in front of the hospital. And how she'd given instructions to the valet staff if they were to find it.

"I have it here," she said.

She relayed her work schedule for the next couple of days. As much as I wanted my ring back, I also needed to thank Tricia in person.

Before heading to the hospital that evening, my husband and I stopped at the florist to pick out a fall arrangement as a small token of our appreciation. We arrived in the lobby at 8:15, well before Tricia's shift ended at 10:30.

But the receptionist informed us that Tricia's shift had ended early. As my husband and I turned to leave, the woman at the desk waved us back. Another of Tricia's colleagues had reached out to her. She was twenty minutes away and was coming back.

Less than a half-hour later, my husband and I watched as Tricia — still dressed in scrubs and black Converse — jumped from the cab of her pickup truck. After a quick greeting, she disappeared inside the building and returned minutes later with a specimen cup — and my wedding band securely tucked inside. I laughed and cried as we hugged.

"You are an angel," I said, handing her the potted plant, a card tucked between its velvety leaves.

A short while later, as my husband and I drove through the hospital parking lot toward the exit, a bright orange sign staked in the ground alongside the curb winked at me beneath the streetlights.

"Kindness… a gift you give yourself," I read aloud.

I recalled the placards then — signage displayed throughout the interior of the hospital touting the medical group corporate-wide philosophy.

Kindness matters.

Human kindness has no off season.

Indeed. While my ring no longer fits on my finger, the simple band hangs from a chain looped around my neck. It is a daily reminder that even the smallest act of kindness can make all the difference in the world.

— Chris Maday Schmidt —

75

Jedi Training

*Perhaps more than any other factor, kindness gives
meaning and value to our life, raises us above our
troubles and our battles, and makes us feel
good about ourselves.*
~Piero Ferrucci, The Power of Kindness

I knew that Walt Disney World was supposed to be magical, but I was initially not so enthusiastic, especially given how much I was spending on the vacation. However, during that trip, I was converted. A cast member gave my family an experience that showed us what makes Disney, well, Disney. With thoughtfulness, inclusion and some "magic," she helped make our Disney experience one to remember!

Being huge *Star Wars* fans, it was important that we visit Hollywood Studios for our sons to experience Jedi Training. Sign-up was "first come, first served," and there was no way we were going to miss watching them in a lightsaber duel with Darth Vader! So, early on our second morning, my three sons — Nicholas, Nathan, and Ryan, ages eleven, nine, and five respectively — stepped up to a cast member to register for "training."

The cast member asked if I was signing up all three boys. I replied, "No, just Nathan and Ryan." I did not get to explain to her that Nicholas was on the autism spectrum and had significant attention and sensitivity issues that would prevent him from participating. These issues resulted in uncontrollable vocalizations and body movements ("flapping") that

Nick sometimes couldn't control.

We'd experienced the worst of these behaviors the day before in the Magic Kingdom. After he was accidentally splashed while watching boats careening down Splash Mountain, Nicholas had multiple meltdowns and refused to go on any ride that was on water. He was in sensory overload. Plans to ride Jungle Cruise, It's a Small World, Pirates of the Caribbean, Splash Mountain and any other ride that involved water were nixed. We were hyper-sensitive after that and we decided, perhaps incorrectly, that Nick would not be able to participate in Jedi Training.

While the cast member was taking our information, Nicholas had difficulty waiting for us to finish. He started showing behaviors from the previous day. I was giving information about the boys while simultaneously calming him down.

I waited for the cast member to give us weird looks and question what was going on. Surprisingly, she did not and remained patient.

After taking our information, she asked us to return for training at 1:30. I was so impressed. I remember taking note of her name: Hoda. I thought, *How cool! It rhymes with Yoda, and she works in the* Star Wars *area. I won't forget this.* Little did I know that Hoda would give my family a lot more reasons not to forget her.

We returned promptly at 1:30, and the kids got into their Jedi cloaks. It was awesome! While they were being taught the ways of The Force, they were ambushed by a gang of stormtroopers and Darth Vader. Each Jedi trainee then had to show their worth and engage in a lightsaber duel with Darth Vader. Nathan and Ryan expertly used the powers of The Force and defeated Lord Vader. Nicholas excitedly watched from the sidelines.

Upon concluding their training, Hoda returned to give the kids certificates to memorialize their accomplishment. When we brought Nathan and Ryan up for their certificates, Hoda handed them their Jedi documents but also surprised us with a certificate for Nicholas!

While taking our information earlier that day, Hoda saw and overheard me working with Nicholas. She explained she had a cousin on the spectrum. She understood the challenges that came with having a child with autism, especially in Disney World, and this was a small way to recognize that. Our eyes filled up like swimming pools.

But it didn't end there. Hoda asked if we could wait because she wanted to do "something special" for us. With a lemonade stand nearby to visit, and the kids overheated from training, we agreed. We were not prepared for what was to come.

Hoda returned and said, "Follow me." She walked us past long lines of people waiting for the Star Tours ride.

"Wow! We're going to the front of the line!" my kids shouted. But that didn't quite happen.

Instead, we followed Hoda through an intergalactic sliding door that led into an empty holding area. A few minutes later, the sliding doors opened, and in walked three stormtroopers and Darth Vader! She had arranged for us to have our own private photo session with *Star Wars* characters. Our boys were over the moon. Nicholas looked like he had just received the keys to George Lucas's universe.

Once the shoot was over, Hoda introduced us to the manager of the Star Tours ride.

"Hoda told me about your family, and I'd like to do something special for you, too," he said.

What more could these people do for us? we thought.

We followed the manager out of the waiting area, past more throngs of people, and into a boarding area for the Star Tours ride! There, he said he knew that kids with autism had difficulty in crowds, and he knew overstimulation was not fun to deal with. So, not only did he want us to skip waiting in lines, but he also wanted us to experience the ride with no crowds. He placed my family into a 100-plus-seat ride with no one else!

Humbled, and not knowing what to say, we rode Star Tours crowd-free. I'll never forget the huge smile on Nicholas's face and the pure joy my other boys were experiencing. We laughed and screamed through the whole ride, overwhelmed with emotion in response to the acts of kindness we were experiencing in "the happiest place on Earth."

When the ride ended, the manager met us again and asked, "What else can we do for you?" We told him that they had already done way too much. Nevertheless, he gave us VIP passes to the popular Toy Story Mania ride and to that night's performance of Fantasmic.

As we walked out of the park that night, we passed a Guest Services office. I could not leave the park without telling Disney what Hoda and her colleagues had done for us. It was the least we could do to say, "Thank you." I went inside, and a cast member feverishly took notes as I narrated this experience that profoundly changed our vacation.

In fact, as I write about this experience eight years later, I can't help but think about how many events have occurred in my life since then that I can barely recall. But, because of the thoughtfulness, kindness, and unselfish actions people took on my family's behalf that day in May 2013, I can recall every detail as if it happened yesterday.

Hoda changed me. I became much more optimistic about my son's future knowing there are Hodas in this world. Additionally, her actions have challenged me every day since to consider how I can be more like her and take steps to make someone's day a bit more "magical."

— Steve Filipiak —

76

Wait for It

*Kindness is igniting a light in someone else for no
reason other than to watch them enjoy the glow.*
~Author Unknown

As an engineer's daughter, I was a disgrace. I couldn't unclog a drain, mow a lawn, or decode a fuse box well into adulthood. It's not that I don't like things working; getting them there is just not in my nature. More the creative, artsy type, I became a graphic designer, and then a college writing tutor. I broke more things than I fixed, and Dad was forever there to take care of whatever had gone wrong. He'd always say it was fun, even as he ran into kinks, like it was a game to him. That was his gift and my incredibly good fortune.

One summer, he wanted to do an oil change on my car. I *hated* car work — the grime, the fumes, and my unshakable anxiety that something was going to bust and leave me immobile for days or stranded somewhere. But I was fine with assisting him, handing him his tools, collecting the dirty towels, oil bottles, and garbage, and bringing him cold water.

Well, there were kinks that day — a runaway washer, some dripping fluid, headlights that needed buffing — and Dad's "fun" went on for hours in that July sun. It was evening, and we were both achy. Mind you, Dad had done all the back-breaking work; I had only my early-onset osteoporosis to thank for my pain. Personally, I was eager to go inside, take a hot shower, and get some carb-bomb ready in a microwave minute. Not Dad.

"Let's go out for dinner. We can take the car for a test drive. I'm feeling like sushi." Wait, what?

Dad didn't mean at the sushi joint around the corner but "his" sushi place half an hour away where he'd gone with his best friend for years. You mean I'd have to actually get dressed? But Dad had spent his day working on my car out of his good heart and know-how. It would be nice for me to tag along with him for dinner — and pay for it, too, probably.

The restaurant was dim and serene, as many sushi restaurants are. It was late, so we had our pick of tables. The hostess seated us and brought us tea, and Dad and I chatted about the car. Minutes later, a server came to take our order.

After the usual greetings, he ventured, "Are you May? Do you still tutor writing?" It hit me that he indeed looked familiar, but I couldn't find his name anywhere in my mental contact list.

"Uhh, yes, I do," I replied. And as I pretended to know exactly who he was, things did start coming back to me. I remembered sitting with him, usually in evening appointments, as he struggled first with his composition assignments, and then with research and chemistry papers. He became a regular for a couple of semesters until he finished his coursework and moved on.

Clearly, my student had no problem holding onto the memory. He turned to my father and proceeded to gush, "I used to only go to May. She was so kind and patient with me. She helped me in every class, and she always made me understand how to write better until I could do it."

It turned out he'd been my student nine years earlier, so I felt a little better about not recalling him right away. Still too embarrassed to ask him his name, I was beyond flattered to hear that I'd had such an impact on him.

Over dinner, the conversation between Dad and me turned from the car to my work, and how, like this young man, my students had come and gone through the years. When we finished, my student came over to take our plates and asked, "Would you like anything for dessert?"

"Oh, no, we're full, but thank you," Dad answered. "Just the check, please."

"No, sir, that's okay. Your dinners are on me." Wait, what?

Dad and I immediately started declining his gracious offer, but he persisted. "I always wanted to be able to give you something to thank you for everything you did to help me, but I never did. I never went back all these years. Please, let me do this as my thanks to you now."

So, we accepted his gesture… and left a very big tip.

I hadn't thought of my tutoring and teaching as a gift to my students, just like Dad probably didn't consider tinkering with my car a gift to me. Still, I was quietly ashamed that I'd even thought to selfishly refuse Dad's invitation at first. The thoughtfulness of this former student reminded me that gratitude and kindness always prove to be the right choice.

On our way back to my newly maintained car, Dad chuckled, "Hey, May, thanks for dinner!"

The engineer's daughter had found grace.

— May Jampathom —

Worth the Effort

77

Dennis

*Be kind, for everyone you meet is fighting
a harder battle.*
~Plato

"Turn off the talk-to-me sign on your forehead," said my husband as he headed to the restroom. He remained bewildered by how strangers would gravitate toward me to share their life stories, yearning for consolation or advice. Just before midnight, we routinely walked to the only local coffee shop that stayed open twenty-four hours for a quick jolt of caffeine to stay alert as we labored into the wee hours. Cold canvassing to start a business at twenty-six years old meant grueling ten-hour days, frozen fingers, and numb toes.

At the witching hour, the colorful characters and homeless in the neighborhood would surface for some warm java and free leftover bagels and donuts. I was intrigued by the faces. My imagination raced to fill in the stories of who they were and how they got there. Their tattoos. Their tattered clothes. Their defeated expressions.

I knew my husband worried about my impulse to hug and interact with strangers. I understood this to be a reasonable concern, but, again and again, my instinct would take over. As he reluctantly headed to the restroom, I looked down and vowed to keep a low profile that night. I cradled the cup of aromatic brew warming my hands, but then my eyes naturally glanced up. I locked eyes with a man whom I had noticed would routinely sit in the same corner. His wavy brown hair was matted down, his hands were worn, and his expression looked heavy with untold stories.

The corners of my mouth instantly curled, and he smiled back, whispering a muffled "Hi." He was missing several teeth, but his smile just beamed. His tired hazel eyes revealed a kind character. He continued, "I see you here every night." Thus began an animated exchange of ordinary chitchat that felt natural and comforting.

Then my husband entered, rolling his eyes in disappointment when all he wanted was a quick and uneventful cup of caffeine before returning to work. He stood and stared staunchly while waiting for me to get up. Like a mischievous child, I turned and snuck one more grin and goodbye to my new friend. We would run into each other again and again, and although we didn't get a chance to engage in conversations, we always nodded a greeting with a covert smile.

About twelve years later, I was handling the marketing for a city transportation system and was asked to do a photoshoot of their buses and building. I hastily made my way to the mechanic garage to request props and volunteers to stage each photo. The staff was very cooperative, but one man in particular went above and beyond in helping me. As I was packing my gear, he came over to me and said, "You don't remember me." Dates and names evade me, but I recall faces with ease, so his comment challenged me. Determined to prove him wrong, I put down my briefcase and calmly looked into his eyes. It was like my mind was fast-forwarding a movie and pausing at the pivotal scene of the plot. "It's you!" I yelled as I spontaneously threw my arms around him. We hugged and laughed like reunited family.

I learned his name was Dennis. A secretary in the building I was very friendly with divulged the backstory. Dennis's parents were abusive drug-and-alcohol addicts who had inflicted cigarette burns on his tongue. She suspected he had been in and out of foster care until he came of age and managed to find his version of peace on the streets. He had chosen to turn his life around, was hired and certified to work as a bus driver, and had proudly obtained a brilliant new set of teeth. I barely recognized him with his trimmed hair and freshly pressed uniform.

We stood in the garage appreciating our uninterrupted time and filling in what had taken place since our nights at the donut shop. "I have never forgotten you. You were the only person who smiled or talked to me," he said. I was struck by the reality of how many faces remain unperceived as we dash through our days. To me, each one has a compelling story that helps me better understand and appreciate my life and connection to others. That seemingly insignificant smile had given us both an indelible gift.

No, my dear husband, I will not turn off the talk-to-me sign on my forehead.

— Barbara Espinosa Occhino —

78

Money Well Spent

Our job on earth isn't to criticize, reject, or judge.
Our purpose is to offer a helping hand, compassion,
and mercy. We are to do unto others as we hope
they would do unto us.
~Dana Arcuri, Harvest of Hope

It was late spring, and we were living in a rural part of Tennessee in a house with a few acres. I have always loved to garden, and this morning seemed like the perfect time to be working on the extensive flowerbeds surrounding the old house we were remodeling. It wasn't long before my two boys and the dogs were outside running around, and I was elbow-deep in mulch, soil, and weeds.

The world always seemed to fade away as I was gardening, so I jumped when I heard a soft voice.

"Hello?" the girl said hesitantly.

I thought of her as a girl, but she was nearly grown, seventeen or eighteen years old. She was thin with long, dark hair past her shoulders.

"Hello," I answered back with a smile. She did not smile back.

I looked behind her at the driveway.

Had I missed seeing or hearing a car drive up?

The driveway was empty except for my own vehicle.

"Could I have a glass of water, please?" she asked, looking at the ground.

"Of course," I said, taking off my gloves. After a quick check on my little ones happily playing on the swing set, I went into the house and came back out with a cold bottle of water.

"Thanks," she said to the ground.

She drank most of the bottle with the first swig and then turned as if to walk back down the road.

"Hold on a minute," I said.

She hesitated but then turned around.

"Did your car break down?" I asked.

"No," she answered.

"Do you need some help?"

She shook her head and took a deep breath that ended somewhere between a sigh and a sob.

"Where are you going?" I asked.

"I need to get to the bus station," she said.

It took me a minute.

"You're walking to the bus station from here?" I asked.

She shrugged.

It was thirty miles from our house to the bus station in Clarksville. I suggested she sit down a minute or two to rest.

"I only have a few hours to get to the bus station," she answered. "I can't wait around."

"How about I drive you there?" I suggested. "It would just take me a few minutes to get the boys ready."

Tears welled up in her eyes, and she nodded.

"You're not running away, are you?" I asked.

There was a flash of anger, and her eyes sparked.

"No, my dad threw me out, so I'm going to live with my grandma in Memphis. But she can't come get me, so she has a ticket for me at the bus station."

"Well, let's give your grandma a call," I said. "She's probably worried."

Within a few minutes, the young lady was dialing her grandma on my phone. As soon as I talked to her, she confirmed the whole story. It had been a bad year for this family. The girl's mother had died suddenly in an accident. Her dad had been coping with a lot of anger, and the two of them were not getting along.

It took me a couple of minutes to get the boys ready. As a second thought, I grabbed some extra cash from our emergency stash in my top dresser drawer.

It wasn't long before we were on our way. The boys were chatty and had a million questions for our pretty stranger. She was a good sport with them. About thirty minutes later, we pulled up to the bus station. Nothing about this place looked great. It was in a rundown part of town, and there were some questionable-looking people hanging around.

The young lady looked uncertainly around the parking lot.

I reached over and squeezed her hand.

"We are doing this together," I said.

I grabbed one boy's hand, and she grabbed the other's. We marched right into the station.

There was a ticket there for her to Memphis, but the bus wasn't scheduled to arrive for another two hours.

"Anyone hungry for a burger?" I asked.

My boys erupted into cheers.

Before long, we had burgers, fries and shakes from a local fast-food restaurant and had found a shaded spot in the riverside park. The boys played happily on the playground.

I watched the girl slurping down a chocolate shake and slipped $50 into her hand.

"No," she said, almost panicking. "I can't take your money; you've already done too much."

"It's okay," I said. "It's just a little money in case you need something. You can always pay me back."

She launched herself at me and gave me a gigantic hug.

While the boys played, we talked about her mom and dad, how life sucks, and that nothing is fair. Before long, it was time to catch the bus to Memphis.

We waited together until the bus pulled up, and I got another bone-crushing hug before she boarded.

I gave her grandmother a quick call to let her know her granddaughter was on the way.

About a year later, a car pulled up in our driveway. I was in the flowerbeds again. The young lady whom we had helped a year ago jumped out of the car, along with her grandma. The girl was all smiles and sparkly eyes. She had a new hairstyle. She gave me a huge hug before she said anything. If it was possible, her grandmother gave me a bigger hug.

Things were better, and she was visiting her dad and her mother's grave. She had been living in Memphis, and her grandmother seemed thrilled.

She handed me an envelope, and when I gave her a questioning look, she giggled.

"It's the money you loaned me," she said.

Her grandmother went on to explain that her granddaughter had saved up money from babysitting around the neighborhood to pay me back.

I gave them both another big hug.

"I wasn't really expecting you to pay me back," I answered. "In fact, it would have been fine if you hadn't."

"Well, you didn't have to help, and you did," the young lady said. "I'll never forget what it meant to me that you helped me that day. You gave me back some hope that life isn't all bad."

It was nice that she brought the money back, but mostly I was just glad to know that she was doing well. Maybe someday she'll show a little bit of kindness to someone else in need.

— Theresa Brandt —

79

Kindness Never Goes Out of Style

Kindness makes the world a better place. When we do something for someone else without expecting anything in return it makes people happy.
~Giovanna Tucker, Random Acts of Kindness

When I was a young hairstylist and worked inside a JCPenney salon, a lady came in one day who looked broken and tired. "Can I help you?" I asked.

She was almost in tears as she replied, "My sister is really sick, and her hair is a mess. I've been to several salons, and no one will help me because she can hardly walk. I'll have to bring her inside in her wheelchair." The woman went on to tell me that she had managed to wash her sister's hair before they left home, which was hard for her to do, and she stressed that all she needed was for her sister's hair to be cut.

"I'll be happy to help you," I said. I offered to help her get her sister out of the car, but the woman said, "No, I'll get her in." She must have told me "thank you" a hundred times as she headed out to get her sister.

While I was waiting on the women to come in, I walked over to my station and moved my hydraulic chair out of its space because I knew it would be easier for this woman to just roll her sister right up to the spot.

When she came back in, I was not prepared for what I saw. The sister was near death, and my nineteen-year-old self had a hard time holding back the tears.

But I composed myself, and Lord, you would have thought I had given them a million bucks simply because I moved the chair to make things easier on them.

I cut and styled the sister's hair, and the three of us chatted and laughed. It was truly a moment I knew I would never forget.

Before the women left, the woman who'd originally approached me asked me to write down my name and phone number for her, so I gave her my salon card, which already had all the information on it.

What's crazy is that during the chaos of getting the sister in and out, I never even asked the women their names.

Two weeks after this encounter, I received a phone call from the salon at a local funeral home, and they said they'd received a request for me to come over and style the hair of a woman who had passed away. I was so puzzled, and I had no clue who she was. I even asked, "Are you sure you've called the right person?"

They assured me they had. They said, "We have your business card, and there's an envelope here for you."

So, I made arrangements to go to the funeral home and style the woman's hair, still wondering who she could be.

When I walked into the funeral home, there was that precious young woman whose hair I had cut after everyone else had turned her away. A bouquet of flowers was sitting by the envelope with my name on it. I styled the woman's hair, and then I opened the envelope.

Inside were two $100 bills along with a handwritten note. It read, "Dear Lesa, we will probably never cross paths again here in this life, but I wanted you to know what your kindness meant to my sister and me. You see, we had been turned away that day and actually treated rudely by several salons. Watching someone die is hard enough but feeling like no one cares when you are at your lowest is terrible. My sister had been a hairdresser for years, and one of her final wishes was that her hair be cut before she died. Not important to some, but she had begged to have it cut. Your kindness to us that day was something that touched my sister, and she said when we left, 'It's my request that this Lesa do my hair when I'm gone, and I know she will because she's what kindness is.'"

Well, I ugly cried over that. I took the flowers, turned the card around and wrote on it, "Your hearts weren't the only ones touched that day." I signed it simply "Lesa" and left the bouquet for the funeral home to place with the woman's other flowers.

I tried to give the money back, too, but the funeral-home folks said that the deceased woman's sister was adamant that I keep it.

What she didn't know, but God did, was that my car needed work done, and I didn't have the extra money for it that week. And how much was the work going to cost? Two hundred dollars.

I have that letter packed up with some of my special things from childhood and college years, and I've never forgotten that incident.

Kindness. It never goes out of style.

— Lesa Shirley-Sheffield —

80

A Lost Ring Finds Kindness

The ripples of the kind heart are the highest blessings
of the Universe.
~*Amit Ray,* Yoga and Vipassana:
An Integrated Life Style

I t was one of those December nights when it gets dark outside early. Nights like that make me procrastinate. So, instead of doing what I was supposed to do, I was scrolling through Facebook.

That's when I came across a post from my local school district. It was a picture of a class ring from the 1960s that had been found in a nearby lake. It was from a local high school. "Do you know who this ring might belong to? We would love to return it to its owner, if possible!"

I thought about another Facebook group I follow, one that posts about the history of our town and had many members who went to high school around the same time as this ring's owner. Perhaps one of them had lost it. Without much thought, I pressed the "Share" button and added a little note: "Anyone missing this or know someone who is?" Then, I posted it to the group.

It was a little moment of kindness on that dark night that I hoped would reunite the owner with their ring.

But I still had to deal with real-life responsibilities: making dinner for the family, helping with homework, folding some laundry, getting the kids to bed. It was several hours before I was able to check on the post I had shared, that little act of kindness. Maybe someone had responded to my post.

When I opened it, I was stunned.

In the few hours since I had passed along the photo of the ring, the post had blown up.

There were suggestions to contact the high school and check if they had any records that could help. People pulled their yearbooks off their shelves to see if they could find a match. Someone else tried to track down information on an ancestry website.

For that academic year, there was only one person whose initials matched those on the inside of the ring. But another post pointed out that there was an obituary for that man. My hope that this little post would help the owner get the ring back was not to be. *Oh, well,* I thought. *I guess that's the end to this story.*

Except the posts kept going.

"I think I may have found his daughter-in-law on Facebook," one person said.

"Who has the ring? I have an e-mail address for his son," another one posted.

She even included a note she had received from the son regarding her inquiry. "What a surprise and gift, especially this time of year. Christmas was his favorite holiday."

The school district's original post also had plenty of responses on it from more people searching through yearbooks, and there was a note from his daughter-in-law. Someone from the school district had already responded, asking for a way to reach her and get the ring sent to their family.

I could only stare at the screen. All I had done was press that little "Share" button. What followed was a roller coaster of emotions, swinging between defeat and hope that there might be a happy ending to this story. How could so much have come from this one little post in such a short amount of time?

I shared the story with my own family with tears in my eyes. It had been a rough year for all of us with the pandemic, and things were not normal. We were planning for a small Christmas with our loved ones on a tiny computer screen from their homes thousands of miles away. We were stressed out about work and school, about tough decisions that needed to be made and holiday celebrations that weren't going to be all that festive.

And yet, this one post that I had quickly shared as a little act of kindness had somehow spurred on a group of other people to perform their own acts of kindness to reunite this ring with a family we didn't know. It was like a bright, twinkling light during those cold and dark December nights.

The ring reached the family two days before Christmas.

— Jenny Cohen —

It Gets Better

The words of kindness are more healing to
a drooping heart than balm or honey.
~Sarah Fielding

ometimes, a kind word from a stranger during a stressful moment can mean the world to someone. When I was
raising my daughter, there were many times when I could
have used a hug or compassionate word when I was at my
lowest point.

My daughter Rachel had severe ADHD as a child and the most
embarrassing and trying moments as her mother came when we were
out in public. I would try to quickly get my shopping done while
simultaneously trying my level best to avoid a meltdown when she was
begging me for a toy or candy bar. All parents have been there — trying
to remain calm while their child is having an epic tantrum. Shoppers
stare or surreptitiously walk by the aisle believing that, surely, they are
catching a murder in progress. The snickers, stares, and not-so-subtle
comments, "If that were my child…" made me pray for the ground to
open and swallow me whole. I would have done anything to escape.

My daughter is now twenty-four and proudly serving in the U.S.
Navy. She has grown and matured into an amazing young woman.
Most people who hear my stories of her struggles growing up do not
believe me when they meet her as an adult. This is a testament to the
saying, "It gets better," because it really does. To be honest, I didn't
think it ever would at the time I was going through it myself. Those

old memories of her extreme rages feel not-so-distant when I encounter a child's mirror-image behavior in a store. The ear-piercing screams of an inconsolable child cause flashbacks that I would rather forget. More often than not, I continue shopping, never stopping to offer any kind of assistance or words of encouragement to the parent. Until recently.

Last week, I was shopping in our local Target. My daughter happened to be with me as she had just arrived home for a much-needed visit while she was changing duty stations in Japan. As we were walking through the aisles and stocking up on things she needed, we heard the start of a child's meltdown that would last more than fifteen minutes. I decided to walk over to investigate the situation, already picturing the scene in my mind. No doubt, the wails of the young boy could be heard clear across the store.

My daughter came up to me and said, "Mom! OMG, is that what I sounded like when I was little?"

"Yes, Rach, you sounded just like that," I replied.

We tried to continue our shopping, but the screams and the sound of the boy pleading with his mom continued for what felt like an eternity. Several more minutes went by, and the boy just wouldn't stop. I felt compelled to follow the screams. As I approached the aisle, I could see several people peeking down the other end of the aisle, whispering to each other and shaking their heads. They would walk away and then turn around with their carts to peek back down the same aisle and continue their whispers.

I arrived at the aisle to find a twenty-something mother standing in the middle of the aisle calmly telling the boy, "No." She was not going to get whatever the boy so desperately wanted. He was grabbing at her folded arms, pleading, trying to get her to move, his face red and blotchy with tears. He hurled himself onto the floor and beat at his mom's legs with his arms while screaming at the top of his lungs.

I was mesmerized by the mother's composure and thought she was doing an excellent job of ignoring his behavior while trying to remain calm during this trying situation. Then I saw the sheer embarrassment and terror in her face, a flashback to my past. I knew what was going through her mind: "Please, make it stop!" She knew people were watching her, and her eyes said everything that I had ever felt in those moments.

I then did something I had never done before. I walked over to the mom and put my arm around her shoulders. I told her she was doing a great job and that everything would be okay one day. I then called my daughter over and introduced her to the young mother. I explained that my daughter had been just like her son when she was that age. I told her that my daughter had had severe ADHD when she was young, and her temper tantrums had been off the charts.

"I know exactly what you are dealing with right now, and I know how you feel," I said. I looked at her and added, "It does get better. Believe me, it really does."

She hugged me back and squeezed me so hard that I knew she was grateful for the kind words of a stranger. At that moment, I could see relief wash over her. Her son stopped screaming for a minute and looked at us with a perplexed expression. His momentary silence gave us a chance to share a few words. The mom went on to tell me that her son had severe ADHD and was also autistic. I told her, "If nobody has told you yet, you are an amazing mom, and you can and will get through this difficult time with your son." I told her to hang in there, keep up the good work, and know that her son would thank her for being his mom someday.

Parents who have a child with special needs, or a learning or behavioral disorder, just need a kind word or a compassionate gesture to know that everything will be okay. Sometimes, that's all it takes.

— Michelle Padula —

82

Two Quarters

Seeing the world through the eyes of a child
is the purest joy that anyone can experience.
~Constance Zimmer

"Go back, Mom! Go back!" shouted my six-year-old daughter, June. "Go back!" I quickly peered into the back seat, worried I had forgotten something. I was relieved to see the girls safe and snug in their car seats, but June's expression was one of pure panic.

"Mom, we have to go back," she insisted. "Someone needs our help!"

As I looked back from the driver's seat, I saw a young, disheveled man playing his guitar. His scrawny, scruffy dog rested next to him near an old, tattered cardboard sign that read, "Homeless, please help."

We'd encountered homeless people in the past and had talked about their needs and struggles. I frantically searched for some cash, quickly realizing that I only had credit cards.

"I'm sorry, sweetheart, but I don't have any cash," I said.

"I have some, Mom!" June replied. She opened her little pink unicorn purse and pulled out a five-dollar bill.

"Oh, good. I'll pay you back when we get home," I responded with a sigh of relief.

"No, Mom," she insisted, "*I* want to help him. I don't want you to pay me back. I want to give him *my* money."

As we drove down the crowded rows of the parking lot, I reassured her that we would get to him. When we got there, I called out,

"Excuse me, sir!"

He cautiously walked toward our car and answered, "Yes, ma'am?"

"Here you go, sir." June stretched out her entire body to hand him her five-dollar bill through the window and explained, "I want you to have this."

He smiled and hesitatingly asked, "This was your money?"

"Yes! I want you to have it," she proudly answered.

"Thank you," he said, touched by her thoughtfulness.

We shared a smile, and as we drove away, my younger daughter Scarlett began to cry. I hadn't noticed that she had emptied her purse and was holding two quarters in her tiny hands.

"Mom, I wanted to give all *my* money to him. I wanted to help," she said, weeping and feeling like she had missed out.

I replied, "Sweetheart, it's only two quarters…"

Before I could finish, she interrupted, "Mom, he needs help!"

I sighed and turned around.

"Excuse me, sir." Now very confused, the gentleman returned to us. "I'm sorry to bother you again, but my other daughter wanted to give you *her* money." He peered into the van window to see my pig-tailed four-year-old grinning ear-to-ear.

"I want to help you!" she said proudly.

Now with tears in his eyes, he said in disbelief, "You? You want to help me?"

"Yes! Yes!" she replied, nodding happily.

Then June proudly handed him her little sister's two quarters. He tightly clutched the coins in his dirt-stained hand. He held his hands to his chest and said, "Thank you. Thank you so much. I… I… I just can't believe *you* wanted to help me."

We all smiled at each other one last time, with tears now running down his face and mine. I watched June put her hand on her heart, close her eyes, and tell her little sister, "It feels so good to help someone, doesn't it, Sisterbaby?" Scarlett agreed. With big smiles, they sank back into their seats.

— Charmin Gans —

83

Change of Heart

Schedule kindness in your day. Watch how small acts
of kindness can change your mood, bring someone else
joy, and give both of you a positive benefit.
~Germany Kent

I was preparing baked beans and mixing up potato salad to go with our Saturday night barbecue when our daughter Rikki stormed in the front door and marched to her room. I glanced out the window and saw our neighbor Lexi walking back to her house across the road. My mother's intuition told me this situation might need some direction.

"Rikki, come in here. I need some help with dinner."

She came out of her room and stood beside me. She had an obstinate look on her face — the kind kids have when they know they are wrong but have convinced themselves they are right.

"I noticed that Lexi came over but didn't stay long. I've noticed that a lot. She is your age and in your class at school. Why doesn't she stay longer?" I watched her out of the corner of my eye as I continued to prepare food.

"I don't like her," Rikki whined. "I wish she would stop coming over here all the time. She dresses terrible, and sometimes she doesn't smell good. Her nose is always runny, and her hair is yucky and tangled. None of us like her."

I knew that "none of us" meant the popular crowd she ran with. It was a lot for a fourth-grader to deal with — trying to fit in and be everything society had convinced them they should be. It might be a scandal if one of the girls in that crowd knew Lexi was playing with Rikki.

"That's not her fault, Rikki. I don't know what her family is like, but maybe she doesn't have anyone to help her. Some kids don't have the extra things that you and your friends have. That doesn't make them any less worthy than you."

Rikki replied that she knew that, and those things were not the real issue. "I just don't like to play with her, Momma. She doesn't like to do the same things that I do."

I told her to go on outside and play. I couldn't force her to like someone. What I didn't know, however, was that Rikki's dad had been watching while he was grilling. He didn't like the fact that Rikki had ignored Lexi, so he decided to intervene. He called Rikki and me outside and asked what was going on. He wanted to know why Lexi was leaving with her head down and looking so sad.

"She just comes over here, Daddy. I don't invite her or anything. She just walks over here."

Looking at me for further explanation, I told my husband that Rikki didn't like to play with Lexi, and that was all there was to it. He studied us both for a moment before he spoke.

"Momma, can you watch the grill for a minute? Rikki and I are going to make a little trip, and we'll be right back." Of course, Rikki wanted to know where they were going. "Just jump in the truck. You'll know in a minute."

She did as he told her, and they took off on a very short trip to Lexi's house across the road. He invited Lexi to come over, have dinner with us, and play with Rikki. He cleared it with her mother, and soon they were on their way back to our house.

I remember Lexi getting out of the truck all smiles. The girls talked a little, and then they played in the tree swing and played ball with Rikki's younger brother. Soon, I heard them talking and giggling. They were having a great time. I could tell that Rikki had put away all the inhibitions she had been feeling. We gathered around our picnic table under our huge oak tree. I looked at my daughter sitting beside her visitor. They were both beautiful little girls. They were unaware of what the world might throw at them as they matured, but on this warm summer evening, everything was grand.

As dusk set in, Rikki and her dad took Lexi home. This time, they both jumped right in the truck, still talking and laughing. When they came back, I could see a sweet glow in Rikki's eyes. Her dad had talked to her about some things. She began to think differently from that day on. I told my daughter how proud I was of her for being so kind and thoughtful to Lexi.

"I had fun today, Momma. She will probably come back and play again sometime."

Her dad sat down beside us and explained why he had felt so sad for Lexi. "You see, baby," he began, "I know how she felt today when you were sort of cold toward her. I know because that was me when I was in fourth grade. I was the poor kid with hand-me-down clothes, the kid who others looked down on. I also know what it was like to be hungry and see other families grilling out and enjoying things. That feeling never goes away." He went on to tell her that he didn't want her to be that child or adult who looked down on others. He told her he wanted her to be kind and helpful, not judgmental and hurtful. She told him she understood and was sorry. Tears were streaming down her face and mine.

Later that night as I tucked her in, she hugged me and told me how good she felt. "You know what, Momma?"

"What?" I replied.

"I think that Jesus is real proud of me right now. I think He is really proud of what I've done today."

Of course, through tears, I told her that Jesus was proud of her, and so was I.

She smiled and snuggled down into her blue sheets with puffy white clouds on them. Lexi came over a few times after that. The two girls took turns on the tree swing and talked like little girls do. They never became best friends, but they did become good friends and find some common ground.

Today, Rikki has a heart of gold. She is the first to welcome those whom others might turn away and is generous in helping others. She has the ability to love the unlovable and encourages her own children to do the same. I truly believe that day made a major difference in the person she has become today. She is a nurse and has worked through COVID with all the strength she can muster. I know she recalls this memory from time to time, always with a grateful heart. I think Jesus is still very proud of her, and so am I.

—Georgia Hendrix Shockley—

84

Tag, You're It

How beautiful a day can be when kindness touches it!
~George Elliston

My teenage granddaughter, Amanda, helped me make 100 tags. We laminated them, punched a hole in each one and tied a string through each hole. On one side of the tag, we printed, "TAG! YOU'RE IT!" On the other, "A kindness has just been done for you. Keep it going by doing a kindness for someone, and then leave this tag with them to pay it forward."

It was such fun finding ways to use the tags over the coming days. I cleaned the mud from my granddaughter's band shoes right before a band trip and left her a tag. She had cleaned out my refrigerator (a task I dread) and left a tag on the milk jug. We eventually used all our tags. We enjoyed sharing different ways we had thought of to use them.

One evening, I went to pick up meds for my husband. As I waited in line, I began counting my money. I was terribly embarrassed when I realized I was five dollars short! I had grabbed just my wallet, leaving my purse at home.

"I'm so sorry, ma'am," I whispered to the cashier. "I don't have enough cash. I'll have to return later."

An elderly lady in line behind me stepped up and handed five dollars to the cashier. "Oh, please, let me help you out!" she pleaded, as she handed me one of my homemade tags. "I have just been waiting for a chance to use this. Be sure and read both sides!"

I was astounded. One of my tags had gone full circle and made it back to me! What could I do but smile, thank her, and promise to pay it forward?

— Christine M. Smith —

85

A Debt Finally Paid

Because that's what kindness is. It's not doing
something for someone else because they can't,
but because you can.
~Andrew Iskander

The first night of our honeymoon in Las Vegas, my new bride and I dined at a charming Italian restaurant named Battista's Hole in the Wall. It was a meal to fondly remember forever, including the elderly accordion player — Gordy — who came to our tableside and, learning we were from Ventura, played and campily sang "California, Here I Come."

Fifteen years later, we returned to Battista's, this time with our ten-year-old daughter and seven-year-old son. Again, Gordy performed "California Here I Come." Again, the meal was wonderful.

We were enjoying ourselves, in no hurry to leave, but after a while the kids grew impatient as we waited for the check. Ten minutes became thirty, and now the adults were also impatient.

"Where's the check?" I grumbled.

"Where's our waiter?" my wife echoed.

"Where's the bathrooms?" the kids needed to know.

Gordy came by a second time but still our waiter remained AWOL. Eventually, I caught the attention of a different waiter. I asked if he could get our check. He disappeared.

We left without paying.

Before you get the wrong idea, let me explain. Our waiter turned up and told us that the two gentlemen at a table across the room had paid for our dinner but requested he not let us know until after they had gone. They saw a happy, young family, the waiter explained, and simply wanted to do something nice without us having to thank them.

Wow. Those two men gave us far more than an expensive meal free. They gave the four of us a warm memory that we talk about to this day. More importantly, those two gentlemen gave us a life lesson in random acts of kindness and giving. Coffee and a sandwich for a homeless person; texting a donation to an earthquake relief fund; a new backpack, books or shoes for a disadvantaged child — almost always my daughter and son recall that long-ago Las Vegas dinner as part of their motivation to give.

My wife and I have felt similarly. While the Hole in the Wall dinner bill has been "paid forward" in full many times over in many ways, I have always felt the act itself has not been squared, a proper and worthy "thank you" not given.

Nearly fifteen more years passed since that memorable summer evening. Somewhere along the way, I must have stopped looking for the perfect occasion to anonymously say, "Put their dinner on my MasterCard." It's funny how sometimes you find what you are looking for once you stop trying so hard.

As I was waiting for my take-out order at our favorite BBQ and grill one recent evening, a U.S. soldier dressed in desert camouflage fatigues walked in. He wore a backpack that looked about three times as heavy as a middle-schooler's, which is saying something, yet effortlessly stood tall and erect. "MORGAN" said a name patch on the pack.

"Hi," I said. "I want to thank you for all you do."

"I appreciate that very much, sir," the authentic American hero humbly replied, smiling warmly as we shook hands. I wanted to say more, something less trite, but a table for two was ready, and the hostess led the strapping soldier and his visibly proud mother away. As I watched them walk off and be seated, it struck me that the soldier was probably older than my twenty-year-old son but younger than my twenty-three-year-old daughter. His mother would be about the same age as my wife and me.

I hope they ordered an appetizer each, soup *and* salad, tri-tip *and* prime-rib entrees so big even a hungry serviceman couldn't eat what his mother didn't finish, plus dessert.

And afterward, I hope they had to wait a while, enjoying each other's company and some laughs even as they grew a little bit impatient wondering where in the world their waiter was with the check.

— Woody Woodburn —

Small Things, Big Impact

The Bambi Incident

We can only be said to be alive in those moments
when our hearts are conscious of our treasures.
~Thornton Wilder

A s I was packing up some boxes in an effort to clean out some things, I found a beat-up box of small toys. I didn't know I still had them. I had planned to pass these items on to my grandchild, but after several moves, I thought they had gotten lost along the way.

My daughter always loved small toys and carried them everywhere. It was the era of "Polly Pocket"—small dolls with tiny houses who had little toys of their own. When my daughter was about three years old, the movie *Bambi* was re-released. It became her favorite movie. Then her favorite toys became all the Bambi characters: Thumper, the rabbit; Flower, the skunk; the wise, old owl; and, most especially, Bambi, the fawn. The Disney characters went with her everywhere. She carried a little purse with them in it, and she could recite the lines of the movie for each character.

One day, when I got home from work, a tragedy had befallen Bambi. He had lost two of his four legs to our dog, who had picked up the toy and chewed the legs to bits. I tried to make all the legs the same size because my daughter's worry was that Bambi couldn't walk now. So, I "operated" on Bambi and bandaged his legs so they would "heal." As a nurse, that was the only thing I could think of to make her feel better about her constant companion. She still carried Bambi with her, but she was very disappointed that I couldn't make Bambi all better because that is what moms do, especially moms who are nurses. Unfortunately, this was one boo-boo that Mom couldn't fix.

The next day, I went to work, and the mother of one of the kids asked me how I had enjoyed my time off. She had a child who was terminally ill. She listened as I told her of the Bambi tragedy and smiled. She said her girls were very attached to a few things, and she understood my daughter's heartbreak. She told me that one of her daughters had loved a stuffed animal that fell apart, and someone had made her a new one just like the old one. It was lying on the bed next to the tiny girl who was my patient. I had observed how attached she was to her stuffed animal, and in fact we made sure her animal had an oxygen mask just like hers.

Her mom told me, "I think I have one of those Bambi toys at home. My girls don't play with them. When my husband comes in and I go home, I will look for it."

I remember thinking that would be the last thing on her mind. She had a terminally ill child and another with the same disease. So, I forgot about Bambi given the circumstances that mother was facing. I never expected her to remember to look.

I was off work for a while after that, and Bambi became a distant memory for me. But my daughter was still very upset at the bandaged legs of her favorite toy. When I returned to work, a package was waiting for me. Inside was a perfect, unbandaged Bambi and a note from the mom of my patient, the much-loved little girl with the oxygen mask. While I had been off work, the girl had passed away. I hadn't been able to say my final goodbyes or be there to support the family. I had taken care of her for several years and felt the loss deeply.

Inside the package, the note said, "Thank you for caring for my daughter. I found Bambi and a few more of these characters that I thought your daughter would enjoy. I am sure we will see each other again when my other daughter needs to come in, but enjoy your daughter and love her, as I did mine." I couldn't stop the tears after I read the note. Even today, I can't stop them. It is the cost of being a nurse to children.

It occurred to me again when I found these toys how fortunate I was to have known this family and their kindness. They were losing a child, and eventually would lose another, both of whom I took care of in my career as a pediatric nurse. But what an extraordinary family to think of someone else while they were going through the most difficult thing that life could have given them. It may have been a small Bambi toy, but I was given an extraordinary kindness. And if, by the grace of God, they read this story, they can know that I passed the Bambi characters on to my grandson, who I think will treasure them like my daughter did.

I took care of many terminally ill children throughout my years as a pediatric nurse, and I never forgot what "The Bambi Incident" taught me. It has been many years now, and I will always remember the seemingly small gesture that brought my daughter happiness. It was made even more precious, forever remembered by one nurse who had the privilege of knowing them and their girls.

—Kathleen E. Jones—

87

A Can-Do Attitude

All God's angels come to us disguised.
~James Russell Lowell

For some weeks, I had noticed an elderly woman walking past our house, pushing a grocery cart filled with trash bags. I couldn't help but feel sorry for her as she shuffled along. Occasionally, she would pause and pick up a can from beside the curb. She would carefully tuck it into one of the sacks and continue on her way.

I wondered what circumstances had brought her to this point in life. Did she have no family? Was there no one to look after her?

One evening, I could stand it no longer. As she walked by, I went out to the street and stopped her.

"Ma'am," I said. "Can I ask you something?"

She turned to look at me with beautiful, dark eyes that twinkled in her wrinkled face. I knew then that she was no ordinary homeless person. There was a dignity and, yes, even a joy about her. Suddenly, I felt embarrassed to ask her my questions, but I persisted.

"I've seen you for a few weeks picking up cans," I explained. "Do you sell them to help buy groceries?"

"No," she said with a smile. "I do this to help the children."

I must have looked bewildered because she went on to explain.

"I had cancer — twice — and both times I went to a big hospital in another town. They cured me. But while I was there, I met the children, and I've never forgotten them. I don't have any money, but

I can still walk, and I pick up these cans to sell them for money for the hospital."

She told me that she spends many hours a week collecting cans; at least two businesses save cans for her. When she has enough, she loads them all into a friend's pickup, and the two of them take them to the city where the hospital is located. There they get cashed out.

She reached out and touched my arm.

"It's what God wants me to do," she said. "I've been blessed in my life. I wanted to do something, and this is something I can do. It doesn't cost me much — only the cost of the gas — and it helps the children."

I reached into my purse.

"No, no. I don't want your money," she replied with a wave of her hand, backing away a bit.

"But I want you to take it," I told her. "Use it for gas or however you want."

She smiled an almost toothless grin and finally took the bills I held out. She gave me a hug. I watched as she began walking down the street again, pushing the cart of cans, stopping occasionally to retrieve one or two. At the corner, she turned, smiled, waved and was gone.

And I knew then I wasn't watching just a little old lady going down the street. I was watching one of God's angels — one who was helping His children in her own simple way without expecting any reward other than the knowledge that she was doing something for the children she'd come to love.

And I realized then that not all angels have halos and wings. Some have grocery carts.

— Joyce Ashley —

88

A Humble Thank You

Love and kindness are never wasted. They always
make a difference. They bless the one who receives
them, and they bless you, the giver.
~Barbara De Angelis

The city circle was quiet when my van pulled up to Two's Company café. It was 8:00 A.M., and the mom-and-pop businesses wouldn't be open for another three hours. As the film crew of student moviemakers hopped out of the van and started unloading a ton of equipment, I sat in the driver's seat reading a book.

I learned a long time ago that I was not wanted or needed on the set. Sometimes, that made me feel a bit sad. These kids used to need a parent's advice, help and caring. Now, as older teens, they were making their own decisions, helping each other and supporting their friends through whatever assignments they were given. I was the designated driver. That was my title. Anything else that I might be able to impart to them was not required and, I dare say, unwelcome.

Emptied of its movie-related contents, the van now became the snackmobile and place to leave personal items. My job, as the driver, was to stay within calling distance with the keys so that if anything was needed I could open the van.

Knowing that I could crawl into a corner somewhere and finish reading the book that a friend asked me to critique, I got out of the cargo holder and looked for a place to sit down. It was early, but the

California sun was already beating down, and I didn't want to sit in the heat. Against a wall, in the shade, just twenty or so paces away, I spied a beautifully carved park bench. I noticed that a man was sitting on one end, but there was plenty of room for at least two more bodies. Walking over, I set my drink on the ground near the leg of the bench and sat on the end seat so that I could rest my elbow on the arm.

The man on the other end looked at me oddly but remained seated. I quickly discovered that he'd probably spent the night on the bench. His clothes were unkempt, his hair was matted, and I was soon confronted with a stench of body sweat, greasy food and urine. I looked at him and smiled, and he smiled back with a mouth of mis-shapen and blacked-out teeth. That was it. He wasn't bothering me, and I surmised I wasn't bothering him.

We both sat there for over an hour. I was reading. He was intently watching the filming. He then stood, walked in front of me and bowed. I looked up, not knowing what was going to happen next. In a slightly shaky but clear voice, he said, "Thank you."

I tilted my head, examining his dusty face and cracked lips.

"For what?" I questioned.

He looked at the ground as he whispered, "Usually people won't even look at me, let alone sit by me. Thank you for treating me like a human being."

I honestly didn't know what to say as he turned, picked up a small, dirty backpack, and walked quickly around the corner. I was shocked. I hadn't done anything spectacular; I shared a bench. That's all it was to me.

After several seconds of inner turmoil, I unexpectedly realized that my actions had truly meant something to this soiled and beaten-down man. To me, he was just someone who wanted a place to sit out of the sun. That's exactly what I had wanted. We were no different. Doesn't matter who we were, what we did in our lives or where we lay our heads at night. Both of us just wanted to be treated like a human being. Is that so hard?

— Candace Carteen —

89

Mystery Man

An act of kindness may take only a moment of our time,
but when captured in the heart the memory lives forever.
~Molly Friedenfeld,
The Book of Simple Human Truths

There was a lot of food left on Dad's plate. We sat across from each other at Perkins, one of his favorite places to dine. He always ordered two sunny-side-up eggs with hash browns, toast, a cup of fruit and coffee. It had become a tradition for us to stop for something to eat after getting results from the doctor.

Our chats at these brunches covered a lot. Dad always asked about his granddaughters, my job and my husband. He liked to be caught up on how we were all doing. We'd crack jokes and talk about what we were reading and the latest movies we'd watched. At some point, he'd ask me to go over the parts of the appointment he hadn't heard or understood clearly, and I'd consult my notebook to fill him in. We'd celebrate little treatment triumphs with a clink of my apple juice cup and his coffee mug.

As the months passed, I found our chats leaning more toward his memories of his childhood and life as a young adult, his failures and aspirations, and about the big and small ways he'd loved my mother. There was an urgency, a need to share these precious memories with someone, to try and cover the details of all the things we hadn't talked about during the forty-two years he'd spent being my father.

Months of chemo and radiation robbed him of his appetite, adding it to the long list of things that cancer had taken from him: his extra pounds, his hair, his strength, the laugh lines around his eyes, a sense of calm, of comfort... of hope. Now, most of the toast remained along with the eggs as he attempted to shove down a few pieces of hash browns, no longer bothering to dip and swirl them in egg and then ketchup as I'd seen him do so many times before.

My throat tightened. I tried hard to think of a joke from our bank of favorites, but nothing came. I tried to think of something from the appointment that was positive, something to hang onto, but we both knew there was no pretending anymore. With his PSA flying upward, blood transfusions becoming routine, and the results of the last MRI that lit up with spots full of the demon along his left femur, clinging to his spine, and taking up space at the base of his brain, we knew. We knew we were losing, and with that knowledge came sorrow that snuffed out joy until it was just a dark shadow.

I looked at my dad across the table — bald and weak, such a kind and humble man, wearing his favorite yellow sweater that was now too big — and I was profoundly aware we were beginning our "lasts." Was this our last breakfast together? Our last joke to share? Our last stories to tell each other? Would it be our last fall season together? Our last Christmas to celebrate? We didn't know exactly what would be the last of anything, but we both knew we were in that territory.

My father put down his fork, and his eyes locked with mine. The man I'd sat across from so many times, so full of chatter and laughter, so ready to listen and care, said nothing, his eyes searching mine, his expression so solemn I couldn't stand it. It was the first sign of retreat I'd seen since all this started, the first sign that this positive, kind, quick-to-laugh-and-say-hello, happy-go-lucky fellow was reeling from the blows and getting ready to put down his battle gear. I reached across the table and took both his hands in mine.

"It's okay," I said, as tears filled our eyes. "It's okay." As we sat there holding hands across the table, my strong, selfless father let me see his fear and sadness, and it hurt more than if I'd been physically struck. Knowing there was nothing I could do was the worst part.

"I love you," I said, meaning it and praying it would soothe him in some small way. He closed his eyes, and his nose started running along with the tears. He bowed his head slightly, squeezing my hands and offering the slightest nod. Determined to regain his composure, he took back his hands, cleared his throat and asked for a tissue. I fished one out of my purse and passed it to him.

He blew his nose and straightened up a bit.

The waitress appeared, asking if she could get us anything else.

"Not hungry today, honey?" she cooed at my father.

"No, not so hungry," Dad said quietly, wiping feebly at his nose.

"I'll box that up for you, okay?"

"Okay," Dad said, never one to waste food even though I knew he wouldn't be able to eat it later, or tomorrow, or the day after that.

The waitress returned to box up what was left of his meal as we watched in silence. Dad's face was blank and tired.

"We're ready for the check, please," Dad almost whispered, slowly reaching into his pocket for his wallet.

"It's already taken care of, honey," the waitress said.

"What's that?" Dad said.

"It's already taken care of," she repeated a little louder.

"Beth…" my dad addressed me weakly, as he always insisted on paying when we stopped for breakfast despite my protests. And, after realizing it let him feel like a gentleman taking his daughter out to eat, I had stopped objecting.

"Dad, it wasn't me," I said, just as puzzled as he was. We looked at each other.

"What?" Dad said again.

"I didn't pay. It wasn't me."

"Who was it?"

"I don't know. Can you tell us who paid the check?" I asked the waitress.

"It was that guy," she said, nodding toward the window across from our table. "The one out there."

I caught sight of the back of the man she indicated. He was tall with broad shoulders and a quick pace that was leading him away from us toward his car. He was dressed in dark green scrubs with sneakers and had on a surgical cap. He didn't look back.

"Do you see him?" Dad asked. And as I turned back to reply, I was struck by my father's face.

His smile was huge, filling his whole face. His eyes were suddenly brighter than I remembered them being in months. He was a boy again, thrilled with this treat, and the happiness radiating from him shoved out the darkness of the moments prior, lifting him up and comforting us both. He stood slowly, and I took his arm.

"Wow! How about that?" Dad said, unable to stop smiling.

"How about that?" I said, smiling with him and sharing an uplifting moment of his life that I'd remember forever.

Kindness really does touch us and fill us… even on the worst days.

— Beth Rice —

A Knock at the Door

The ornament of a house is the friends who frequent it.
~Ralph Waldo Emerson

My mother's long journey with cancer was coming to an end. It was her wish to die at home, surrounded by loved ones. But, as with all things in life, it was complicated. For weeks, the hospice nurses would come and go throughout the day, staying only briefly to administer medication or help with other needed tasks. I was my mother's primary caregiver, with my father and sister taking turns to help.

I think back on the last days of her life with such sadness. She was cognitively failing as well, which made everything so much harder. She was not herself, and yet there were cherished moments of clarity. Family came and went, helping when they could. Their visits were bright spots in that dark time.

At night, I was often alone with my mother, with her sleeping in her hospice bed and me wide awake. I was terrified she would pass away if I fell asleep, and I soon began a destructive pattern of sleeping intermittently during the day, giving all my energy over to my mother's care and lying awake at night, watching her, waiting to see if she needed anything. Making sure she was still there.

Inevitably, it all caught up to me. As her condition worsened, I was barely sleeping at all, day or night. Honestly, I don't know how I was able to keep it together. However, I was determined to make sure my mother was as comfortable as possible for as long as possible.

One day, there was a gentle knock at the door. At this point, I was used to strangers coming into our home from the hospice services, but I knew immediately the woman on the other side of the door was not a healthcare worker. I opened the door to an older woman, dressed smartly in a green dress with matching shoes. She introduced herself as "Nancy, from the church" who had heard about my mother's condition and wanted to see if we needed any help. Something about her — her honest, kind face perhaps — simply broke me. She seemed so motherly, so instinctively helpful, that I opened the door and let her in.

Nancy took one good look at me and said something I will never forget, "It's time for you to rest. You have to take care of yourself, too." It was something my mother would have said.

I could feel whatever defenses I had built up over the last few weeks begin to break. I was so tired. Beyond exhausted. This total stranger was ordering me to take a nap, and I did just that. I quickly introduced Nancy to my mother, who was barely awake herself, and my father who had come home from work moments after Nancy arrived. I went upstairs, climbed into bed, and slept for six straight hours.

When I woke, it was nighttime. I could smell dinner cooking in the kitchen and heard my father's booming voice and the tinkle of strange laughter. I accessed the cameras on the home-security app and saw my father and Nancy sitting at my mother's bedside in the living room. They were talking and laughing, and even through the grainy footage, I could see a faint smile on my mother's face. I took a long, hot shower and, for the first time in weeks, I felt I was able to breathe freely.

When I finally went downstairs, Nancy had left. My father was in a good mood, the first in weeks, and my mother was sitting up, her eyes wide and alert. "Your hair looks nice," she said. It was one of the last things she ever said to me.

Nancy's arrival that day was unexpected but desperately needed. The rest I had that day gave me the strength I needed to endure the worst: my mother's passing two days later. I never saw Nancy again, but I am eternally grateful for her act of kindness that day.

Those who have been through similar experiences will know how isolating it is, how emotionally and physically draining it can be. It's like being a step out of time, and, for one moment, a total stranger was able to help me reset myself so that I could be there fully for my mother as she came to the end of her own journey. It was a truly selfless act of kindness, one I will never forget. Thank you, Nancy. Wherever you are.

— Melanie R. McBride —

A Very Happy Birthday

Let us be grateful to people who make us happy,
they are the charming gardeners
who make our souls blossom.
~Marcel Proust

Birthdays were a huge deal at my workplace. Co-workers went above and beyond to shower the person of honor with food, decorations, affirmations, love and, yes, embarrassment on their special day. As one who prefers to go unnoticed and cringes at being the center of attention, I was horrified to walk in on my birthday to see my desk adorned with glittery streamers, confetti, and a hot pink sash with the words, "Kneel! I'm the Birthday Princess," which I was forced to wear for the duration of the day.

Although humiliated by the display, I felt immensely loved. I thoroughly enjoyed the gorgeous bouquet of flowers and delectable chocolate cake my co-workers gave me.

Several months after my birthday celebration, our office welcomed a new member to the team. Hired as our office manager's assistant, Laura was also tasked with establishing a human resources department. Possessing an ambitious vision and receiving carte blanche from our manager, she immediately enacted major changes — which were not well received.

Laura rubbed many members of our office the wrong way. Our office swiftly morphed into a catty environment, rife with gossip and passive-aggressive bullying, predominantly at Laura's expense. I knew it wasn't right but will shamefully admit that I also participated in gripe sessions, frustrated by her actions.

When Laura's spring birthday neared, it was evident that no one wanted to celebrate. The birthday card and collection pot to purchase goodies never made the rounds. I understood why no one wanted to go all-out in celebrating Laura's birthday, but it bothered me nevertheless. As an exceptionally shy and introverted individual, being left out or ignored was nothing foreign to me, and it pained me to think of the deliberate effort to ignore her birthday. Although she drove me crazy, too, I knew her time in our office had not been easy.

Stopping by Bath & Body Works on the way home from work, I picked out some body sprays and lotion. At our local grocery store, I selected a bouquet of rosy-pink tulips and a birthday card in which I wrote a heartfelt note highlighting some of Laura's qualities I genuinely admired, such as her ambitious spirit, creativity, and strong inner drive. Arriving an hour early to work the morning of her birthday, I transformed her corner of the office. With butterfly streamers pinned to the rafters above her desk, neon birthday bows taped to every surface, and an array of other obnoxious birthday ornaments littering her desk, her work area morphed into a rainbow of glee, with her gifts, card and flowers arranged in the center.

I watched Laura spot her decorated work area when she arrived. She stopped dead in her tracks. I expected a smile or maybe a delighted chuckle but her face showed no emotion at all. Was she humiliated? Annoyed? I couldn't tell. After a few seconds of staring blankly, she placed her purse in her drawer, sat down at her desk and booted up her computer, seemingly ignoring the bows and confetti.

Later that morning, convinced I had unintentionally ruined her birthday, I asked Laura if she had plans for lunch. When she said she didn't, I asked if she'd join me for Mexican food at the Qdoba close to our office. After accepting, she asked if I was the one who left the birthday surprises. Face flushing, I 'fessed up. She nodded and continued with her day.

I really didn't know what to say when we sat down for lunch, so I was relieved when she began to talk. "You know, I wasn't going to say anything, but..." she began. *Uh-oh.* My pulse quickened. Laura went on to explain how birthdays were no small deal in her family. From decorations to special homemade cakes, endless singing to an array of positive notes and affirmations, her parents and siblings took birthdays to the next level in an effort to make each other feel ridiculously adored. Having relocated to the area only recently with all her loved ones over a day's drive away, she was extra lonesome and fully aware of the hostility she experienced with co-workers.

She admitted that she hadn't wanted to come to work today. She spent the entire commute crying, feeling dejected and forgotten. Laura tearfully expressed the great impact my efforts had on her weary heart, which craved a gesture of kindness and love more than she knew.

Hearing Laura speak, not even Muhammad Ali could slap the smile from my face. Getting to know this wonderful woman I worked with each day but hadn't taken the time to get to know, it became evident how similar we were. Same sense of humor, same insecurities, and same shameful enjoyment of cheesy reality TV shows, for starters. The friendship that began in Qdoba that spring afternoon continued to grow over the years, blossoming into a lifelong friendship.

This priceless friendship was initiated by nothing more than a small act of kindness. It's an ever-present reminder to never squander an opportunity to reach out to those seemingly on the outside. A reminder that when feeling leads to doing something for another — whether a friend, sibling, co-worker or stranger — there's likely a very good reason for it. And, lastly, a reminder that birthdays are no small deal.

— Emily Marszalek —

From a Child

*Because it proves that you don't need much to change
the entire world for the better. You can start
with the most ordinary ingredients.*
~Catherine Ryan Hyde, Pay It Forward

Several years ago, in doing research for a new book, we wound up in Honolulu headed for the University of Hawaii and its collection on Micronesia, my passion at the time. My wife and I stayed at a comfortable hotel on the ocean, ate a delectable meal, and slept soundly our first night. The next morning, we skipped breakfast and headed out in the morning rush hour. As many know, Hawaiian rush hours are long and frustrating. After many stoplights, all red, we found ourselves at one of the main intersections, stopped behind a big yellow school bus. It was warm, and our windows were down, so we could hear the laughter and banter of the children on the bus as we patiently waited for the light to change.

Then we noticed a young man sitting on the ground with a cardboard sign propped up on his knees. It was too far away to read the lettering, but we assumed it was a plea for help because of an unknown situation in which he found himself. He looked pretty rough, with a longish beard, ragged hair, and unkempt clothes that had seen better days. He was obviously down on his luck.

Suddenly, he got up, put his sign on the ground and walked toward the stopped school bus. As he approached, a little girl reached out with a brown paper lunch bag clutched in her fingers, probably lovingly put together by a family member. As the stranger came closer, she handed him the bag. There was no conversation that we could hear, no words exchanged, but he took the bag and very gently kissed her little hand. Then he went back to his perch, the light changed, and we slowly edged forward. But not before we could see the tears on his cheeks.

I am ninety-four years old now, and there are few moments in my life that have affected me more than that little hand giving a total stranger her most precious gift: her lunch bag.

— Robert Willett —

Lesson for a Lifetime

No one who achieves success does so without the help
of others. The wise and confident acknowledge
this help with gratitude.
~Alfred North Whitehead

I stood beside the hospital bed where my husband lay pale and scared, still dressed in the clothes he wore to the emergency room at 2:00 A.M. It was now late afternoon. The local ER had transported him to a large hospital two hours from home, and after a day of testing, the doctor stood at the end of the bed with lab results and a diagnosis — acute myeloid leukemia.

The diagnosis answered questions — why antibiotics and steroids had not helped Russ's immune system fight an ongoing respiratory infection, and why his hands and legs were covered in a rash as if someone had dotted them with a red pen. But the doctor's announcement created even more questions, some I was afraid to ask. Russ had the first one. "Will I be in the hospital over the weekend?"

The doctor raised his eyebrows and hesitated as if to prepare us for the upcoming shock. "You'll be here at least a month. We'll move you to the leukemia floor." Then he looked at me. "You're welcome to stay as much as you can. The rooms are private. He'll need you here."

A month! My mind started spinning. My mom had fought breast cancer. My aunt had lung cancer. Both had died. But neither had been admitted for a month of treatment! Exactly how bad was my husband's diagnosis? And how were we supposed to halt life for an entire month?

It was March. The end of a school year was approaching. My days with my high-school seniors were limited. How could I prepare four weeks of lesson plans and hand my kiddos off to a substitute to release into the world? A month! Could we afford being in the hospital that long? Our insurance was good, but we'd still have to pay our portion of the medical expenses. My meals wouldn't be covered, and parking was so expensive! My head couldn't do the math.

A nurse entered the room. "Russ, your room is ready on the eighth floor."

She helped my husband into a wheelchair. I grabbed his few belongings and followed.

Room 8834 was surprisingly large with a fifty-five-inch, flat-screen TV and a wall of windows overlooking a park of trees sprouting green buds. The nurse showed us the private bathroom and a spacious closet. "You'll be more comfortable in your own clothes. Here's plenty of room to store them." Then she turned toward me. "Bring whatever he'd like from home — a laptop, books, his favorite snacks. When you come back, stop by the valet desk on the first floor and buy a weekly parking pass."

She left, and the quiet settled around us in this unfamiliar room that was now our temporary home. I didn't know how we were going to do this, how my husband was going to endure seven days of round-the-clock chemo infusions. How can a person survive that much chemo? Did I have enough sick leave to cover a month, maybe longer if he needed me once he was discharged?

"You should go home and rest. Come back tomorrow," Russ said, giving me a list of items to bring back.

Reluctantly, I left his room. On the first floor, I passed the valet and noticed a poster advertising the parking pass the nurse had mentioned. I estimated the month would cost one hundred and twenty dollars. I continued to the parking garage and found my car where I'd left it hours earlier. I drove to the exit, took the parking ticket off the dashboard, and inserted it into the meter: fifteen dollars. I shoved my debit card into the slot and rolled forward as the gate lifted. I drove home with a million worries to keep me company. Even though the parking pass would be a significant discount, the cost nagged me throughout the drive. How silly to fixate on something so trivial when my husband faced a potentially terminal diagnosis. Maybe I was trying to find the one thing I could control in an out-of-control situation.

The next morning, I packed the car with everything I imagined we'd need for our extended hospital stay and headed to school to write sub plans and see my students. Because we live in a small community, they would have heard about my husband's diagnosis. I would assure them he would be fine, although I didn't know that, and that I would be fine. I'd encourage them to be their best selves for the substitute — and for me — while I was on family leave.

When I entered my classroom, the chatter stopped. I could feel my students assess me as I walked to the front of the room, so I put on a smile and continued to my podium. Sitting on top was a green envelope with "Mrs. Sargent" written on the front. I looked over the frames of my reading glasses at twenty-eight faces, some smiling, some trying to resist.

"What is this?" I asked. I picked up the envelope, stuffed so full that the flap barely closed. "You guys…"

The kids grinned as I opened the card and coins and dollar bills fell out — fives, tens, twenties. My throat tightened with emotion. How had these kids collected that much money? Some of them came from families that couldn't afford to pay for school lunch. Others worked two or three part-time jobs.

"I can't take this," I said. But their eager faces gave me no choice. There was pride in their eyes.

"We were going to get you flowers," one student, Jesse, said. "But we decided to give you the money and let you decide what to do with it."

I held up the stack of cash. "This would buy a lot of flowers." I quickly estimated the amount. My voice cracked as I told them how I had obsessed over parking. "Kiddos, you just covered my parking costs for the month."

As the adult in the room, I felt guilty for accepting cash from teenagers, but I could not refuse it. More important than the envelope in my hand was the kindness in their hearts and the lesson they had taught themselves: how wonderful it feels to meet someone's need and to make a difference. I cherished that recognition on their faces and prayed this wasn't a lesson for the day but for their lifetime. Whether I would be with my seniors at the end of May, or they would finish the year with a substitute, I felt hopeful of one thing: It didn't matter who released them into the world. They were ready.

— Karen Sargent —

The Joy of Doing for Others

94

It's Not Hard to Be Kind

Never look down on anybody
unless you're helping them up.
~Jesse Jackson

One day, my mother and I were out having a girls' day, and we decided to go to a seafood restaurant. We got there just as the lunch rush started, so there was a line to get in. I looked over to the side and spied a very thin lady with no coat and a chemo shunt in her arm. She was holding a sign that read: "Homeless and hungry. Please help."

I looked around at everyone, and no one looked like they cared in the least. I knew that if I didn't do something, it would haunt me forever. I went over to her and asked if she would like to come out of the cold and get something to eat. She looked for a second like she was unsure I was talking to her. She put her head down and said in the lowest voice, "Yes."

I helped her to her feet and walked her up to my mother, who was in line. We stood there together until we were seated. When the waitress came, she looked at the woman as if she were a disease waiting to attack her. She asked what we wanted to eat but completely talked over this woman and acted like she didn't exist.

Then the owner came over and asked if we wanted this woman to sit at our table. I assured her we did. She then asked what her name was, to which I replied that we hadn't gotten to ask that yet because the waitress had run over as soon as we sat down.

Then she said something that put me over the top. She said, "Well, you did right by getting her food instead of giving her money."

This was the last straw for my mother and me. I talked loud enough for everyone to hear when I told her, "This woman is sitting right here. She is not invisible, and she is not deaf. She is just as good as anyone in here, and I will not allow her to be treated any differently than any other customer in here."

I called the waitress back over and told her to take the woman's order and get her a cup of coffee.

After the waitress left, we got to talking, and I found out that her name was Judy. She had been released from the army on a medical discharge because she had cancer. When she came back home, she could not find a job because of her cancer and she lost her house. She was supposed to get a ride to a shelter, but her chemo took too long, and she missed the bus.

When the food came, she took out some plastic bags from her purse and started putting food in them. I asked her why she was doing that, and she said so she could eat that night. I told her not to bother because she could order a to-go plate. I also told her we would give her a ride to the shelter so she didn't have to sit in the cold. She thanked me in a quiet voice, looked down, and started eating.

I could only apologize to her for the way those people had treated her and thank her for her service to our country. After we ate, I left the waitress her tip on the receipt and wrote, "Kindness costs nothing."

I think about Judy every so often and wonder if she won her battle with cancer and got back on her feet. I really hope so.

If you are ever given the opportunity to help someone in need, do it. The feeling you get out of it is worth more than you'll ever know. It's priceless.

— Donna Faulkner Schulte —

95

A Bunch of Bananas

For it is in giving that we receive.
~Francis of Assisi

Seeing dozens of homeless people was a natural part of my daily commute in Spokane, Washington. They congregated along the streets where traffic was most congested, begging for assistance from drivers stopped at red lights.

I tried my best to ignore them. It wasn't because I didn't care or have compassion for their plight, but because they scared me. I assumed many suffered addiction or mental illness. Only weeks before, I had heard in the news that a young woman had been dragged from her unlocked car by a homeless man while at a red light along the very street I drove on. Besides, what could I do to help? I had no money to give. Working a minimum-wage job, I had my own trouble making ends meet.

Then one evening, as I was stopped at a red light, a homeless gentleman caught my eye. An older fellow, he sported a bushy white beard, broad shoulders and a barrel chest. In scribbled black handwriting, his cardboard sign read "War vet. Anything helps." I instantly thought of my dad, a Vietnam veteran who was not well-received upon his return to the States. His life after service was arduous. If things had gone differently, I reasoned, that could be my dad seated on that corner. They looked roughly the same age and sported the same milky white hair.

I felt sad for this man. But what could I do? I was broke. And, as a single young lady, the thought of engaging with a homeless older man was inconceivable. When the light turned green, I zoomed past him and headed home.

The next day, I observed the same gentleman seated at the same corner holding the same sign. Only when the car behind me honked did I realize I had been staring at him.

I continued to watch this man night after night for weeks, pondering the string of events that had led to his current state of affairs. Where was his family? Did he serve in Vietnam like my dad? Where did he sleep at night?

One evening, I could ignore my heart no longer when I peered at him stationed at that corner. Looking around my car, I wondered what I could give him. I had no cash in my wallet. No change in my cupholders. I had only one item. Nestled in my passenger seat was a bunch of newly bought and perfectly ripe bananas, my favorite snack. I felt pathetic offering this poor man nothing more than a two-dollar bunch of bananas but decided to anyway. Ignoring my fearful, pounding heart while stopped at the light, I rolled down my window and made eye contact. He immediately walked to my car.

"I'm sorry. All I have is bananas. Would you like them?" I asked sheepishly.

The man's face lit up like a kid on Christmas, his wide grin revealing many missing teeth. "I *love* bananas. They're my favorite fruit," he stated gleefully. "Have to get your potassium!" he declared while chuckling. Handing him the bananas, I also smiled. Seeing this gentleman's immense gratitude for something as trivial as bananas motivated me to do more.

Stopping at the grocery store on my way home that night, I purchased a feast for kings: a foot-long sandwich layered with three kinds of deli meats, granola bars, chips, peanuts, applesauce, carrots, beef jerky, water, Gatorade, and other goodies. My joyful anticipation overcame my concern regarding how I would pay my now hefty credit-card bill at the end of the month. Hauling the plump grocery bags to work the following morning and storing them in the breakroom fridge, I could hardly wait for the workday to end so I could deliver them to the man.

But he wasn't there. He had been here every day for almost a month. Where was he? Was he okay?

He wasn't there the next day either. Day after day, I looked for him on my commute home, but he never returned.

I felt so guilty. Something in that man reminded me of my dad. And yet I ignored him each day. When I finally made an effort to help, he was nowhere to be found. If I had acted even one day sooner, he would have enjoyed the feast and known that someone out there cared. He would have felt loved. I had missed my opportunity. I felt terrible. Selfish. Regretful.

That jolly man's childlike joy at receiving a bunch of bananas showed me how even the smallest act of kindness can bring joy to not only the recipient's soul but the giver's soul. It also taught me the heart-wrenching lesson of how easy it is to miss an opportunity to have an impact in someone's life if I wait to act. Needy people are all around me. I can't help them all. But I believe when I open my eyes and listen to the whispers in my heart, I will be directed to those I can help. Although I don't have much to give financially, I have time and love to give in abundance.

I often think of that gentleman on the corner in Spokane and hope that, wherever he is, he is alive and well, warm and safe, with unlimited access to his fill of bananas.

— Emily Marszalek —

96

Better than Goat Yoga

Kindness is a passport that opens doors and fashions
friends. It softens hearts and molds relationships
that can last lifetimes.
~Joseph B. Wirthlin

My friend, Kristen, told me she had something planned for us to do to celebrate my forty-fifth birthday. She wouldn't tell me what we were doing. We're both adventurous, so I thought it might be skiing, or a winter hike. Or maybe snow biking or goat yoga.

All Kristen said was to dress comfortably for the outdoors — not much of a clue.

Our first stop was at a local flower shop. All the ladies there stared at me — three sets of sparkling eyes, three grins from ear-to-ear. One lady handed Kristen a large bouquet of assorted flowers. Flowers? Why was she giving me flowers?

As requested, I stood outside the shop to pose for a picture. I sported a curious smile as my mind reeled.

I placed the flowers in the back seat and noticed that each stem had a ribbon. I realized the bouquet must not be for me. It must be meant for multiple people. But for whom?

We got in the car. I looked at Kristen expectantly. "Can you please tell me what we're doing?"

"We're going to celebrate your birthday by performing random acts of kindness."

I was stunned. Her gift to me was blessings for others — strangers at that.

Our next stop was Aldi, where we put quarters in twenty shopping carts. We also put quarters in gumball machines at the local drugstore. I imagined the surprise of little kids walking into the store pulling on their mom's arms, begging for a trapped prize. After noticing the quarter, the mom would shrug her shoulders with a "Why not?" The children would leap with joy when their toy dropped out of the hole.

Kristen then pulled into the Burger King drive-through. My stomach was telling me it was lunchtime. But instead of feeding our own bellies, we fed others. Kristen ordered five cheeseburgers and five fries. She also paid for the person behind us. She then drove across the street to a non-profit donation center. We went around back where there were stacks of donations that needed to be sorted.

Kristen told me to give all the burgers and fries to the staff unloading and sorting the donations. A bearded man dressed in a winter hat, work gloves and boots walked towards our car, ready for a long day outside working in the chilly January weather. I handed him the warm bags and explained my birthday present, hoping he and the others would consume the food given to them by strangers. He uttered a simple "Thank you" but it was the follow-up smile that warmed my heart as I hoped the food would warm their souls.

Kristen then handed me a stack of colored index cards on which she had written inspirational quotes. "What are we doing with these?" I asked.

"You'll see."

We pulled into the parking lot of the local library where Kristen provided the details of her plan. Each of us took a stack of cards to place in random library books.

I thumbed through the cards. So many beautiful quotes — each one an opportunity to bless an unsuspecting bookworm. My goal: try to match the right quote with the right book. I prayed as I walked the aisles. I even prayed about what page to place each card in. I didn't want the blessing recipient to return the book before finding their inspirational quote at page 201.

One of my favorite aspects of the birthday celebration had to do with the flowers. As we drove around town, I got to bless people with a flower — from the elderly gentleman at the drugstore to the young woman walking into Aldi. It was a simple flower, but it was also a key directly to a person's heart.

Our town is known for numerous railroad crossings, which in turn provide ample opportunities to get stuck waiting for a train. I asked Kristen to park the car. I jumped out as snowflakes were falling and enthusiastically ran up to people's cars as they waited for the train to pass. Thinking back, I probably should have approached the cars in a calmer fashion. It took some convincing — the sight of the flower usually did the trick — but eventually each driver rolled down their window. Hopefully, the unpleasant experience of getting stuck at the train crossing was softened by the petals of a flower.

The day of random acts of kindness was my friend's gift to me. But that gift was shared by countless others. Sometimes, we got to see them receive the gifts. Most of the time, we didn't. We didn't see the joy or amazement of the kid with the gigantic blue gumball, the Aldi shoppers, the hungry Burger King patron, the other donation center workers, or the unsuspecting library patrons. It truly was the birthday gift that kept on giving. Maybe now when those same people get stopped by another train, they will remember the flower and won't care so much about the inconvenience.

When Kristen said she had planned something for my birthday, I thought it would be for me — something fun to do or a gift to keep. My gift wasn't the type of exciting event I'd guessed. There were no snow bikes or goats. But it was even better spreading the gift of kindness to others. My gift wasn't something tangible I could hold and keep. But I will hold the day in my heart for years to come. I envision the countless strangers who shared my birthday gift — one of the best gifts I ever received and gave away.

— Diane DeCaprio —

97

Entertaining Strangers

*Let brotherly love continue. Be not forgetful to
entertain strangers: for thereby some have
entertained angels unaware.*
~Hebrews 13:1–2 KJV

Rushing, rushing… always rushing! That was my life, rushing from one appointment or obligation to the next… until the day I met Jim.

That day started like most days for me. My husband, John, had an appointment at the veterans' medical center in Long Beach, California at 10:30 A.M. and a second appointment at another VA facility thirty miles away at 1:00 P.M.

On this hot summer day the freeway was packed, and an accident was holding up traffic. As we inched along, I realized we were probably going to be late for the morning appointment. It is difficult for John to walk very far, let alone hurry. So, when we got there I pulled right up to the entrance and let him out. Then I zoomed down the drive to look for a parking place.

"Come on, God, help me find a parking place… please!" Divine intervention was the only way I was going to find a place to park as I surveyed the cars filling every spot. I turned left and started down the next aisle and then slammed on my brakes as an older man crossed in front of me, leaning on his cane. Finally, I saw someone backing out of a parking spot and rushed to pull in as soon as the other car was clear.

I grabbed my purse and ran up to the medical center. I found John waiting, and we took the elevator up to the fourth floor. By now, we were half an hour late, so we had to wait until they could work him in. It was a lengthy wait, and we weren't finished until after noon.

Now, we were in danger of being late for the second appointment! "You wait here on the bench by the door," I told John. "I will go get the car and pick you up."

"Okay," he agreed and sat down on the bench while I rushed off to get the car.

I found the car, and as I backed out, I saw the same older gentleman I nearly hit in the parking lot earlier now walk *behind* my car! What was he still doing out there?

I started to leave the parking lot, but my conscience wouldn't let me. I glanced at my watch — yes, we still might be able to make the appointment if we left right now — but I couldn't leave until I knew the man was okay.

I drove up and down the aisles looking for him but didn't see him. Maybe he had found his car and I could go pick up John. But then, as I drove down the last aisle, I saw the man sitting on the curb, wiping his face with a handkerchief.

I rolled down my window, and the hot air rushed in. "Are you okay?" I called out to him.

"No," he replied without looking up. "I can't find my truck, and I've been walking all over this lot. I just had to sit down. I don't know what to do."

I checked my watch; it was 12:20. Although time was ticking away, I felt like God had literally put the man in my path twice and wanted me to help him.

"Why don't you get in my car, and we'll drive around to find your truck."

"I don't want to bother you," he said, shaking his head.

"It's no bother, and it will be a lot cooler in here," I assured him.

"Okay, thanks," he said as he tried to get up.

"Let me help you up." I jumped out and went around the car to give him a hand. "My name is Judee. What's your name?"

"My name's Jim, and I sure do appreciate this. I didn't know what I was going to do. It's so hot out here!"

He struggled to his feet, and I helped him into my car. "I'm so embarrassed," he told me as I got back in the car. "I'm eighty-six years old and normally very independent, but today I just couldn't remember where I parked!"

"Don't feel bad," I told him. "These parking lots are huge, and sometimes I don't remember where I parked either. Now, what color is your truck?"

"It's white, and I remember the front was facing toward the street."

There were probably hundreds of white cars and trucks in the lot. This wasn't going to be easy.

"Don't worry, Jim," I told him as I began driving slowly up and down the packed aisles. "We'll find it."

We didn't find his truck in that lot, so I drove out and into the next lot. As I looked to the left, I saw my puzzled husband stand up when he saw me drive by. I was going to have some explaining to do when this was over!

We drove slowly through the second parking lot and then the third one. We were heading down the last row when suddenly Jim shouted, "There it is! Right there, facing the street."

I stopped the car and got out to help him. "I told you we'd find your truck, Jim."

He took my hand and got out, leaning on his cane. "Gosh, I was never so glad to see that old truck!" he exclaimed. "How can I ever thank you?"

"Just give me a hug, and we'll call it even."

He hugged me there in the parking lot and walked away to his truck. I waited to be sure he got in okay, and just before he climbed in, he turned and waved goodbye. "God bless you, dear," he called out, giving me a wink and a big smile.

As I drove back to the entrance to pick up my husband, I reflected on this encounter and felt tears running down my face.

"Thank you, God, for slowing me down and helping me remember

The Joy of Doing for Others | 297

what is really important to you."

"Who was that man, and why are you crying?" John asked me.

"It's a long story," I told him, "but I think God just sent me an 'angel to entertain.'"

—Judee Stapp—

98

Those Forgotten Wallets

We were born to unite with our fellow men,
and to join in community with the human race.
~Cicero

"Mama, crunchy French toast!" my three-year-old son squealed with a huge grin on his face. It was Saturday, and we were at our favorite breakfast spot, enjoying each other's company. My husband had to work, and I had planned for this to be a morning out with my son. I had filled a backpack with a ton of toys and everything we needed to keep him occupied while I enjoyed a cup of freshly brewed Earl Grey tea and a hot meal.

We were seated next to a wonderful man who started up a conversation with me about being in town for a conference. He said my son reminded him of his grandson back home. He asked if I needed help with anything, and I responded, "No, I'm fine, thank you." But I couldn't shake this feeling he was there to help me, like a guardian angel. He had this unique energy.

When our meal was finished, I went to grab my wallet and discovered I had left it in my other bag at home. How was I going to pay for this meal? Tears began to cloud my eyes. The man at the next table immediately asked if everything was okay, and I whispered, "I forgot my wallet, and I have no way to pay for this meal." The man called over the server in front of me. Because of my tears, I was barely able to see that he had pulled out his credit card and handed it to the server. When I realized what he was offering, my jaw opened. I started to protest, but he put his hand up and said, "My wife has been in your shoes before. Please just enjoy this breakfast with your son. I know how hard motherhood can be."

At that moment, I truly felt his sincerity, and it comforted me like an invisible hug. I cried more, but they were tears of relief as I picked up my son to give him a hug and pack away his toys to leave. It suddenly dawned on me that I also had no money to pay for the parking valet. When I turned around, the nice man who had helped me was gone. I called over the restaurant manager and began to explain what had happened with my restaurant check and how I couldn't pay the car valet. He smiled sweetly and said, "I know! That kind gentleman who bought your breakfast also paid for your car valet. You are good to go. The man said to enjoy your day with your son."

My jaw opened for the second time within fifteen minutes. Not only had that kind man paid for breakfast, but he had also taken care of my car valet fee and tip. All I could do as I walked my son out to my car was thank that man over and over in my mind. His kindness overwhelmed me. I hoped for the chance to do the same for someone else.

My chance came one week later while my son and I were shopping at a grocery store. I found myself next to a woman at the self-checkout realizing she hadn't brought enough money to pay for her groceries. So, I walked over to her and said, "Will you allow me to help? I'd be happy to pay for your shopping." She stared at me for a moment in disbelief. Then her eyes widened, and she replied, "All of it?"

I smiled and answered, "Yes. Last week, I was in need, and someone did the same for me. Please, let me do this for you." Still looking shocked, she thanked me and told me that all this shopping was for her sick mother who was stuck at home without food. She needed to get it all to her before a big work meeting that she couldn't afford to miss. Had she gone home to get her wallet, she would have missed her meeting and been in trouble with her boss. As we stood there bagging her groceries together, I could see the weight lift from her shoulders. It brought me so much joy. The woman left the store giving me a big smile and another heartfelt thank you.

I returned to my self-checkout station to pay for my shopping and found the store manager there with a bouquet of flowers for me. He said, "Thank you for restoring my faith in helping someone when they need it. I will look to paying it forward, too." I left the store with a spring in my step and a beautiful bouquet of flowers. What a wonderful ripple effect of kindness. It's true! No matter what you give, you will always receive more in return.

— Emma Cohan —

99

A Generous Tip

*Connecting with others is rewarding; it makes us feel
like we're not alone in the world.*
~Jonah Berger

ur flight didn't leave until Sunday night, so I worked my usual Sunday day job, playing piano during brunch at a golf resort located down in the valley. I loved my job and adored my customers, most of whom faithfully dined every Sunday.

That morning, I'd told my customers that my sweet daughter had loaned me money for an airline ticket so I could fly out with her and my grandchildren to see my father for what we believed would be the last time.

One of my favorite customers came over before she left and gave me a huge farewell hug. In the process, she slipped a bill in my hand instead of dropping it in my tip basket. Her voice sounded stern. "This is for your trip. It's not to pay bills and not to reimburse your daughter for the plane ticket."

My eyes watered as I stared at the fifty-dollar bill in my hand. "Thank you, but I can't accept this. It's way too much money."

Every Sunday, this woman left me a more-than-generous tip, but this seemed extravagant. When I refused the bill and tried to hand it back, she gently pushed away my hand. "I know you'll find the perfect use for it. Have fun. I'll see you when you get back."

I was struggling to make ends meet, so that extra fifty would have come in handy for bills or groceries. Yet my customer's words kept echoing through my head. After talking it over with my husband, he agreed. I should take the fifty with me and honor my customer's wishes.

Our plane took off late, and when we landed, my daughter and I dashed through the airport with two young children in tow, terrified of missing our connecting flight.

When we reached our gate, my daughter raced to the restroom with my grandson while I kept an eye on my granddaughter. From the waiting area, a soft whimpering filled the air, which soon turned to full-blown sobs. I spotted a young mother with tears streaming down her face rummaging through her carry-on bags. When her son spotted us, he raced over, grabbed my granddaughter's hand, and started swinging it back and forth as if they'd been best friends forever.

"Is that your mother?" I asked.

"Yes," he answered. "She's sad because she lost our stuff."

I gazed at the packed room, astounded by how everyone ignored this woman. People gazed at the floor or kept their eyes glued to their books or magazines. I walked over and put my arm around her. "Are you okay? Can I help?"

Between sobs, the woman told me that she'd lost her purse somewhere along her trip, and it held her plane tickets, credit cards, cash, and ID. She'd reported the purse missing, but no one had turned it in. Thankfully, the airline had arranged it so she could continue her flight, but that was all. She had a three-day layover in the next city where she and her son planned on sightseeing before continuing her trip and meeting her husband. Without her purse, she could not pay for a taxi, food, or a motel, and had no way to contact her husband and let him know what had happened.

I'd flown alone with my young children many times and could not imagine being in her situation. I helped her search her carry-on luggage one last time and then headed for the counter where I told the clerk what had happened.

The attendant made several calls, but the purse had not been turned in. As they announced that our flight was boarding, fresh tears of panic filled the mother's eyes, and I told her not to worry. I got goosebumps when I realized my customer had been right — I had found the perfect use for the money she'd given me.

I grabbed the woman's hand and slipped her the money. Ecstasy filled me as I reassured her that, once she reached her destination, she'd have enough for a taxi, food, and a phone call to her husband who could book a motel room and smooth everything over for her. Thanking me over and over, her sobs turned to tears of joy as we boarded our flight together.

On the plane, my daughter ended up sitting near this woman, and I overheard their conversation. "Please, give me your mom's address so I can pay her back when I get home."

"Nope," my daughter said. "Maybe someday you'll get the chance to pass the favor on to someone else in need. That would make my mother happy."

Receiving with grace — something I'd always struggled with — took on a whole new meaning for me that night. If I had refused the money or gone against my customer's wishes and paid bills before I left, this young mother's story would have had a much different ending.

And I have never felt so humbled, blessed, and grateful that I had been given something to give.

— Jill Burns —

100

The Courage to Say Yes

You cannot do kindness too soon, for you never know
how soon it will be too late.
~Ralph Waldo Emerson

My baby Reese started screaming as we watched my eight-year-old kick and punch while he tested for his coveted black belt. Through high-pitched shrills, I struggled to hold him in my arms as we pushed our way through the crowd to the side of the studio.

I looked up, and that's when I saw it. There was a woman on a flyer with a bright white smile surrounded by her daughters. "OUR MOM NEEDS A KIDNEY" it said above the photo. "My name is Vonchelle Knight, and I have polycystic kidney disease," it said below. "I am a single mother of two girls and have been on the transplant waitlist for eight years."

As I continued to read, I was mesmerized. My eyes couldn't get to the next word fast enough. My eyes brimmed with tears as I thought about how desperately this momma needed a kidney. And that's when I felt deep in my gut, *It's me. I'm going to be her donor.* In the middle of that busy taekwondo studio, God was calling me to donate my kidney to a woman whom I had never met.

The drive home was not a typical Saturday kind of drive home. I trembled at the thought of speaking aloud what I was so convinced of just moments before. I glanced over at my husband who was driving.

"Hey, babe?" I asked nervously. "I need to tell you something."

He looked at me, unsure and a little afraid of what might come out of my mouth next. After all, I do like to keep him on his toes. "Yeah, what is it?" he asked intently.

"I think I want to donate my kidney to a stranger."

I thought he might swerve right off the road. By the look on his face, he clearly thought I had lost my mind. I was a busy mom of two boys working a full-time job as a sales account manager. I had a calendar filled with sporting events, group fitness and volunteer church hours. This girl's plate was definitely full. What was I thinking to add anything else to my already crazy, busy life?

"Where is this coming from?" he asked earnestly. I was excited and slightly terrified as I explained the flyer I saw. I told him I wanted to at least call Vonchelle's nurse and get more information. He was reluctant, but we both agreed that I would pray about it. And pray I did.

Several weeks later, the results were in. We were a perfect match! It felt like Christmas morning as the nervous excitement filled my body. Thoughts swirled in my head as I realized I had the ability to give this momma a new lease on life. Vonchelle had already waited eight years and obviously didn't have any family members who could donate. I wrestled with the thought, *If not me, then who?*

In the nervous excitement of my recent test results, the holiday season was upon me. What else seemed to be on me, actually surrounding me, were the clothes and toys we hadn't touched in months. I could feel my face getting red-hot and the onset of heart-racing anxiety as I looked around at the plethora of things we needed to donate.

As I sat on the floor, putting into bags the piles of half-broken toys and clothes that clearly didn't fit my kids anymore, I had an epiphany.

Anytime I realized I had something that I didn't need, I knew I had to give it away. I thought, *Okay, I have all these bags of stuff... but that's not all I have. I have a perfectly healthy kidney. How can I keep it knowing someone else needs it?*

"January twenty-fifth," I said.

My husband looked at me, confused. "What do you mean, January twenty-fifth?"

I slowly swallowed the lump in my throat as I stammered nervously, "I mean… that's the day the doctor can do the transplant. That's the day I'll be donating my kidney to Vonchelle."

I said it out loud, which meant it was happening. I was really going to do it. His eyes filled with tears as he stared at me reluctantly. "Well, I can't say I'm not nervous, but I know God has called you to it. So, I know He will see you through it."

A quiet peace filled me up more each passing day. Vonchelle's daughter worked at my son's taekwondo studio, so I arranged a meeting with her to share the news. "I saw your mom's flyer a couple of months ago," I anxiously told her. "And you're never going to believe it, but we're a match! Can you take me to her?"

After a few moments of attempting to grasp the words leaving my mouth, she shouted, "Yes!" And, with celebration and tears, we were off.

So, there I was. After months of anticipation, I sat on a cozy, leather couch in a dark living room. I was in a woman's house whom I hadn't yet met but felt like I already knew. As she walked through the door, her daughter signaled for me. My heart was beating out of my chest when I walked up to her.

"I saw your flyer at my son's taekwondo studio," I stuttered. "I've gone through all the tests and…"

She gasped, "And you're my donor!"

She fell into my arms. We held each other, crying more tears than I knew were possible. We talked into the night, and I clung to every moment. It was incredible.

When I think about my kidney donation, I also think about that morning at the studio. What if my baby hadn't been crying, and I hadn't walked off to soothe him? What if I didn't slow down long enough to read Vonchelle's story? And what if I hadn't stepped out in faith and said, "Yes"?

All I know is this: I don't need to do anything special to be used by God. I simply need to say, "Yes."

— Amanda Hayhurst —

Thank You, Ma'am

*Remember there's no such thing as a small act
of kindness. Every act creates a ripple
with no logical end.*
~Scott Adams

One afternoon, I had to drive through downtown Houston during rush hour. As I was heading home on I-10 just outside the loop, I came upon a construction slowdown. The loop is a freeway that runs a full circle around the downtown area of Houston and has an exit to I-10, putting more traffic onto the freeway.

As I approached the final stretch inside the loop, traffic came to a halt. As we inched slowly forward, the road gradually narrowed down to two lanes from four lanes. In Houston, during rush hour, that's a huge problem.

I was obviously going to be late for my next client appointment, but there was nothing I could do. So, I turned up the music and started singing while people all around me were honking their horns, cutting each other off, and cursing.

As I inched forward, I noticed an 18-wheeler sitting on the right side of the road with the left blinker on. He was obviously trying to merge into traffic. I was nearly a half-mile from the truck, and as we continued to inch forward, no one slowed down to let him in.

I devised a plan to block traffic and allow the truck driver to enter my lane. I knew that I would have to block both lanes, or the people in the left lane would quickly move in front of me and continue to block the truck driver. So, as I got closer, I moved across the line so that I was in the middle of both lanes. When I got directly behind him, I flashed my lights as I turned my car almost sideways to be certain to block both lanes.

Horns were blaring, but what happened next stunned everyone to silence.

The truck driver pulled his 18-wheeler into my lane and stopped his truck. He then stepped out onto the step on the side of his truck, turned, looked directly at me, took off his cowboy hat, tipped it to me and took a full bow. He then got back into his truck and drove on.

His reaction made me feel so good that I still get "God Bumps" when I think of how that small gesture on my part got such an awesome reaction. I also feel certain that I am not the only person who witnessed that bow and was affected deeply by his act of kindness and gratitude.

— Krystalya Marie' —

Meet Our Contributors

Monica Agnew-Kinnaman was born in 1918 and served in an anti-aircraft artillery regiment in the British Army during WWII. She is a long-time resident of Colorado and is the author of three children's books (*Samson's Adventures*) and a memoir of dog rescues. This is her seventh story published in the *Chicken Soup for the Soul* series since age ninety-four.

Janet L. Amorello is the mother of a young man diagnosed with autism. She lives in central Massachusetts with her husband, son and chocolate Lab. She can be followed on Facebook under "Blending with Autism."

Monica A. Andermann can be found on any sunny day sitting on her front porch, writing. Her work has been included in such publications as *Woman's World*, *Ocean*, *Sasee* and *Guideposts* as well as many *Chicken Soup for the Soul* books.

Elizabeth Blosfield is an East Coast-based journalist and creative writer. Her previous work has appeared in *Thought Catalog*, *Buzzfeed*, *Medium*, *Rèparition Journal* and the *Chicken Soup for the Soul* series. In her spare time, she loves running, traveling, and watching true crime documentaries.

Sophie Bolich is a teacher and bilingual journalist living in Milwaukee, WI. She received her B.A. in journalism and M.A. in Spanish Language, Literature and Cultures from Marquette University. In her free time, Sophie enjoys running marathons, writing poetry, painting, skateboarding, baking and tending to her small jungle of house plants.

Theresa Brandt shares her life with three handsome sons and the best boyfriend in the world. She writes for the local paper and loves to cook, garden, read and spend time with family and friends. Theresa loves animals and has several furry friends that add unlimited joy to her life. E-mail her at tbbrandt1972@yahoo.com.

Jill Burns lives in the mountains of West Virginia with her wonderful family. She's a retired piano teacher and performer. She enjoys writing, music, gardening, nature, and spending time with her grandchildren.

Candace Carteen started writing at the age of eight. Her stories can be viewed in many anthologies and magazines published over the last fifty years. Being a mother to one son and widow to a beloved husband has allowed her to experience many varied moments. Know her life by reading her words. E-mail her at ccarteen@gmail.com.

Brenda Cathcart-Kloke lives in Denver, CO where she enjoys writing and sharing true inspirational stories. This is her seventh published story in the *Chicken Soup for the Soul* series. Her other interests are spending time with her family, reading anything and everything, and oil painting landscapes.

Elizabeth Chenault is a small-town girl from southwest Missouri. She home schools her three children. She loves photography and art in all forms. She also enjoys music and being outdoors. She hopes to publish a pictures and poetry book someday.

Emma Cohan lives and writes in Los Angeles, CA where she shares a home with her husband Greg, their son, and their Bernedoodle, Lucky Buttons. In between writing and shuffling her son to activities, you will find her nose buried in a book with a cup of tea in hand. Contact Emma via her website at emmacohan.com.

Jenny Cohen is a freelance writer and editor, and lives in Michigan with her husband and sons. She enjoys knitting, reading, museums with her kids, and coffee with extra cream.

Linda J. Cooper writes songs, poems and speeches that enable people to creatively deliver tributes at parties and special events. She has been published in *Hilton Head (SC) Magazine* and is pleased to be included once again in the *Chicken Soup for the Soul* series. E-mail her at ljcooper@ix.netcom.com.

Stephanie Daich sees life as a gift. When she isn't writing, she fills her time with family, nursing, and hobbies. Her career has opened doors for her to serve a diverse range of the population. She refines her character by training MMA with world champions. Stephanie often escapes into the mountains or hits the pavement on a run.

Darcy Daniels is a writer, teacher, and patient advocate. She loves to garden, make jam, and take walks in the woods. She is bursting with pride for her two daughters Wendy and Penny, and happily married to her husband Michael. Her favorite quote (right now) is from Mother Theresa: "Do small things with great love."

Angela Dawson is a Bristol-based flash memoir writer and post-menopausal married mother of three. She wild writes with intimate circles of mid-life women. In this tender space they listen, write, speak their naked truths and bear witness. Together they reawaken, liberate, and reclaim their instinctual soul voices.

Diane DeCaprio is a school psychologist in the Cleveland, OH area. She is also pursuing dreams in the fields of writing and martial arts. Diane would like to thank her rockstar friend, Kristen, for making this story possible and her writers' group, the Little Red Writing Hoods, for growing her writing skills.

Rose Demarest (she/her) is an award-winning author who believes that love is love and kindness never goes out of style. An avowed word nerd, she is a fan of the Oxford comma and using they as a gender-neutral third-person singular pronoun. She and her husband live in New Jersey, along with four cats and three dogs — all rescues.

Elizabeth A. Dreier received her Bachelor of Arts in English/creative writing from Ohio University in 1983. She earned her teaching license in 2005 from Notre Dame in Cleveland. Now retired from teaching, Dreier writes a humor column for *Mahoning Matters*.

Melissa Edmondson is a real estate paralegal living in the North Carolina mountains with her wonderful husband Richard, four cats, and three dogs (all rescues). She is the proud mother of four perfect grown children. She enjoys writing whenever she can find the time (and whenever she can get a cat off her laptop).

Mary Eisenhauer has spent her career in corporate human resources but has been an aspiring writer since she was a girl. She has two adult children and lives with her husband and two dogs in New England. She plans to continue writing short stories and articles.

Betty Farkas-Hart was born and raised in France and has been living in the U.S. for almost twenty years. She lives in Florida with her husband, children, and cats. She enjoys taking her family to Honeymoon Island whenever she can! They relax and enjoy the water and the beautiful scenery that Florida offers.

Joy Feldman, a retired executive secretary, vigorously works out. She studies and practices organic gardening and the violin, writes poetry and articles. Her award-winning biographies and poetry have been published in local newspapers. She enjoys sharing her garden's bounty, writing, museums, live theatre, and family.

Steve Filipiak received his Bachelor of Science from Salem State University. He is a human resource director and resides in Virginia with his wife and three boys (but was born and raised outside Boston). Steve enjoys theater, writing, hiking, golf and always promoting the importance of inclusivity.

Sherry Furnish is a graduate of Taylor University and Olivet Nazarene University. After thirty-four years of teaching seventh grade English, she retired in 2020. Happily married, she has three daughters and six grandchildren. Sherry enjoys raising goats and Great Pyrenees.

Dr. Charmin Gans received her Doctor of Chiropractic from Logan College of Chiropractic in 2000. She is the proud mother of two wonderful daughters and practices with her husband in Missouri. She enjoys time with her family, photography, traveling, chocolate, professional speaking, and helping others reach their full potential.

TG Gilliam started writing at the insistence of family. This is her second story published in the *Chicken Soup for the Soul* series. She has a blog detailing visits to old dance halls and has self-published a book titled *Ghosts I've Met: Encounters with Spirits, Angels and Creatures of the Night*, as well as a book of self-care massage techniques.

Lynn Gilliland was an electrical engineer for a large corporation. He and his wife have two daughters and five grandchildren. He has been active in judging science fairs at all levels for fifty years, and since retirement has been writing personal essays for local magazines. He has had eighty pieces published.

Holly Green is a wife, mother of two, grandmother of four, retired nurse, and author of four novels: *What Julia Wrote, Linger, Exactly Enough* and *Swan in Winter* under her pen name Anne Ashberg. She has written nonfiction under her own name: a book on domestic violence and numerous articles on family and parenting issues.

Rob Harshman taught social science at the secondary school level for over thirty years. He has co-authored fifteen textbooks and written numerous short stories. Rob's interests include photography, travel, and spending time with his grandchildren. He is currently writing a series of mystery stories for children.

Amanda Hayhurst is currently pursuing her Master of Arts in Christian Studies from Dallas Theological Seminary. She is married, a mom of two busy boys and a guardian to her cousin, a teenage girl. Amanda enjoys writing, cooking, and taking spontaneous adventures with her family. E-mail her at amandahayhurstwriting@gmail.com.

Carol Goodman Heizer lives in Granbury, TX, and is an eight-time published author. Her work has appeared in several editions of the *Chicken Soup for the Soul* series. Her latest books include *Losing Your Child — Finding Your Way*, *Seasons of a Woman's Life*, and *Snapshots of Life from a Writer's View*.

Linda Hemby is an award-winning author who has authored seven historical fiction novels and four nonfiction books. She's a member of the NC Scribes read and critique group. At age seventy-nine she found and married her soul mate, living proof that it's never too late to find true love.

Laurie Higgins is an award-winning journalist who writes about health, food, gardening, and family. She is a regular contributor to *The Cape Codder* newspaper and *Cape Cod Health News*. She and her chef husband live in Brewster, MA. Laurie enjoys hiking, photography, camping, cooking, and spending time with her grandchildren.

Dana Hinders received her B.A. in Journalism from the University of Iowa. She is a full-time editor and part-time freelance writer living in rural Iowa with her husband and teenage son. She'd like to thank her mom for encouraging her love of reading and storytelling. E-mail her at danahinders@gmail.com.

Kayleen Kitty Holder is the editor of *The Devine News*. She is also a children's book writer. Follow her on Facebook to read more of her work, contribute to the yearly gift drive, or another cause that's dear to her heart. Help her family find a cure for her three-year-old niece and other angels battling A-T. Donate at www.atcp.org.

Born and raised in California, **Miryam Howard-Meier** moved to Alaska out of high school where she worked on a commercial salmon vessel; later moving to Washington State where she raised a family and worked in juvenile corrections. Upon retiring, she moved to Israel and has pursued writing about her many adventures.

Toni Hoy received her B.A. in Communications, with honors, from Thomas Edison State University in 2009 and is an author and freelance writer. Toni is a mother of four who won multiple awards for children's mental health advocacy including Angels in Adoption, a congressional award. She enjoys nature and exploring Tennessee.

David Hull is a retired teacher who lives in Holley, NY. He enjoys reading, writing, gardening, and watching too many reruns of *Star Trek*. E-mail him at Davidhull59@aol.com.

Formerly a graphic designer, **May Jampathom** has been a college writing tutor since 2007. In addition to working with her students, she enjoys dabbling in her own writing and reading. May is grateful for the kindnesses life has granted her: time with her treasured friends and her loving parents, brother, nieces and nephew.

Diane DeMasi Johnson lives in the Pacific Northwest. She is a freelance writer and has been published in regional parenting magazines across the country, as well as *Chicken Soup for the Soul: Dreams and Premonitions*. Now that her boys are grown, she spends her non-writing time training her new puppy.

Kathleen E. Jones, a former nurse and a freelance writer, often writes about the patients she cared for. She is currently working on a book about her career, tentatively titled *Pieces of my Heart*. The book chronicles the journey of caring and loss she experienced, and what it taught her about life.

January Joyce, a retired civil servant and grandmother, spends her rocking chair years caring for little ones while crafting essays and stories. After working relentlessly for decades, her pajama-clad self couldn't be happier.

Kiesa Kay, poet and playwright, writes and plays old time fiddle at her cabin in the Appalachians. Her plays have been presented in six states. She's on the literary maps of both Kansas and North Carolina.

Ric Keller is a former U.S. Congressman, author, speaker, TV commentator, and attorney. He received his bachelor's degree from East Tennessee State University, where he graduated first in his class, and his law degree from Vanderbilt Law School. He lives in Central Florida with his wife, Lori. Learn more at rickeller.net.

Jennifer Kennedy lives in suburban Philadelphia with her husband, sons and rescue dogs. She is grateful for Chicken Soup for the Soul's kindness. Through their charity program, Jennifer has used the books her stories appear in to raise thousands of dollars for special non-profits. E-mail her at jenniferkennedypr@gmail.com.

Kelly Kittel is the author of the award-winning memoir, *Breathe: A Memoir of Motherhood, Grief, and Family Conflict*. She has been published in many magazines and anthologies and speaks about grief and loss. Check out her TEDx talk "Why We Should Share Our Stories" at inyurl.com/y2etqdcp or visit her website at www.kellykittel.com.

Don Lambert has written about and promoted the Art of Kansas on state and national levels for more than fifty years. He received a B.A. in Journalism from Kansas State University in 1972 and an M.A. in American Studies from the University of Kansas. Art exhibits he organized have been in nearly 400 museums across the country.

Charlotte Lewis is a retired accountant who lives in Southwest Kansas. She is the matriarch of a five-generation family. Charlotte has self-published several novels. Her story was written in memory of Marvin G. and M. Emmabelle Johnson. Learn more at charlottelewisonline.com.

Singer, songwriter and worship leader **Allison Lynn** is drawn to the power of the story to grow hearts and communities. Allison and her husband, Gerald Flemming, form the award-winning duo, Infinitely More. Their ninth album of original music will release in 2022. Learn more at www.InfinitelyMore.ca.

After healing from a golf ball–size lump in her breast with a Krystagraph (Symbol/Colored-Drawing) during one brief session, **Krystalya Marie'** created the *One-Minute Energy Tune-Up*, series of books using Krystagraphs for healing all types of ailments and has helped thousands of people worldwide with these amazing healing gifts.

Emily Marszalek graduated with her B.A. in International Studies from Whitworth University in 2013. She enjoys the simple pleasures in life with her best friend, Nick, and their two Goldendoodles in the Pacific Northwest. She is proud to be an American and proud to be a follower of Jesus Christ.

Nicole Ann Rook McAlister is a writer, homemaker, and crafty mother of two. She calls the Pine Barrens home; here she hides away in her log cabin and spends her time gardening, reading, painting, and crafting. She enjoys camping in the Pines and exploring the beaches during off season.

Melanie R. McBride is a freelance writer and editor with an M.A. in English Literature. A book lover, she hopes to one day publish a novel of her own. Melanie currently lives in New Jersey.

Kim Johnson McGuire received her Bachelor of Arts in Literature from the University of California, Santa Barbara. She works as a Pilates instructor and enjoys traveling, golfing, and reading. Kim lives in Grover Beach, CA with her two quirky, but kind, cats. E-mail her at kimmycat2@msn.com.

Caroline S. McKinney is retired from the School of Education at the University of Colorado where she taught children's literature, literacy and writing classes for over twenty-five years. She was also a teacher and Literacy Coach for Boulder Valley Schools. She loves her eight grandchildren, making quilts, Italy, and her dog, Milly.

Casey McMullin is a poet/artist from Pennsylvania who believes in the power of nature, loving the little things, and finding solace in absurdity. They volunteer for *Eclipse Lit*, a literary magazine devoted to mental health and healing. Their work can be found in *Quiddity* ("Orphean Epilogue") or @casmcmullin on Instagram.

Amy Mewborn is a 1992 graduate of East Carolina University. She teaches high school English in eastern North Carolina. Of course, writing is her favorite pastime — especially when she is blogging or posting at thepeacanseeker.com. She loves new followers! Besides writing, she reads, gardens, and enjoys family and friends.

Paula W. Millet is a retired high school educator and ovarian cancer survivor. Holding a B.A. in English and an M.A. in Humanities, she has always been fascinated by the human experience, which has become the inspiration for her novels. She currently lives in suburban Atlanta, GA. Follow her blog at paulamillet.com.

Geri Moran is a writer and craft artist who lives in New York. She believes her mission in life is to make people smile through her stories and handcrafted items and laugh with her humor. She is honored to have a story included in the *Chicken Soup for the Soul* series for a third time.

Marya Morin is a freelance writer. Her stories and poems have appeared in publications such as *Woman's World* and Hallmark. Marya also penned a weekly humorous column for an online newsletter and writes custom poetry on request. She lives in the country with her husband. E-mail her at Akushla514@hotmail.com.

Eve Morton is a writer living in Ontario, Canada. She teaches university and college classes on media studies, academic writing, and genre literature, among other topics. Her poetry book, *Karma Machine*, was released in late 2020. Learn more at authormorton.wordpress.com.

Sheree Negus, as a later bloomer, received her Bachelor of Arts, with honors, in 2000. A single mom, she met the love of her life and is happily married to a funny and clever man and added another son to her family. Now a retired teacher, she is newly accepted in an MFA program for creative writing.

Barbara Espinosa Occhino was born in Cuba and lives in Connecticut. She is married, has two daughters, a granddaughter, and a marketing agency. She volunteers as a student mentor and in the arts. Barbara has a Rutgers University B.A. in communications and thrives on anything creative: dance, theatre, nature, travel, writing, and people!

Molly O'Connor is a graduate of creative writing at Carleton University and Algonquin College. She spends her time writing, walking, singing, and capturing photos of wildflowers. She has published nine books and her stories appear in six other *Chicken Soup for the Soul* books.

Kelly Okoniewski is a poet, writer, and copy editor. Her poetry has most recently been published in *WestWard Quarterly*. The greatest joy in her life is being a mother to her amazing son. She loves to read, cook, exercise, and take walks in nature. Kelly lives in Garnet Valley, PA with her husband and son.

Caitlin Q. Bailey O'Neill has been a writer by trade since high school and by passion since the first grade; she has previously been published in eight *Chicken Soup for the Soul* anthologies. She is the proud mom of two children on earth and one in heaven.

Alina Ottembrajt has devoted her life to the care of her son who has a severe developmental delay and medical complexities. At the age of sixty she realized that she needed to achieve some of her own dreams. Being included in the *Chicken Soup for the Soul* series has encouraged and inspired her to write stories that encourage and inspire others.

Michelle Padula is an avid animal lover, Navy mom, photographer and aspiring writer. She resides in Chesterton, IN with her wife Paulette, dogs Bella and Piper, and two rescue kitties. Her adult daughter Rachel is an active-duty sailor stationed in Japan. Her previous story "A Gift from Heaven" was published in 2021.

Voula Plagakis has written for *ELLE*, *ParentsCanada* and a variety of online and educational publications. She enjoys savouring things like the crema on an espresso and a last glimpse of nature's goodbye kiss, the sunset. She lives in Montreal and is currently at work on a series of vignettes about her childhood.

Mary T. Post resides in rural Oregon with her husband of thirty-three years. They have four grown sons, two daughters-in-law and one grandson. She enjoys hiking, gardening, and cooking. As a life-long Lutheran, Mary enjoys writing stories that weave together her faith with ordinary (and oftentimes humorous) life experiences.

Michael T. Powers, whose writing appears in thirty-three books, is a youth pastor, international speaker, and an award-winning photographer and high school girl's coach. Preview his book *Heart Touchers,* or join the thousands of world-wide readers on his e-mail list at HeartTouchers.com. E-mail him at Michael@faithjanesville.org.

Evan Purcell is an American teacher working with young learners in Almaty, Kazakhstan. He has also taught in Bhutan, Zanzibar, China, Russia, and Ukraine. He writes YA adventure novels and is currently working on his first web series.

Linda Holland Rathkopf was a cabaret singer, is a playwright (Member of Dramatists Guild) and fine artist/illustrator. Her plays have been produced in six states, her writings have been published in anthologies, and her artwork has been displayed in galleries around the country. Learn more at lindarathkopf.com.

Beth Rice did not become a journalist like she'd planned, but her dad wouldn't let her give up on writing. She works as a content writer for DutchCrafters.com and is the author of the children's book, *I'm Adopted, I'm Special*, as well as *The Tale End: Stories from the Vet*. She enjoys reading, theater, movies and running.

Anne Russ is a writer, workshop leader and ordained pastor in the Presbyterian Church (USA) living in New York. She creates Christian community on her online platform "Doubting Believer." She is married and has a daughter in college who is majoring in musical theater.

Karen Sargent is the award-winning author of *Waiting for Butterflies* and *If She Never Tells*. A retired English teacher, she writes for multiple *Guideposts* devotionals, leads book launches for authors, and enjoys teaching writing workshops. Learn more at KarenSargent.com.

Chris Maday Schmidt believes it's always the write time for real-life fairytales brimming with hope for new beginnings, humor in the messy middle and heart for happy endings. She's been published in *Woman's World*, among others, and is working on her first small-town romance series. Learn more at info@chrismadayschmidt.com.

Donna Faulkner Schulte hails from Fayetteville, NC. She has published *Santa's Search for the Perfect Child* and *The Lover Club* in addition to writing poetry. Donna is married and has three daughters, seven grandchildren and three great-grandchildren. She is a big advocate for helping those in need as well as the homeless.

Crystal Schwanke has enjoyed freelance writing since 2004 and lives in the Atlanta, GA area with her husband, daughter, and rescue pup, Josephine. She loves reading, trying new coffee shops, collecting kitchen gadgets and cookbooks, and cramming in as many online courses as possible, across a variety of topics.

Kori Sciandra earned her Bachelor of Arts in Journalism from Buffalo State College in 2010. She is a writer living in New York with her husband and two children. She values her time with her family and plans to continue writing for various publications, including *The Batavia Daily News*.

Lesa Shirley-Sheffield is a busy hairstylist in Carrollton, GA. She has been married to her husband of nearly thirty years Matt, and a mother to Will and Ivie. Her love of loving others was instilled into her by her precious mother Margie, who passed from this earth in April of 2019. She was the best at showing God's love to everyone.

Georgia Hendrix Shockley began writing at the early age of eight years old. She graduated from Fairview High School and attended Wallace State College, majoring in accounting. Both schools are in Cullman County, Alabama. She loves to write stories, songs, and poems. Georgia treasures spending time with her family most of all.

Shirley Nordeck Short was fascinated by a 1910 Oliver typewriter stored in her farmhouse while she was growing up. She loved using it and began writing stories at a young age. She has been published in *Chicken Soup for the Soul: Answered Prayers*, *Chicken Soup for the Soul: Messages from Heaven* and *Chicken Soup for the Soul: Angels Among Us*.

Christine M. Smith is a mother, grandmother, and great-grandmother currently living in Oklahoma with her husband of fifty-three years. She loves God, family, and especially loves to read and write about both.

Heather Spiva is a writer from central California. When she's not reading or writing, she's shopping for vintage clothing or drinking coffee. And when she's not doing those dynamic feats, she is probably spending time with her family and dog. This is her third story published in the *Chicken Soup for the Soul* series. Learn more at HeatherSpiva.com.

Judee Stapp is a speaker and author who loves to share her life experiences in an engaging and inspiring way. She has had eight stories published in the *Chicken Soup for the Soul* series and a one syllable story in *Short and Sweet*. Judee is a wife, mother and grandmother who loves storytelling. E-mail her at stappjudee@gmail.com.

Danielle Stauber is a stay-at-home mom of three and has been married for nineteen years. She resides in upstate New York and spends all her time with her family or writing.

Tina Szymczak received her Bachelor of Arts degree in 1995. She has two grown boys and has been married for over twenty-five years to her amazing husband, Adam. Tina enjoys public speaking, writing and her full-time job working in early intervention. Learn more at www. spiritedblessings.com.

Tammy Thornton is a full-time writer who loves travelling around the world with her two furry companions, Ragnar and Tiva. She loves reading, learning new languages, dancing until dawn and eating good food, especially when it is cooked for her! She is currently working on two novels, and aspires to live in sunnier climates.

Susan Traugh is the award-winning author of the YA novel *The Edge of Brilliance* and the special education series *Daily Living Skills*. Her work has appeared in scores of books and magazines. Susan lives in Oregon with her now-grown children and husband, Steven. Learn more at www.susantraugh.com.

Dorann Weber is a freelance photographer and has a love for writing — especially for the *Chicken Soup for the Soul* series. She's a contributor for Getty Images and worked as a photojournalist for many years. In her spare time, she enjoys reading, hiking, and spending time with her family in the Pinelands of South New Jersey.

Robert Willett is a retired banker living in Florida. After retirement he began writing and has had five books published as well as a number of articles in various publications. His work primarily deals with military wartime characters. His travels have taken him to lesser known destinations such as Bishkek, Kyrgyzstan, and Russia.

Glenda Wood received her bachelor's degree in communication from Florida State University and spent her career in political communication. After retiring she forged two more careers — one in real estate and another teaching English primarily to students with English as a second language. She loves travel and writing.

Woody Woodburn lives in Southern California and spends much of his time writing, reading and running — he is a "Streaker" who has run a minimum of three miles every day since July 7, 2003.

Mary Jo Wyse is the iMOM content writer at iMOM.com. She has an MFA in creative writing and an M.A. in English. Besides writing and reading, she loves to be active outside, taking walks and working in her garden. She lives in Michigan with her husband, two kids, and their new puppy.

Meet Amy Newmark

Amy Newmark is the bestselling author, editor-in-chief, and publisher of the *Chicken Soup for the Soul* book series. Since 2008, she has published 179 new books, most of them national bestsellers in the U.S. and Canada, more than doubling the number of Chicken Soup for the Soul titles in print today. She is also the author of *Simply Happy*, a crash course in Chicken Soup for the Soul advice and wisdom that is filled with easy-to-implement, practical tips for enjoying a better life.

Amy is credited with revitalizing the Chicken Soup for the Soul brand, which has been a publishing industry phenomenon since the first book came out in 1993. By compiling inspirational and aspirational true stories curated from ordinary people who have had extraordinary experiences, Amy has kept the twenty-eight-year-old Chicken Soup for the Soul brand fresh and relevant.

Amy graduated *magna cum laude* from Harvard University where she majored in Portuguese and minored in French. She then embarked on a three-decade career as a Wall Street analyst, a hedge fund manager, and a corporate executive in the technology field.

Her return to literary pursuits was inevitable, as her honors thesis in college involved traveling throughout Brazil's impoverished northeast region, collecting stories from regular people. She is delighted to have come full circle in her writing career — from collecting stories "from the people" in Brazil as a twenty-year-old to, three decades later, collecting stories "from the people" for Chicken Soup for the Soul.

When Amy and her husband Bill, the CEO of Chicken Soup for the Soul, are not working, they are visiting their four grown children and their four grandchildren.